Knowing *Other*-wise

KNOWING
OTHER-WISE

Philosophy at the Threshold
of Spirituality

edited by
JAMES H. OLTHUIS

FORDHAM UNIVERSITY PRESS
New York
1997

Copyright © 1997 by Fordham University Press
All rights reserved.
LC 97-7412
IBSN 0-8232-1780-9 (*hardcover*)
IBSN 0-8232-1781-7 (*paperback*)
ISSN 1089-3938
Perspectives in Continental Philosophy, No. 4
John D. Caputo, Series Editor

Library of Congress Cataloging-in-Publication Data

Knowing other-wise : philosophy at the threshold of spirituality /
edited by James H. Olthuis.
p.   cm. —(Perspectives in continental philosophy, ISSN 1089-3938 ; no. 4)
Includes bibliographical references.
ISBN 0-8232-1780-9 (hardcover : alk. paper). —ISBN 0-8232-1781-7
(pbk. : alk. paper)
1. Postmodernism.   2. Feminist theory.   3. Ethics, Modern—20th
century.   4. Philosophical theology.   I. Olthuis, James H.   II. Series.
B831.2.K66   1997
190'.9'04—dc21   97-7412
                                                                                  CIP

Gratefully dedicated to the faithful
who have made the Institute for Christian Studies possible.
Without their support,
this book would have been impossible.

CONTENTS

A God with/for the Other

ACKNOWLEDGMENTS

Grateful acknowledgment is made to the following for permission to reprint previously published material:

Chapter 4: Ronald Kuipers, "Singular Interruptions: Rortian Liberalism and the Ethics of Deconstruction" was published in a condensed version in *International Studies in Philosophy*, 28/1 (1996): 11–27.

Chapter 5: James H. Olthuis, "Face-to-Face: Ethical Asymmetry or the Symmetry of Mutuality" appeared in slightly revised form in *Studies in Religion/Sciences Religieuses* 25/4 (1996).

Chapter 7: Jeffrey M. Dudiak, "Again Ethics: A Levinasian Reading of Caputo Reading Levinas," *Joyful Wisdom* 3/2 (1997).

Chapter 9: James H. Olthuis, "Crossing the Threshold: Sojourning Together in the Wild Spaces of Love" is reprinted from the *Toronto Journal of Theology* 11/1 (1995): 39–57 © Toronto School of Theology.

I wish to thank Jamie Smith and Jeff Dudiak for their help in editing and John D. Caputo for his encouragement. This collection of essays was born in the matrix of a multi-year interdisciplinary research project on pluralism at the Institute for Christian Studies in Toronto, made possible by a three-year grant from the Social Sciences and Humanities Research Council of Canada, whose support is gratefully acknowledged.

Introduction: Love/Knowledge: Sojourning with Others, Meeting with Differences

James H. Olthuis

RECENT DISCUSSIONS in the various circles of feminism, postmodernism, and environmentalism have begun to make clear that ontology and epistemology without ethics is deadly—oppressive to women, oppressive to men, oppressive to the earth. This collection of essays joins in suggesting that developing non-oppressive (or, at least, less oppressive) ontologies, epistemologies, and ethics calls for another way of knowing, a way of knowing "the other," a knowing other-wise, a knowing of the heart with the eye of love. Philosophy and ethics need *Geist*, not as the dialectical movement of cognition *à la* Hegel, but as "in the beginning was Love" *à la* Julia Kristeva.[1] What is needed—and what is hopefully adumbrated here—is, in the words of Jacques Derrida, a "thinking of *Geist* which would be other and more originary."[2]

Knowing-otherwise is a response to the crisis of reason in modernity. The impact of the forays of feminism and deconstruction has been to show "reason's *inability to rationally know itself.*" Reason is not able to "come outside of itself, to enclose and know itself from the outside."[3] Although philosophical thinking in the West has been "in essence the attempt to domesticate Otherness,"[4] achieve unity, and erect closure, Jacques Derrida, applying Gödel's incompleteness theorem, has shown that every philosophical text bears the scars of exteriority and alterity.[5] Closure is a pipe-dream, and a dangerous one at that, accompanied by bloodshed and scars in the flesh. For, as Jane Flax observes, "any appearance of unity presupposes and requires a prior act of violence."[6] Indeed, instead of affirming Bacon's doctrine that "knowledge is power," the archeological diggings of a Foucault have demonstrated that, historically, the opposite is more likely: "power is knowledge."[7]

Knowledge is never an indifferent, atemporal, aspatial, translucent matrix. There is no such thing as "Universal Reason—a fixed, trans-temporal structure that in no way depends on the nature of our bodily experience nor on the social contexts, historical events, or cultural practices in which it is manifested."[8] Knowledges cannot be and never were neutral, dispassionate, disinterested—all our modernist Cartesian illusions to the contrary. If this is true, "if reason is an effect not of reason itself but of something unreasonable (i.e., power), then adhering to even an altered, modified reason is no solution."[9]

"A YES MORE ANCIENT"

What now, after reason? Or perhaps, more apropos, what now, before, in, and through reason? Deconstruction, in pointing out not only the impossibility of constructing airtight, knockdown arguments, but also the inevitable bleeding of texts into their margins and margins into their texts, opens within philosophy itself a prephilosophical space. The scars or traces of the other, in disrupting unity and preventing closure, provide exits to this non-pre-philosophical unheard, un-thought, unfelt, unseen, intangible, secret place. In "Violence and Metaphysics,"[10] Derrida says that an "injunction," "an unbreachable responsibility," is announced in this space which interrupts the unity and breaches the totality of philosophy.

In other words, prior to all knowing, prior to any context, decon-struction opens us up to the space of a preoriginary, " 'unconditional' affirmation,' or of 'unconditional' 'appeal'," that "is independent of every determinate context, even of the determination of a context in general." This appeal is a responsibility which "intervenes in the deter-mination of a context from its very opening."[11] That is to say, although Derrida continues to insist (rightly, I think) that "there is nothing out-side the (con)text," he is also emphatic (again, I think, rightly) that there is nevertheless a "wordless word," a "yes" that calls forth and interrupts every context. Indeed, Derrida writes that for a long while the question of the *yes* "has mobilized or traversed everything I have been trying to think, write, teach or read."[12] In *Of Spirit* Derrida claims that before any actual contextual yeses and noes "there is this sometimes wordless word which we name the 'yes.' A sort of preori-ginary pledge [*gage, Zusage*] which precedes any other engagement in language and action." Moreover, "no erasure is possible for such a pledge." We are linked to it "by a faith which defeats any narrative."[13] Indeed, "the promise has already taken place wherever language comes. . . . This would also be a promise of spirit."[14]

Here Derrida begins, in most remarkable fashion, I believe, a re-thinking of *Geist*. Here we have a space of proximity to the other, a place of ethical and spiritual responsibility—prior to, or at least other than, philosophy! *Knowing Other-wise* is an effort to join with Derrida in this endeavor. In another piece, in which Derrida is again dealing with this pre-originary pledge, he talks of "a *yes* more 'ancient.'"[15] For us that "yes more ancient" is love, the love of God. Love is the yes, and although Derrida himself does not explicitly affirm this connection, he reminds us that Angelus Silesius did: *Gott spricht nur immer Ja* (God only always says Yes).[16] Love is the unthought, the unfelt, the unde-cidable, that makes for thinking, feeling, and deciding, the excess that evokes the context and exceeds the closure of any context. It is the unthought, the unfelt, the unnameable, the Spirit, that gives rise to thoughts, feelings, and names, even as it cannot be thought, felt, and named. In the beginning, before "the beginning," was the Yes.

"In the beginning was the telephone,"[17] chimes in Derrida, in per-haps his most ringing metaphor. For me it is also a most happy meta-phor, which I render thus: "In the beginning was the Love of God." Love is a gift/call: a ringing-gift which needs to be answered in order to be actualized. Everyone, by virtue of being a creature, answers. Yet some, hearing, do not hear. Some try to stop up their ears. Others have ears to hear. And at any time in the conversation, the communi-cation can go astray: slippage is possible, love may be refused, aborted, denied, betrayed. The pre-originary gift, the yes more ancient, is an undecidable which heightens the tension: To love or not to love, that is the question. And although a yes is called for, not any yes will do. The yes may be mechanical, halfhearted, or devious. Genuine yeses of love need to be as different as the situations into which they are spoken, as unique as the persons who speak them. There are no pre-scribed, unambiguous responses that are guaranteed to be appropriate in particular situations. The very space needed for genuine response opens the possibility of contamination. Responsible and healing yeses always involve risk, the risk of violence. That is why I refer to these uncharted interstices as the "wild" spaces of love.

The risk of violence is always with us. The truly big question is whether this means that in time violence is always and forever un-avoidable. This seems to be Derrida's position: "[V]iolence may be considered the very condition of the gift, its constitutive impurity once the gift is engaged in a process of *circulation. . . . The violence appears irreducible, within the circle or outside it, whether it repeats the circle or interrupts it."*[18] If the "economy of violence" is inescapable, it becomes existentially and historically impossible, despite our best efforts, despite the call of the pre-originary gift, to ever genuinely meet another in a way that is not appropriation or expropriation. For Derrida, the gift is impossible because it is a function of an economy of reciprocal exchange, a kind of "zero sum game" in which something can be given here only in withholding it there. But what if the gift is possible because it is a function of another economy, an economy of love, an economy in which love expands and increases in its being given?

In an economy of reciprocal exchange, the choice is between the sacrifice of myself or the irresponsibility of sacrificing the other. Neither choice is appealing. In contrast to such a self-other dichotomy, in the economy of love there is return to self that is not at the cost of the other: In truly loving self, I love the other; in loving other, I love self. Both giver and receiver are enriched. A gift of love, then, is not an expenditure without return, but an expenditure without a controlled, manipulated, or contracted return. That risk factor is intrinsic to the dynamic of love. Without the risk (of refusal, manipulation, etc.), a gift is not an authentic gift. Attempting to minimize the risk of an ethical relation by turning it into an economic exchange makes the "gift" counterfeit. A "gift" may turn out to be poison. But to deny that a gift can ever be fundamentally an authentic—as distinct from a "perfect"—gift is to condemn humankind forever to an economy of violence from which there is never any escape. An economy of love—risky and precarious as it is—provides an alternative for genuine meeting, a connection other than violence.

In the context of the current discussion, it is important to make clear that we are not suggesting that love is an indispensable auxiliary to the order of reason, a handmaiden to help reason with matters it cannot know on its own, or a heart knowledge that, after Pascal, "has its reasons, which reason does not know." We are more radically suggesting that there is only one order, the order of love, and that in its form and function reason will always be shaped by the response given to the preoriginary word of love. At the same time, since the gift of love is received only via interpretation—Derrida has also said "in the beginning is hermeneutics"[19]—there is no automatically privileged or authorized interpretation. Thus, although we want to say, along with

Jean-Luc Marion, *ama ut intelligas* (love, so that you may understand),[20] we also want to say, in distinction from Marion, that the
Christian vision of love is one interpretation among others. It is the
interpretation we choose, it is the one by which we live, it is even the
one for which we are willing to die. But it remains, nevertheless, an
interpretation—as witnessed by the many shapes and forms it has received in the course of church history. To say anything else is not only
to pretend to bracket out our subjectivity, but also to risk considering
ourselves to be the blessed possessors of the Truth with all the attendant
dangers of oppression, or complicity in oppression, to which history so
eloquently, and tragically, bears testimony. That is to say, if love is an
undeconstructible gift/call (of God) which holds the world together,
all creatures, all traditions, large and small, bear in themselves the
mark of this free gift, which they can deny and disfigure or accept and
refigure until death. Until the end, we live by the knowing of faith and
not by sight, by grace and not by works, lest any of us should boast.
"We can hear the telephone constantly ringing."[21] May the yes of our
response be: "*Get Geist: de l'esprit*"[22] of love. Let love come! (*Viens!*)[23]

With the Ear of Compassion and the Eye of Love

Philosophy and ethics, we are suggesting, unless they are thoroughly
imbued with a spirituality of love, leave us trapped in an economy of
war, shivering in the cold, lacking the fire which alone is able to warm
our hearts and empower us to see, feel, and honor alterity as alterity.
If viewed other than through the eye of love, difference can be espied
only as deficit or deviance, as a threat to be denied, marginalized, or
annihilated. Reason untransformed by love can only totalize. Reason,
in service of love, forms concepts, not as devices of closure and enclosure of difference into sameness, but as holding patterns for approach,
orientation, understanding, and meeting of difference. If the immense
task of "working love conceptually (and hence, in return, working the
concept through love)"[24] were taken up, philosophy would not be the
love of wisdom, but, in the fashion of Levinas, "the wisdom of love at
the service of love."[25]

In calling for another way of looking at reason's operations, knowing-otherwise also calls into question the Western philosophical tradition of giving pride of place to reason in the acquisition of knowledge.
Since only reason was considered by the tradition to know the proper-

ties of Being, goodness, beauty, and unity, sensory knowing, however necessary and useful, could not be considered knowledge of equal worth to rational knowing.[26] Instead of judging that emotions are subversive of knowledge, or at best irrational urges that need to be controlled by reason, we believe emotions, as emotions, are vital and honorable ways of knowing. Feelings are themselves indispensable thermometers, signals registering how we apprehend, situate, and motivate ourselves in engaging the world. There is also tactile-kinesthetic knowing, as there is knowing a friend, and, to employ a biblical idiom, knowing one's wife. In other words, reasoning is only one of the many ways in which we engage (i.e., know) the world, only one of the ways in which we seek the Eros of connection even as we are evoked by Love, the more ancient Yes. Knowing is the multidimensional, embodied, gendered way human beings engage the world in order to situate themselves meaningfully (spiritually) and come close responsibly (ethically) to the different and other. We also know by touch, by feel, by taste, by sight, by sounds, by smell, by symbols, by sex, by trust—by means of every modality of human experience. Knowing by thinking is no better, no worse, than any of the other modalities. Each modality, according to its own style, is an important and indispensable way in which we actively engage the world. Such diverse modalities are mutually constitutive, and mutually transformative in the process of knowing. Each mode, according to its own style, is a way of knowing that opens up new possibilities for offering love and promoting justice (or for promoting discord and spreading injustice), as we come to know other-wise.

In any human act of engagement, all the ways of knowing are reciprocally interwoven, simultaneously present, even when, as the case may be, one of the ways of knowing stands out and marks that particular activity in a heightened way. Thus, for example, in an act of conjugal knowing, feelings and thinkings are naturally present even though in "good" intercourse the focus is on physical-tactile knowing. When we have "second thoughts" about such acts, the subsumed thinkings come to the foreground, and we have a different kind of act. The simultaneous presence of all the different ways of knowing, potentially or actually, in every human act of knowing also means that the good-enough development of each of these ways of functioning is a condition for the healthy development of each. Reciprocally, this means that not-good-enough formation, or developmental deficits, in any of these ways adversely affects all of the rest. Thus, real or perceived emotional weakness, shame, paranoia, or discomfort with sexuality and corporeality may lead to a retreat into the mind and a flight from the body and/or from another's body, with all kinds of subtle, often hidden consequences.[27]

HONORING ALTERITY/MEETING THE DIFFERENT

The importance of rehabilitating all the ways of knowing increases immeasurably when we realize that, in the West, the reason-emotion opposition was very often aligned, such that reason was paired with male, self, external, culture, and universal, and emotion was paired with female, other, internal, nature, and particular. As we acknowledge the oppressive and discriminatory results of such dichotomizing, we can begin to trace out and legitimate in new ways the place and function of the negative, excluded, or subordinated in the formation of knowledge. No longer will philosophy be privileged in relation in knowledge. No longer can the corporeal body and its processes be disavowed in the production of knowledge and the purely conceptual or mental privileged. Knowledges are "products of bodily impulses and forces that have mistaken themselves for products of mind."[28] The gendered nature of bodies, differences of race, age, and culture all act as co-conspirators in situating, motivating, and coloring the production of knowledge. Criteria for truth and falsity other than correspondence between propositions and reality will need to come into play if our "knowledges" are to be context-appropriate. Knowledges will be retextured as limited, partial outcomes in the service of specific imperatives.

In other words, knowing-otherwise, with the eye of love and the ear of compassion, means the unmasking and dismantling of the "classist, racist, and especially masculinist myth"[29] of the disinterested and dispassionate investigator with his pure, uncontaminated-by-context knowledge. It invites women, with their usually more highly developed emotional sensitivity, to take the lead in ascertaining when and how emotions may contribute to the growth of knowledge. It invites all privileged people—in particular, white males—to open their eyes to the plight of the other, and to be open to the contributions of groups previously oppressed and ostracized—in particular, people of other colors, races, creeds, and orientations. It invites the economic "haves" of whatever color or stripe to share their riches with the increasing number of economic "have-nots." It asks all of us to repent of our domination of each other and the earth. Life on our planet may well depend on such changes of heart. Compassion is still in exile. May we all unstop our ears and hear the cries of pain in our own hearts—and those of our neighbors, our animal and plant friends, our planet—and respond with love to the incessant ringing of Love.

The knowing-otherwise of love opens the space for alterity to be lived with as friend, as partner for growth and enrichment. Other people need not be hell (Sartre); they can be heaven. Alterity can be at home with identity. The name for relations that have genuine room for others is mutuality—mutual recognition, mutual pleasure, mutual empowerment, and mutual transformation. There can, in the words of Emmanuel Levinas, be an ethical relation, "a relation of the same with the other, where the transcendence of the relation does not cut the bonds a relation implies, yet where the bonds do not unite the same and the other into a Whole."[30] Indeed, Levinas purposively reserves "the term religion" for this "relation without relation."[31]

Knowing-otherwise is meeting, not mastery.

Knowing-otherwise is mutuality, not competition.

Knowing-otherwise is of the body, not limited to the mind.

Knowing-otherwise is ethics, intimacy-with, not power-over, the other.

Knowing other-wise is love; opening, not closure; connection, not fusion; drawing nigh, not distancing. Knowing-otherwise is celebrating-with, and suffering-with, the other.

Knowing-otherwise is spirit, shaping love even as we are shaped by Love. Knowing-otherwise is a spiritual process of mutual transformation in which we release/are released into the Mystery of Love out of which everything arises. Knowing-otherwise is to take the risk of loving the other, the risk of meeting in mutuality.

KNOWING *OTHER*-WISE

This collection of essays was born in the matrix of a multi-year interdisciplinary research project on pluralism at the Institute for Christian Studies in Toronto,[32] in which the participants often found themselves needing to interact with postmodern discussions in a variety of fields such as philosophy, literature, women's studies, political theory, theology, and religious studies. Questions of pluralism and toleration are inextricably linked to the questions of difference and otherness, questions that occupy a central place in postmodern discussions.

The spirit with which these essays are imbued issues in an attempt to "know *other*-wise": to be ethically wise with respect to the other, and, to honor the other who is too often excluded from the cultural discourses of power and influence. As such, the book not only signals links between postmodernism and pluralism, but also , and especially, indicates connections between epistemology, ethics, and spirituality, between "knowing" and the "other," between an other and the Other. As the development of these essays suggests, the postmodern critiques and proposals for ethics were already present in—even the motivation for—earlier epistemological critiques of both "foundations" and "transcendentals." To properly appreciate the ethical turn in postmodern philosophical discourse and the approaching spiritual horizon, we do well to begin with the epistemological environs in which these concerns emerged. A brief outlining of each section may help in indicating the spiraling movements we detect between epistemology, ethics, and spirituality.

Philosophy and Its Other

In the opening essay, "Conceptual Understanding and Knowing *Other*-wise," Hendrik Hart traces how logical discourse came to be understood as a privileged grasp of the truth of the world and the sole arbiter of reality. With this move, all other ways of knowing are marginalized: knowing is effectively reduced to logic and rationality, the world is reduced to rational "order," and, in the process, difference is reduced to sameness. Hart wants to remind philosophy of its limits— that there are ways of knowing other than rationality, and that all knowing is fundamentally trusting. I know more than I think. Knowing *other*-wise is a knowing wise of the other, an honoring of alterity, a spiritual attunement with and a nourishing of the interconnectedness of all of life. By tracing modern philosophy's systematic exclusion of faith, Hart also demonstrates that such motives, at the same time, deconstruct the rationale for such an exclusion. In fact, such a project failed to exclude faith. Rather, it replaced all other faith with a fundamental trust in Reason. This exposure results in a new proposal for and opening to spirituality in postmodern philosophy.

The modern delimitation of the person as a subject, and further as a "thinking thing," though purportedly transcendental and universal,

manifested itself to be a white European male named *Res Cogitans*.
And, as I have already noted, this espousal of a universal, neutral
rationality resulted in exclusion and oppression. In her essay "Points
of Convergence Between Dooyeweerdian and Feminist Views of the
Philosophic Self" Janet Wesselius dissects the Kantian transcendental-
logical ego as just such an instantiation of a purportedly neutral subject. In the essay, she draws out similarities between recent feminist
critiques of modernist rationalism and the early twentieth-century critique of Dutch philosopher Herman Dooyeweerd, a critique rooted in
the Calvinist Christian tradition that is the spiritual home for the writers in this collection. The modern philosophical tradition, Wesselius
observes, attempts to exclude all that is *other than* rational, which, for
this tradition, includes both bodies and women. But what Dooyeweerd
emphasized, and recent feminist philosophers such as Wesselius emphasize, is that it is "I" that philosophizes: "I" as an embodied, engendered human being.

Carroll Guen Hart also explores points of convergence between the
reformational philosophical tradition and recent philosophical discussions in her essay, "Taking the Risk of Essence," which explores the
notion of "essence" and "essentialism." The "hidden agenda of essence," as Guen Hart describes it, in both traditional conceptions and
certain feminist employments, assumes that "the many are identical
to the one who is privileged to tell the story" and proclaim what is
permitted the hallowed name of "essence." Wanting to avoid such an
exclusive agenda, other feminist thinkers have jettisoned the concept
altogether. Guen Hart proposes that such a wholesale rejection is based
on a dichotomy that understands essence and difference as mutually
exclusive, and (drawing on Dewey) that a flexible, functionalized notion of essence is a risk worth taking for the sake of solidarity in political
action. The reading she develops is at once a challenge to the Christian
understanding of creation, and one rooted in the Christian tradition.

Ethics and/of the Other

As the previous essays indicate, the questions of plurality and otherness
are questions of ethical import; no longer can a line be so conveniently
drawn between epistemology and ethics. In this section, the authors
thematize the status of the Other in ethics, particularly from the viewpoint of and in dialogue with Emmanuel Levinas.

By reading Rorty through a Levinasian lens, Ronald Kuipers, in his essay, "Singular Interruptions," finds in Rorty points of convergence with Derrida's ethical concern for the other, despite their different paths of criticism. For Derrida, it is singular suffering others that beckon from the margin of our institutions, leaving only traces of their presence, demanding response, and making me responsible. Rorty also hears the ethical call of the other: but it is not the the call of anything exterior. Rather, it is that which is called for by the liberal ideal of inclusion in the public sphere. But, Kuipers wonders, does this concern for inclusion extend beyond the "bazaar" and enter the "gentlemen's club"? For Levinas, and for Kuipers, the call of the Other "interrupts the back-slapping enjoyment that we have in our private clubs." Kuipers concludes that, while Rorty's concern for justice is no doubt genuine, there is still ample reason to be suspicious of his ultimate commitment to a liberal political ethos.

Against the backdrop of modern ethical theory, my essay, "Face-to-Face," ponders Emmanuel Levinas's insistence on the priority of the other. I suggest that an emphasis on the symmetry of mutuality may be less vulnerable to being misread as a plea for selflessness and self-sacrifice. Love of self and love of neighbor are generally understood as mutually exclusive both in modern philosophy, for example, Freud and Sartre, and in modern theology with its Nygren-inspired contrast between selfless *agape* and selfish *Eros*. In contrast, in a model of non-oppositional difference, I am to love others *as I love myself*.

In the following two essays, Jeff Dudiak also engages the work of Emmanuel Levinas. In "Structures of Violence, Structures of Peace," Dudiak offers a helpful exposition of Levinas's understanding of necessary yet violent structures, which we cannot live with and cannot live without, applying this discussion to the traditional pacifism/just-war debate. Each of these positions involves *"un beau risque"* that at once must, but cannot, be taken. This conceptual paradox, whose terms remain irreducible to the coordinates of dialectic, forbids, Dudiak argues, the possibility of a definitive position on this issue, demanding instead a perpetual, and difficult, communal vigilance.

Then, in "Again Ethics," Dudiak engages John Caputo's reading of Levinas in the latter's recent work *Against Ethics*, weaving a "Levinasian reading of Caputo reading Levinas." Despite his debt to Levinas, Caputo insists on keeping himself at a certain distance from Levinas's "seriousness" and "piety." Dudiak's essay inhabits the gap opened up by this distancing, challenges Caputo's reading of Levinas, and proposes that the gap may be smaller than Caputo contends. In short,

Dudiak argues that while Caputo understands Levinas to be proposing an "ethics" in the traditional, metaphysical sense, a way of thinking that Caputo believes Derrida to have effectively deconstructed, Levinas is in fact interested in precisely what Caputo (after Derrida) is concerned about: undeconstructible justice.

A God with/for the Other

In some versions of postmodernity, God is manifested as not the "Wholly Other," but rather as a God for the other, a God traced in the face of the suffering other. The essays in this section explore the domination and oppression of others which have accompanied Western theology, but they also propose new understandings of both God and theology that call attention to the other.

James K. Smith's essay, "How to Avoid Not Speaking," criticizes the Western theological tradition when it claims to speak for God, but in the process excludes (often violently) those who would disagree with its truth claims. However, Smith also questions deconstruction and the apophantic tradition for another kind of violence. He proposes a new vision of ev-angelical theology which emphasizes healing and love as criteria for good (*eu-*) stories of faith, embodied in a plurality of letters and missives from a host of apostles· letters that are not from God, but that nevertheless arrive.

My "Crossing the Threshold" is a critique of the ontology of power, which is inevitably an ontology of violence, and an ontology that is appropriated by most modern and postmodern paradigms. In this ontology, being/power is always power-*over*, and to be human is to be at war with each other. In contrast to this, I propose a vision of love, where the question is not "To be or not to be," but "To love or not to love." Such a mutuality model emphasizes the intersubjectivity of human be-ing as being-with-others and God as God-with-us. Power is no longer qualified by domination, but becomes power-with, celebrating-with, and suffering-with, as paths of mutual empowerment.

All the essays serve, we hope, as points of convergence between postmodern discussions and the reformational or Calvinist philosophical heritage which is the operative spirit "behind" this entire collection of essays. As Alan Olson describes, "it may be that the deconstructive mood of postmodernity is *faith-inspired*—even *faith-obsessed* in an obscure sort of way."[33] Understanding the primordial role of faith in theory formation,[34] insisting that the pretended autonomy of theoretical thought is an illusion,[35] witnessing to the reality of human brokenness, pursuing justice for all (not just "us") in the public arenas of education, media, and politics—all have been compelling themes of the reformational philosophical heritage for nearly a century, beginning with Abraham Kuyper (1837-1920), the Dutch theologian and founder of the Free University of Amsterdam, who also served as Holland's prime minister. These are perhaps a few indications of the sensitivities of this tradition to the concerns of postmodernism, and perhaps, we hope, reason to expect that our resources may be of some small help as we together wrestle with the epochal shifts that shake and disturb us as we precipitously slide into a new millennium. May we all have the ears to hear each other, hands to hold on to each other, and hearts open to each other in response to the call of the Other.

NOTES

1. Julia Kristeva, *In the Beginning Was Love: Psychoanalysis and Faith*, trans. A. Goldhammer (New York: Columbia University Press, 1988). At the same time, I need to note that I do not, as Kristeva does, play a wild, semiotic love over against the symbolic rule of the law of the Father. For me, love is the pre-originary Yes, gifting to and calling for good orderings, that is, good connections.

2. Jacques Derrida, *Of Spirit*, trans. G. Bennington and R. Bowlby (Chicago: University of Chicago Press, 1989), p. 82. For one recent effort to relate postmodern thought and religious discourse, see *Shadow of Spirit*, ed. P. Berry and A. Wernick (New York: Routledge, 1992).

3. Elizabeth Grosz, "Bodies and Knowledges: Feminism and the Crisis of Reason," in *Feminist Epistemologies*, ed. L. Alcoff and E. Potter (New York: Routledge, 1993), p. 189.

4. Rodolphe Gasché, *The Tain of the Mirror* (Cambridge, Mass.: Harvard University Press), p. 101. Derrida and Levinas, in particular, have called our attention to the havoc wreaked by this totalizing motif. For that reason Emmanuel Levinas judges that ontology as first philosophy is "a philosophy of injustice" (*Totality and Infinity*, trans. A. Lingus [Pittsburgh: Duquesne University Press, 1969], p. 46).

5. Jacques Derrida, *Positions*, trans. A. Bass (Chicago: University of Chicago Press, 1971), p. 57. Simon Critchley has an illuminating discussion of "the problem of closure in Derrida" in *The Ethics of Deconstruction* (Oxford: Blackwell, 1992), pp. 59–106.

6. Jane Flax, *Thinking Fragments* (Berkeley: University of California Press, 1990), p. 33. Jacques Derrida's "Violence and Metaphysics: An Essay

on the Thought of Emmanuel Levinas" (in *Writing and Difference*, trans. A Bass [Chicago: University of Chicago Press, 1978], pp. 79–153), is an especially pertinent discussion of such violence.

7. Michel Foucault, *Power/Knowledge*, ed. C. Gordon, trans. C. Gordon et al. (New York: Pantheon, 1980).

8. Mark Johnson, *Moral Imagination* (Chicago: University of Chicago Press, 1993), p. 108. Johnson and George Lakoff are developing a more embodied and contextualized reason. See John and Lakeoff, *Metaphors We Live By* (Chicago: University of Chicago Press, 1980); Johnson, *The Body in the Mind* (Chicago: University of Chicago Press, 1987), and George Lakoff, *Women, Fire, and Dangerous Things* (Chicago: University of Chicago Press, 1986).

9. Grosz, "Bodies and Knowledges," p. 207.

10. Derrida, "Violence and Metaphysics," p. 80.

11. Jacques Derrida, *Limited Inc.* (Evanston, Ill.: Northwestern University Press, 1988), pp. 152–53.

12. Jacques Derrida, "Ulysses Gramophone: Hear Say Yes in Joyce," in *Acts of Literature*, ed. D. Attrridge (New York: Routledge, 1992), p. 287. In his foreword to *Given Time. I. Counterfeit Money*, trans. P. Kamuf (Chicago: University of Chicago Press, 1991), Derrida notes that his "later works were all devoted, if one may put it that way, to the question of the gift, whether it appeared in its own name, as was often the case, or by means of the indissociable motifs of speculation, destination, or the promise, of sacrifice, the 'yes,' or originary affirmation, of the event, invention, the coming of the 'come' " (p. x.).

13. Derrida, *Of Spirit*, p. 130.

14. Ibid., p. 94. For a fascinating discussion of the function of "yes" in Derrida, see Rodolphe Gasché, *Inventions of Difference* (Cambridge, Mass.: Harvard University Press, 1994), pp. 199–250.

15. Derrida, "Ulysses Gramophone," p. 296.

16. Jacques Derrida, *Psyché* (Paris: Galilée, 1987), pp. 640–41.

17. Derrida, "Ulysses Gramophone," p. 270.

18. Derrida, *Given Time*, p. 147. Seemingly accepting that intersubjectivity is essentially and unavoidably violent, Derrida's strategy is to work for "the least possible violence" (*Writing and Difference*, p. 130).

19. Derrida, "Violence and Metaphysics," p. 67.

20. Jean-Luc Marion, "Christian Philosophy and Charity," *Communio* (1992), 463–73.

21. Derrida, "Ulysses Gramophone," p. 270.

22. Derrida, *Of Spirit*, p. 127.

23. For Derrida on the motif "Come," see his "Of an Apocalyptic Tone Newly Developed in Philosophy," trans. J. Leavey, Jr. in *Derrida and Negative Theology*, ed. H. Coward and T. Foshay (Albany: State University of New York Press, 1992), pp. 62–66.

24. Jean-Luc Marion, *God Without Being*, trans. T. Carlson (Chicago: University of Chicago Press, 1991), p. 47.

25. Levinas, *Otherwise than Being*, trans. A. Lingus (The Hague: Martinus Nijhoff, 1981), p. 62.

26. J. G. Milhaven's "A Medieval Lesson on Bodily Knowing: Women's Experience and Men's Thought" (*Journal of the American Academy of Religion*, 57, No. 2 [1989]), 341-72) traces how the emphasis on knowledge = rational has not allowed us to honor "women's experience" of bodily knowing.

27. See, for example, Karl Stern, *The Flight From Woman* (New York: Farrar, Straus and Giroux, 1965), and S. Bordo, *The Flight to Objectivity* (Albany: State University of New York Press, 1987).

28. Grosz, "Bodies and Knowledges," p. 204.

29. Alison Jaggar, "Love and Knowledge: Emotion in Feminist Epistemology," in *Gender/Body/Knowledge*, ed. A. Jaggar and S. Bordo (New Brunswick, n.j.: Rutgers University Press, 1989), p. 158.

30. Levinas, *Totality and Infinity*, p. 48.

31. Ibid., p. 80; see also p. 40.

32. This project was made possible by a three-year grant from the Social Sciences and Humanities Research Council of Canada, whose support is gratefully acknowledged.

33. Alan M. Olson, "Postmodernity and Faith," *Journal of the American Academy of Religion*, 58 (1990), 37.

34. This factor, in fact, prompted Malcolm Bull to describe Kuyper as the first postmodern ("Who was the first to make a pact with the Devil?" *London Review of Books* [May 14, 1992], pp. 22–24).

35. See Herman Dooyeweerd's *A New Critique of Theoretical Thought*, trans. D. Freeman and W. Young, 4 vols. (Philadelphia: Presbyterian and Reformed, 1953-1958). Dooyeweerd with his brother-in-law Dirk Theodore Vollenhoven founded the Dutch society for Calvinist philosophy, inspired by Kuyper.

PHILOSOPHY AND ITS OTHER

1

Conceptual Understanding and Knowing *Other*-wise: Reflections on Rationality and Spirituality in Philosophy

Hendrik Hart

THE RECOGNITION OF SPIRITUALITY

WHEN YOU SURF the Internet's World Wide Web, browse around a magazine rack in a bookstore, listen to rock music, or use the remote control to graze the TV menu, the frequent appearance of spirituality in its many forms is striking. Inside the professional world of academic philosophy, however, there is considerable ambiguity toward today's resurgence of spirituality. The secular academy often seems reluctant to explore this phenomenon. Even where such exploration does occur, the ambiguity remains. For example, Charles Taylor's *Sources of the Self*[1] is not easily appreciated without antennae for spirituality. But the "Index" does not list the term, nor anything close to it. A check of the "Contents" or the "Preface" also yields nothing. Yet on the very first page of the text we read that Taylor uses the stage-setting first part of his book to "explore the background picture of our spiritual nature and *predicament* which lies behind some of the moral and spiritual intuitions of our contemporaries."[2] And the two pages that end the book refer to spirit and the spiritual no fewer than eight times. They are all related to the fact that, as Taylor writes there, "we tend in our culture to *stifle* the spirit."[3] Clearly, even this explicit exploration of spirituality in the West points to a certain reluctance in our culture to come to terms with the spiritual. Taylor himself confesses that he is dealing with something "vague."[4] Against this background, I will discuss some dimensions of the relation between rationality and spirituality, in an

attempt to understand what the renewed contemporary interest in spirituality means for philosophy.

I want to begin with a tentative diagnosis of the problem. Certain
powerful cultural elites in the West are, I think, open to talk about
spirituality so long as such talk remains firmly within the bounds of
reason. But they become hesitant when such talk moves outside of
those limits. The influence of secular naturalism, especially its commitment to rational autonomy, gives rise to a certain timidity with
respect to serious consideration of realities that seem suspect to naturalistic reason. Nevertheless, not all references to spirituality are taboo.
They are acceptable if by terms like "spiritual," "spirit," "spirited," or
"inspiration" we mean something innocuous. For example, a vigorous
team-spirit inspiring a will to perform in every player may be a sports-
writer's explanation for a win by an underrated team. On the other
hand, when talk about spirituality veers toward revealed religion, or
when people suggest that the spiritual dimension of life transcends the
powers of reason, many become resistant. Yet even here the picture
is far from uniform. In Anglo-American philosophy inspired by the
positivistic naturalism of the Vienna Circle one can often almost taste
a disdain for colleagues who take spirituality seriously.[5] European
thinkers oriented to phenomenology, however, discuss spirituality seriously and even make its reason-transcending significance an important
issue. Emmanuel Levinas is by no means an exceptional figure in this
respect. What are we to make of all this?

From the start I want to bypass two possible angles of discussion. I
wish neither to speak of spirituality as related to the occult nor as linked
to spirits in the way earlier philosophy often dealt with ghosts, disem-
bodied personal beings, pure minds, non-physical beings, non-mate-
rial or mental entities or substances. My interest in spirituality is,
rather, related to the meaning of "spirit" in an expression such as "the
spirit of the Enlightenment." In that expression "spirit" is a term of
historical and cultural *orientation*. The Enlightenment is then understood as a complex of values, attitudes, and hopes that *guide and direct*
people in their evaluations, decisions, courses of action, and plans.
Through such a spirit people imbue their lives with coherence as they
relate to other people, institutions, and their culture. Insofar as they
are successful in their aspirations and their life has vigor and meaning,
people can be said to be inspired, for example, by "the spirit of the
Enlightenment."[6]

"Spirit," when taken in this way, is connected to those hopes, questions, struggles, and failures that arise in what may be called the existential boundary issues of experience: life and death, origin and destiny, meaning and happiness, good and evil; what may I hope, what can I trust, how do I know life has meaning, what comfort is there in the face of despair?[7] Such a spirit can inspire confidence in people, but only if it allows them to relate to these existential issues in a positive frame of mind, by which they find value in the things of everyday life: families and marriages, careers, aging, illness, natural disasters, economic hardship, the state of the nation, the decline of religion, dominant powers of marginalization, and others. Boundary issues are inescapably resistant to human control and therefore require a measure of trust in powers and forces also not fully in our control, in order to allow us to be at ease in this world. As we give shape to our lives, these powers also shape us.

This use of the term "spirit," which has little or nothing to do with either personal beings that are immaterial or with the occult, has wide currency among religious and secular people alike. Yet we see today a *spiritual* decline related to the *spirit* of the Enlightenment. How is this to be explained? I hope to gain some insight in this essay into this somewhat paradoxical state of affairs. First, however, I want to relate the meaning of "spirit" I have just sketched to "spirituality."

THE MEANING OF SPIRITUALITY

In brief, I will use "spiritual" and "spirituality" to designate our self-conscious awareness and nurturing of the interconnectedness of reality[8] with the existential boundary issues of life, as we are empowered or inspired to do so by a motivating dynamic or spirit. By "self-conscious" I mean here our awareness, sense, or feeling not only of *ourselves being connected* with, being "part of," the interconnectedness of reality, but also of *our being selves* precisely in terms of this interconnection. In other words, our very selfhood is at stake in our awareness or non-awareness. This self-consciousness or self-awareness need not be active from moment to moment and it can be stronger in some than in others, but without it we would shrivel up spiritually, that is, as selves.[9]

Spirituality thus understood interconnects human responsibility with dimensions of life that transcend human control, especially in the existential boundary situation. It interconnects our shaping and our being shaped. This interconnection means that, without our human responsibility being cancelled, we are also in the grip of powers that transcend us as they guide and direct us. We foster spirituality (1) by growing in our capacity to be aware of the relation between the interconnectedness of everything and a spirit that overreaches our control in guiding us and (2) by taking responsibility for our own role in this interconnectedness. A committed liberal, for example, seeks not merely to be *aware* of the powerfully molding pervasiveness of the Enlightenment spirit, but also to be *responsible*, together with others, for its being pervasive, for spreading its reach. In that way spirituality makes for community. Where a society is a community, in the sense of being more than a group of individuals, a common spirit inspires that society.

The existential boundary issues to which I referred unavoidably affect, color, influence, and shape our movement in history. They give us willy-nilly a perspective on reality. They shape the direction of events and orient us temporally. Spiritual is, in this sense, material: it *matters*. On the other hand, since these existential issues also present us with a dimension of reality that is beyond our immediate control and even understanding, spirituality also is intangible; the existential issues in terms of which we experience this spirituality are beyond what is fully within our grasp. Beyond this tangible horizon we cannot see clearly, even though we can speak in visions of what lies beyond. This invisibility is perhaps what has led people to speak of the *im*material in this connection. Moreover, our efforts to imagine what lies "beyond" may have led to talk about "pure" minds. Nevertheless, I do not associate spirituality with mind/matter contrasts.

Spirituality, then, interweaves human responsibility with realities that overcome us. It has to do with our living consciously self-aware and responsibly in the face of transhuman powers, for we live out of an irrecoverable past and into an uncontrolled future. We live inescapably in the face of death, but with an unquenchable hope to keep life going. We live with our guilt about the massive evil in which we are all implicated and with our own apparent inability to bring this evil to a lasting end. All of this shapes us in the continuities and discontinuities of the generations. All of this makes for tradition and directs history. All of this permeates our bone and marrow. All of this is woven into the synchronic warp and diachronic woof of history. Spiritually alive cultures, spiritually aware people, and spiritually responsible leaders are cultures, people, and leaders whose experience and reality are constantly open to these existential boundary issues and who receive guidance, perspective, and direction in this openness by following a spirit.

When we talk of spirit and spirituality in this way we can speak of the reality of spirits in two fundamental and related ways. In the first place we can acknowledge spirit as the universally permeating presence of such complex, powerful, and influential movements as the Enlightenment, pragmatism, liberalism, Marxism, and Christianity. We call them "movements" because our being oriented to these realities, our being inspired by them, guides, directs, and impels our movement through history. In the second place we can recognize our own spirituality and acknowledge that it makes as much sense to refer to ourselves as spirits as it does to accept ourselves as bodies. We are spirits insofar as we take responsibility for our capacity to live openly in relation to spirits. In other words, we legitimately see ourselves as spirits by virtue of our ability to contribute to reorientation in history, whether that be a calling for a change in spirit in our neighborhood or resisting the mondial spirit of capitalism. To talk about emancipation as the spirit of the Enlightenment is to say that this movement inspired people to seek freedom, that it put freedom in a light that gave perspective to Western culture and allowed the call of future enlightenment to guide and direct people and institutions. We can effectively respond to what we experience when we are open to this spiritual dimension of reality. As agents of spirituality we are spiritual ourselves. We are spirits. Spirits are real, embodied; ghosts are not.[10]

I think it makes eminent sense to speak of human beings as spirits. "The human spirit" is not some entity outside of us, nor is it a separate substance in addition to and temporarily residing inside our bodies. We *are* the human spirit, we in our entirety.[11] It is *as spirits* that we are most authentically ourselves. For in human beings the sense of spirituality I just introduced becomes embodied as spiritual agency. We then accept with vulnerability that we are not enclosed within ourselves but can be open to what lies beyond us, even when this openness reveals to us our powerlessness in the face of realities that can overcome us. Such vulnerability can give rise to a fear of what lies beyond our own limits. We may then try to empower ourselves by rejecting what we cannot overpower except from within our own limits. But in so doing we quench the spirit and thereby embark upon a road on which we move toward our death, since we can live only as spirits.

To sum up: "spirit" and "spirituality" indicate a directing, guiding, leading perspectival dynamic in the historical process of reality in which powers and forces that both transcend human control and take effect in human agency provide a life integrating meaning vis-à-vis life and death, origin and destiny, and good and evil. These latter as boundary conditions of existence also transcend human control. Yet we are responsible for how we relate to them. Consequently, we can speak of people as spirits, and we can also refer to something like emancipation as a spirit or spiritual force. Insofar as people take responsibility for incorporating or embodying, for example, the Enlightenment's striving for emancipation they become agents of emancipation and thereby the spirit of emancipation comes to characterize them as spirit. With these understandings in hand, I suggest we can make some sense of the controversial, ambiguous, and even paradoxical approach to spirituality in our culture. I would even like to suggest that we can get beyond that approach to some degree.

THE DECLINE OF SPIRITUALITY IN THE WEST

One might well ask whether these ways of talking about spirits and spirituality make good sense in our culture, if this same culture often seems to resist spirituality. But if spirituality is unavoidable and if recognizing ourselves as spirits is part of what it means to take our place in history responsibly, we should probably not be surprised at the contemporary return of interest in spirituality. On the contrary, what requires explanation is how our culture ever became resistant to spirituality.

Earlier I referred to the somewhat paradoxical circumstance of a *spiritual* decline in a certain *spirit*, namely, the secular spirit of the Enlightenment. To what can this be attributed? If followers of the Enlightenment themselves can positively appreciate talk of the spirit of the Enlightenment, what makes them at the same time resist spirituality? Even though spirituality is often associated with the occult or with immaterial personal or substantial beings, and though this association may explain some of the resistance, it does not go far enough. For all that would be needed in this case is to avoid the occult or immaterial meaning of spirituality and to amplify the acceptable meaning. Why is this not done? What else is at stake?

I think we are helped to understand this resistance by examining certain key features of the Enlightenment, features concentrated in its emancipatory aspiration. The vision of emancipation has filled the hopes and dreams of all who have become inspired by the spirit of the Enlightenment. In what we now call modernity, however, that emancipatory interest is essentially tied to a human autonomy focused upon the autonomy of reason.[12] Indeed, we can tell the story of the Enlightenment in terms of the gradual rise of the power of reason and the parallel decline of the power of religion. And this story may lead us closer to understanding how, paradoxically, those in the grip of the spirit of emancipation came to regard spiritual talk as a sign of not being emancipated; of how the West's centuries-long process of secularization and naturalization, itself a spiritual process, promoted a resistance to spirituality.

In this process of secularization, human autonomy understood as rational autonomy came to stand for opposition to an essential dimension of spirituality, namely, the acknowledgment of powers that are beyond the control of human power, of realities that are mysterious, of boundary conditions that transcend human understanding. The spirit of emancipation inspired an enthusiasm in humanity that fostered intolerance toward powers or forces beyond the authority of human reason. These powers had been closely associated with the cultural domain of religion. Hence the decline in religion associated with the rise of rational autonomy affected the status of spirituality in the West.

The Enlightenment was undeniably a spiritual movement, in that it gave a direction to human history, influencing every dimension of our lives, permeating the interrelatedness of our complex culture. In its early history the main actors were also religious people, who were therefore inclined to accept spirituality as a natural dimension of the human condition. At the same time, because the Enlightenment inspired a rational autonomy which resists the authority of tradition and religion beyond the bounds of reason, the Enlightenment manifested a spiritually self-impoverishing spirit.[13] For it is now undermined by the spirit-quenching move of denying the spiritual character of perspective on the human journey. Such perspective, in its spirituality, lies beyond our grasp and control and hence beyond the bounds of reason. That becomes a reason for denying spirituality within the Enlightenment. So what the religious originators of the Enlightenment set loose quite naturally bore fruit, for example, in the God-and-

authority-denying forces of the French Revolution and in the denunci-
ation of religion in Marxism.

A relationship with philosophy is not hard to detect here. Throughout Western history, philosophy has been the main exponent of reason
as the integrating spirit of our culture.[14] If we see philosophy in modernity as the most comprehensive and coherent attempt at articulating
the spirit of the Enlightenment, as the promoter of rational autonomy
par excellence, then we can also see the remarkable rise of naturalism
and atheism in philosophy as going hand in hand with resistance to
spirituality. For in the acknowledgment of spirituality and, consequently, of conditions transcending human power, the core of the doctrine of rational autonomy is in danger of eroding. Hence, after Hegel
(who identified spirituality and rationality) and beginning with Comte
(who proclaimed both religion and metaphysics to be behind us), philosophy embarked on a path of limiting and even resisting the spirit in
human affairs.[15] For all that, however, the spirituality of this philosophy remained inescapable. Heidegger's and Derrida's now widely used
designation of metaphysics as onto-theology recognizes this. Richard
Rorty's analysis of philosophy as superjudge of culture also points to
Philosophy's occupation of a spiritual center.[16]

Four aspects of the autonomy of reason in philosophy together provide a key for understanding the resistance to spirituality in the Enlightenment. These four aspects are intimately interrelated. Indeed, it
is their interconnection in the Enlightenment which sheds light on the
(paradoxically) "spirit-quenching spirit" of emancipation conceived as
autonomy. They will help us understand how the paradox of a spirit-
resisting spirit becomes comprehensible in light of the *misleading* character of the spirit of human autonomy. For if spirituality means guidance and if guidance toward autonomy resists the humanity-
transcending components in all spiritual guidance, then the Enlightenment is problematic.

Four Aspects of Rational Autonomy

First I will make some remarks about the doctrine of rational autonomy. It received a celebrated Enlightenment articulation in Kant's
Critiques. A more telling passage than Kant's famous *sapere aude* is
found in the preface to the first edition of the *Critique of Pure Reason*:
"It is obviously the effect not of levity but of the matured judgment of

the age, which refuses to be any longer put off with illusory knowledge. It is a call to reason to undertake anew the most difficult of all its tasks, namely, that of self-knowledge, and to institute a tribunal which will assure to reason its lawful claims, and dismiss all groundless pretensions, not by despotic decrees, but in accordance with its own eternal and unalterable laws." In a footnote to "matured judgment" Kant writes about "the sincere respect which reason accords only to that which has been able to sustain the test of free and open examination."[17] This is a declaration of the autonomy of reason. Reason's only laws are its own, eternally and immutably. And all knowledge is subject to reason's laws if we want to count it as knowledge.

Kant, of course, still struggled to establish the legitimacy of religion. To do so he needed a practical as well as a pure (theoretical) form of reason.[18] But his Enlightenment challenge to dare to know was to become a challenge interpreted more and more in the spirit of the passage cited. That spirit is present as well in *Religion Within the Bounds of Reason*.[19] Though it took some time to get there, that spirit would eventually lead to a rejection of religion and, beyond that, to the now discredited verification principle of logical positivism. In that principle, philosophers pronounced rational closure on any reality that reason could not itself rationally authenticate. The originally anti-authoritarian spirit of the Enlightenment led to an intolerantly authoritarian reason. A. J. Ayer's exuberant *Language, Truth, and Logic* celebrates that intolerance with candor.[20] Free and open examination of what may lie beyond the limits of reason is impossible in this context and hence spiritual freedom is quenched.[21] Reason, as a spirit that promised freedom, quenched the spirit of freedom in closing down all avenues of exploration beyond its own bounds. And since spirituality requires openness, the spirit of the Enlightenment contributed to the resistance to acknowledging any spirituality beyond the bounds of reason. To be sure, there remained, within the enclosure of reason, room to look for guidance in relation to life's boundary situations. But that residue of spirituality appears to be cramped, restrictive, and bound.

Second, the doctrine of rational autonomy has been widely interpreted as a doctrine requiring the ultimate authority of science. The requirement lies in the conviction that genuinely rational foundations for autonomy can be acquired only through scientific reason as the purest, most advanced, and methodically controlled form of rationality.[22] Kant, of course, did not grant science this monopoly of authority. Even for Spencer, the messianic English apostle of positivism, science and religion each still has its own authority. But, as in the case of Kant, Spencer's statements sow the seeds of growths he himself did not intend. Telling citations from three consecutive paragraphs of his *First Principles* make it apparent that scientism, though unintended, lurks around the corner: "What is Science? To see the absurdity of the prejudice against it, we need only remark that Science is simply a higher development of common knowledge; and that if Science is repudiated, all knowledge must be repudiated along with it. . . . To ask the question which more immediately concerns our argument—whether Science is substantially true?—is much like asking whether the Sun gives light. . . . Science must be judged by itself; and so judged only the most perverted intellect can fail to see that it is worthy of all reverence. Be there or be there not any other revelation, we have a veritable revelation in Science—a continuous disclosure of the established order of the Universe."[23]

When this spirit takes hold of philosophy, the authority of science easily leads to the reduction of knowledge to technical, logical-conceptual, mechanical data and information.[24] Where this spirit informs people, the Enlightenment becomes suspicious of any meaning that cannot authenticate itself in the forum of science. Reason as such does not need to be interpreted in these narrow terms. Many modern concepts of reason, however, contain elements which, if taken to their logical conclusion, open the door to scientism, since in science we find the epitome of knowledge construed as rational knowledge. In such a climate of objectivity and logical rigor, where the validity of anything subjective or non-rational becomes suspect, people are tempted to deny any spirit at all.[25]

Third, the rise and influence of scientism has implications for more than just human knowing. What can be accepted as reality in a world dominated by reason can easily become identical with what can be rationally known. Scientism then leads to forms of naturalism which practice closure: the universe itself is limited to what can be scientifically known. Spencer still dealt with the relation between science and religion by letting both end in the inscrutable mystery of the unknown, to which each had its own distinct approach.[26] In Stephen W. Hawking's *A Brief History of Time* we find an expression of our era's confidence in the ultimate containment of both God and the universe within a single principle of physics. Hawking calls this "the ultimate triumph of human reason—for then we would know the mind of God."[27] In such a view the very possibility of conceiving that something might be beyond conceiving, of entertaining the idea that there might be realities beyond reason, has become, if not unintelligible or unimaginable, at least unworthy of serious consideration. Reason has swallowed up the universe, not in the sense that there is only reason, but in the sense that there can no longer be a universe except the universe of reason. And the genitive in "of reason" here is both possessive and objective: the universe is reason's creation out of its own resources. Reason as spirit—that is, reason as the one and only *guiding* principle—leads us to the conclusion that beyond reason's grasp there is nothing. The unknown and the mysterious, the acknowledgment of powers transcending human power—all crucial elements in what I have described as spirituality—have virtually disappeared.[28]

The *fourth* aspect further clarifies the waning of spirituality under the spiritual guidance of reason. I refer to reason's self-authentication. Anti-foundationalism came to terms with this in its discovery that the doctrine of reason founded on rational certitudes amounted to rational self-delusion.[29] However, the passage from Kant previously cited proclaims that reason has only rational foundations. In that passage Kant promotes the idea of *self*-founding.[30] Insofar as the critique of reason is a call to *self*-knowledge, the self which knows itself is the transcendental logical ego, that is, a purely rational self, a form of reason. Anti-foundationalism unmasks this as self-contradictory. The notion that nothing can count as knowledge unless it is demonstrably founded on certitudes self-evident to reason or is logically demonstrable to reason is a notion that cannot meet its own criteria. It is a self-referentially incoherent notion. It leads to its own destruction. In terms of our discussion this means that its spiritual direction is a spiritual dead end. *Foundations for* reason cannot be found *within* reason. Consequently, the transcending of reason is needed for the survival of reason.[31]

A self-founding and self-authorizing reason eventually closes down or forecloses on any and all openness to any beyond, to any transcendence or mystery. As principle, that is, as spiritual directive, as indicator of a path through time, as a place from whence to begin confidently our journey to a destiny unknown, self-founding reason leads to a profoundly skeptical questioning. This questioning happens in response to the irresistible openness of spirituality. The spirituality remaining in a spirituality within the bounds of reason breaks open the doctrine of rational autonomy. The doctrine itself is, namely, incomprehensible to reason. As *spiritual* principle it lies, at least in part, *beyond* comprehension.[32] Evidence for this is found in an absolute principle of verification which is itself unverifiable. Such a principle of reason is *rationally* incoherent. As *spirit*, rational autonomy requires complete openness. As *rational*, however, rational *autonomy* requires *self-*founding. Such incoherence spiritually *leads* to *doubts* about rational autonomy. The spirit in reason turns against rational autonomy. People who are confronted with a need to turn away from self-founding reason often become struck with a deep fear of relativism. For any principles beyond the dogmatic absolutes of reason strike many of the Enlightenment faithful as the arbitrary relativism of having no principles at all. In that fear there seems to be no awareness that the principles that need to be abandoned then still function, ghost-like, to assess the alternatives.

The self-founding of reason was exposed as self-referentially incoherent not only in anti-foundationalism, but also in the analysis of autonomous reason's prejudice against prejudice by Hans-Georg Gadamer.[33] This in its own way shows us the misguided journey on which our culture embarked in following Descartes' cogito or Kant's transcendental logical ego. Prejudice against prejudice is similar to anti-spiritual spirituality. These mislead us into thinking that we can autonomously and rationally create a world out of reason's own resources, without awareness of the inner paradox. Gadamer thus arrives at rational autonomy's incoherence along a different path than anti-foundationalism, but thereby provides independent corroboration for this crucial point.

A Misleading Spirituality

In the preceding section I tried to show that if the role of spirit is that of providing perspective, giving guidance, *leading* us in a certain *direction*, then, because the spirit of the Enlightenment had *misleading* elements, it was a misleading *spirit*. It motivated people to seek freedom via rational autonomy and in that way promoted intolerance toward any spirituality other than rational spirituality. The result was a pulling down of the blinds, a closing down of our horizons, a hollowing out of spirituality so that only reason remains.

In a sense, of course, it is characteristic of broad spiritual movements that they resist competing spirits. But in this case much more is at stake. In following this spirit we are reduced to our rational egos and lose touch with our inner selves as more than rational. Thus we lose ourselves as spirit and no longer connect with the spiritual character of our journey. In our self-characterization as *rational* animals (cogito, transcendental logical ego) we came to see our reality as most authentic in our rational *theories* of reality. In thus denying our reality as spiritual agents in history we began to lose touch with spiritual reality. For spirituality cannot be confined within the self-sameness of the universal and immutable order of theory. Spirituality requires the openness of narrative, of stories that move with time. For since spirituality guides the movement of history through the agency of people who themselves develop spiritually, its truth cannot be caught in the arresting of temporal movement in frozen theoretical propositions. But the rational commitment to the propositional character of truth led to a devaluation or even denial of the truth-character of narrative.

Even though philosophers still seem largely reluctant to accept the reality of spirituality, the misleading character of the Enlightenment spirit is beginning to surface in philosophical literature. Gadamer's emphasis on truth in art as play, beyond the bounds of scientifically methodical reason, though still significantly oriented to reason, contributed a great deal to a new openness in philosophy. In the North American climate the critique of the Enlightenment spirit, without forsaking the Enlightenment as a whole, is palpably present in works such as Richard Rorty's *Philosophy and the Mirror of Nature*, Alasdair MacIntyre's *Whose Justice? Which Rationality?*, and Charles Taylor's *Sources of the Self.*[34] The decidedly spiritual overtones in the latter two works is not altogether surprising, given the religious orientation of the authors. Rorty's explicit discussion of "spirit" is, however, uncharacteristic of contemporary atheist-secular philosophy and is, therefore, even more telling of the crisis in Enlightenment spirituality, especially when coupled with his insistence that our own Enlightenment society has no firmer footing than that of a toehold in hope and trust.[35]

That the Enlightenment is not considered spiritually dead, however, is evident from Thomas McCarthy's recent address to the 1994 meetings of the Eastern Division of the American Philosophical Association, "Enlightenment and the Idea of Public Reason." He argues, in language characteristic of what I have called spirituality, that the idea of public reason "may serve as a critical and guiding, regulative idea, much as it did for Kant two centuries ago." However, in his address on the same occasion, "The Enlightenment's Projects Reconsidered,"

MacIntyre argues for the failed spiritual character of that movement's hope for cultural unity.[36]

The philosophical Enlightenment is perhaps most seriously challenged today in France. Emmanuel Levinas's early ethical critique of totalizing ontologies, Michel Foucault's exposure of the potentially destructive political abuses of the power of (rational) truth, and Jacques Derrida's plea for engagement with what a phallogocentric spirit has marginalized in our culture have given powerful articulation to a postmodern deconstruction of the rational-philosophical edifices of the Enlightenment. In their critiques these authors reveal, as I read them, the moral and spiritual down-sides of the Enlightenment, which remained largely hidden in North America. North American movements such as anti-foundationalism and anti-realism, though critical of key elements of rational autonomy, have tended to remain abstractly philosophical. The focus for discussion is often limited to a demonstration of the rational untenability of anchoring our universe in a self-validated rational image of that universe projected as truth: the permanent neutral framework, the God's-eye view.[37]

Perhaps this still overly rational-philosophical character is due in part to the influence of philosophers and historians of science on the development of anti-foundationalism.[38] Karl Popper's critique of the principle of verification and Thomas Kuhn's demonstration that science does not progress linearly toward a universal truth played an important role here.[39] Both authors, however, have a recognizably spiritual tonality. Popper referred to his fundamental attitude toward science as a confession of faith,[40] and Kuhn spoke of the history of science in terms of revolutions he characterized as conversions in commitment.[41] The French philosophers, however, have argued phenomenologically, traced genealogically, and exposed rhetorically the marginalizing effects of realism and foundationalism. Their focus is on the moral effects of a totalized conceptual sameness, which relegated the difference of the other to the status of the neglected and the voiceless. They have pointed out that rational emancipation has led to ethical oppression and thereby moved the philosophical critique of Enlightenment beyond the confines of academic philosophy.[42]

Anti-foundationalism and postmodernism are not alone in providing critiques of the Enlightenment's rational autonomy. Combined elements of these two movements integrated into a program with a character all its own can be found in the work of feminist philosophers, especially those interested in epistemology as conceptualized in modernity.[43] Women's firsthand experience of having been marginalized as irrational beings has stimulated their tracing of links between the Enlightenment's failures and a patriarchal and phallogocentric spirit of rationality that goes all the way back to the Greek foundations of Western culture. Feminists emphasize how patriarchal reason not only denatured and devalued many functional sides of reality (such as subjectivity, emotion, and spirituality), but also sidelined people (such as women, servants, people of color, the poor, and people of different sexual orientation).

Genevieve Lloyd's *The Man of Reason* is one of many accounts of the prejudiced, white, male, privileged character of reason in the history of philosophy.[44] Andrea Neye's *Words of Power* works similarly, though in a more confined but also more damaging context, namely, the history of logic.[45] And Nancy Tuana's collection of essays in feminist philosophy of science from the feminist philosophy journal *Hypatia* convincingly portrays the damaging effects of male bias in the language of so-called rationally objective scientific controversies.[46] Though this epistemology-centered feminist discussion is strongly oriented to Anglo-American and Australian literature, it is not as ethically unaware as the largely male discussions of anti-foundationalism and anti-realism.[47] Here, too, however, there are differences from French feminist philosophy, such as that of Luce Irigaray or Julia Kristeva, who travel a more literary and psychoanalytical route, though their critique of a male and logocentric Enlightenment is as strong.

It seems fair to say that in our times anti-foundationalism, postmodernism, and feminism have the spiritual effect of demythologizing what has become one of the central myths of the secularity of the Enlightenment, namely, that in "rational man" humanity is emancipated from spirituality, because we no longer need to go beyond reason in our human journey. The combined critique of these three movements effectively means that philosophy itself has begun to pay attention to its own history in this respect and to acknowledge that it contains the anti-spiritual seeds of a misleading spirituality of ahistorical and neutral reason, rational autonomy, and rational emancipation. What does this all mean? If philosophy begins to pay attention to difference that cannot be contained within its traditional framework of universal sameness, does this mean that philosophy can remain autonomous?[48] Does it furthermore mean that if philosophy becomes open to spirituality, we can nevertheless continue to contain the spiritual in the rational? How different will philosophy be if it continues to expose itself to its anti-spiritual tendencies?[49] How will a conception of reason that gives it boundaries affect the rational enterprise internally? If what transcends reason cannot be contained within reason, can reason nevertheless be in touch with what transcends it? If so, how? If not, why not?[50] These are questions to which an open inquiry into the misleading outcome of the Enlightenment spirit of emancipation through rational autonomy should lead. I am inclined not simply to give up on reason altogether. At the same time, I am suspicious of continuing to allow reason, even with the freedom to be playful, to characterize all knowing. What way is open for me?

A PLACE FOR RATIONALITY

A return to spirituality perceived as a revolt against rationality would mislead us as much as the spiritualization of rational autonomy. It does not seem worth the effort to explore the history of rationality and its place in our future unless we can acknowledge from the beginning the reality and significance of what we know as reason: our capacity for inference, concept formation, theory construction, and the development of science and technology. How would we ever explain the centuries of veneration accorded reason in our culture unless we are prepared to acknowledge its potential promise? This is itself a spiritual issue, because it is an issue of where our attitude toward reason will take us in history. A choice, for example, between reason as a precious gift to be used with care and responsibility and reason as self-made tool of human autonomy is a choice between spiritual humility and spiritual arrogance, a choice between science as life-enhancing service and science as the road to supremacy and progress.

My initial approach is to regard reason, rationality, conceptual understanding, reasoning, thought, and science as aspects of *one kind* of knowing. Thus I do not regard "rational knowing" as a pleonastic expression. Knowledge comes to us in more and other valid and valuable forms than the form of rationality.[51] I will return to this. For now I want to devote a few words to an understanding of rational knowing that would, on the one hand, show it as worthy of respect, while on the other hand it would caution us not to overestimate it.

From the history of rational knowing in the West we can form a concept of reason as our capacity to reach a conceptual understanding of regularity and structure in reality which gives us a general grasp of things. The healthy contemporary exposure of the marginalizing effects of *reducing* things to their sameness or seeing their *essential* nature in their *now conceived* sameness—a metaphysics of presence— should not prejudice us against the undeniable reality of *some measure* of sameness, an order of sameness even, in things. Rationally knowing the world is a potentially valuable human project of constructing conceptual insights—subject to a logic of reasons—into sameness. That construction moves through imaginative, perceptive, disciplined observation of structures of regularity and sameness in our world to what we call concepts, insights, understandings, and theories. Within these constructs we can gain a grasp of things in general, which gives us a measure of power in dealing with reality. However, the concepts we thus construct are likely misconceived if we take them as accurate, objectively real reflections of an assumed actual, single, universal framework of properties shared by whatever "fits" our concept. Few, if any, of our concepts will likely "correspond" to real natures or essences "out there." That's fairly obvious when we think of a concept like "humanity." How likely is it that any of our current Western concepts truly "grasp" in their core reality any and all human beings that have ever lived? In the world of mathematics such grasping seems more likely. But even here the difficulty in finding agreement on logical definitions of mathematical primitives indicates that conceptual grasping is not likely to succeed in full and universal enclosure throughout time. The "world of order" which reason constructs is a helpful instrument, though not a "realistic" picture of an immutably universal order of nature itself. [52]

Though we may certainly assume that concepts of categories, for example, do give us a real grasp of real relations, we cannot ignore the fact that the imaginative as well as logical ordering of perceived patterns makes for a measure of idealization not matched by reality, as though our rational conceptual order is the same as the order of things. Concepts are not *true* in that "corresponding" sense. If they are true in our experience this can at most mean that with their help we have been able to make better adjustments to real relationships in our real experience. They help us to control disease, improve crops, spread wealth, and do many other wonderful things that could not have been done without them. Concepts give us a grasp of things with a wide enough scope to develop widely applicable methods and technologies of access. But they are not neutral; they do not just stare us in the face; they are not unavoidable.

It seems more likely that the order of our theories is not found as such in the world out there, but is rather the result of hard human work. In science, for example, we idealize regular patterns. But those idealizations are more likely shaped by our (often legitimate) desire for an increase of our own power or control over things we understand than by a disinterested view from a distance. If, as is now widely acknowledged, there is a point of view from which we perform our idealizations, it is not furnished by the things themselves.[53] The long history of science shows us that with our reason we did much evil and caused much grief in addition to the achieved gains. I have tried to point to some of the grief in the previous section. However, there can be no problem with also acknowledging rational knowledge as potentially salutary knowledge. It gives potentially beneficial powers to our culture, even though such power can be, has been, and is being abused. As Westerners we have come to depend on it. We can no longer do either without scientific reason or without its continued improvement. Hence we face a serious call to responsibility in knowing how to deploy our rational powers. The power is there. Foucault has emphasized this over and over. The power is not as such evil, nor is it automatically good. Only what we do with it in our spiritual journey determines the good and the evil.

A single or simple recipe for the good uses of reason is not only beyond the scope of this essay, but also not readily available. It seems clear, however, that what many Enlightenment faithful fear must, nevertheless, be done. I have in mind the relativization of reason. Alasdair MacIntyre has made it very clear that reason is historical and plural.[54] The history of the many concepts of reason and rationality and of their various influences makes the absolutization of reason as autonomous an unlikely story. But if that should lead us to a deconstruction of rational autonomy and to a perception of this as a relativization of reason, many traditional outlooks on philosophy induce a fear of such relativization.[55] The question is: why? Relativism need not in itself be bad, if we mean by it that relativizing reason acknowledges its historicity, plurality, mutability, and limits; that its "truths" are helpful conceptual constructs in a limited context. Given the widespread criticism of the Enlightenment's naïve optimism about a neutrally and objectively founded universal and autonomous reason without prejudice,[56] such relativism might be seen as an improvement over ahistorical, absolute, autonomous reason, especially when the earlier naïve optimism is also perceived as having been oppressive.[57]

An acknowledgment of relativism is not identical with subscription to a doctrine of arbitrary and individualistic subjectivism. The relativism I am talking about simply accepts that reason is subjective, historical, limited, and plural. That does not make reason arbitrary, but calls rational people to responsibility. However, many remain critical and skeptical about this relativization. [58]

It also seems clear that we must give up our rational stranglehold on the *limits* of knowledge and reality. By this I mean more than that reason must be relativized. For I now have in mind the release of many *different* kinds of knowing besides *rational* knowing, as well as the different kinds of reality to which such different knowing gives us relationships. In the final three sections, devoted to a brief development of this theme, I will begin by sketching a view of what I call knowing *other*-wise. Then I discuss the many faces of knowing. I will conclude with some remarks about that kind of knowing through which we gain access to the world's spirituality and can thus take responsibility for our own spiritual agency.

KNOWING *OTHER*-WISE

A plausibly traversible path into the area of multiple ways of knowing, possibly attractive to anti-foundationalists, feminists, and postmoderns alike, is the wide agreement that rational-conceptual knowing is a knowing of what is the same in things, a knowing of a general structure things share with other things of their kind. If that is so, would this mean that what is different in things that are in other respects same, what is unique in each, what is other about them, is an inscrutable mystery? If all our knowing is rational, and if rational knowledge knows sameness, how is difference known? Or, if we insist that difference is knowable, do we need to acknowledge the reality of knowing in a non-rational way? Suppose rational knowledge is the knowledge exclusively of thinking or reasoning, then what might Michael Polanyi mean by saying that we *know* more than we *think*? By this Polanyi meant to say not only that we cannot possibly *think* of *all* that we know, but also that some of what we do know is not *accessible* to thought, in the sense that concepts do not suffice to grasp it. We know it, but cannot think it. [59] Is there knowing beyond reasoning?

In considering this possibility of knowing that is not the same as rational knowing, I am conscious of the fact that I am working here within the domain of thought, of rational knowing. So I am speaking in general, or conceptually, of a knowing that may not be general or conceptual. In that way I would, in this context at least, not get beyond rational knowing. This is as such not entirely objectionable, insofar as such other knowing will also have dimensions of sameness. That's true of difference in general. When we conceptualize difference, we grasp what is the same in the different. Difference as a concept is not, in that sense, different. Yet I also wish to get beyond this conceptuality. I will try to achieve this with the use of examples that point beyond themselves. To clarify my view that all modes of human experience— not only reasoning, thinking, and conceptual understanding—lead to knowing, I will try to appeal to examples of such knowing, to our experience of knowing which we can recognize as different from ratio-nal knowing.[60] I want to appeal to our awareness that all modes of experience are revelatory. They give us their own entry into openings into which light may shine and meaning may penetrate, in which sounds may be heard that make us hear new meanings. All dimensions of experience may help us know truth not as simply (conceptual) re-presentation of or (semantic) co-respondence to reality as *it* presents *itself* to us, but, more richly, as the result of our call to embody what-ever guidance we receive concerning the directions that point to a way in which reality can flourish.

The crucial thing is that in order for us not just to know other*ness*, differ*ence*, alter*ity*, that is, for us not just to have *concepts* of what is uniquely and individually other, different, and alternative in *general*, and so for us to know an other as uniquely other, we must know that other with a knowledge which itself is other and fuller than just con-ceptual knowledge. The knowing must be other. The other we know in philosophy is a same (other). We must know the other otherwise, more fully than just conceptually, in order that in knowing this other we become wise in relation to that other, relate wisely to that other. This is what I am calling "knowing *other*-wise." The "other-wise" means both "differently" and "leading to *wisdom* through the *other*." The other can make me wise as *irreducible* even to others *of its own kind*, that is, in being otherwise than *only* a same; as irreducible to others different from itself; and above all as other than I can conceive and than I am as rational animal. The wisdom potentially derives from my becoming exposed to what lies beyond the rigid conceptual bound-aries of rational sameness in which I try to control things in my grasp and power. I am being opened up to relating to things on their own terms. I am taken out of the isolation of my rational self-reduction to becoming a self vulnerable in open relations.

Levinas has developed a rich image of a relating that flows from what happens in the ethical dynamics of meeting face to face. Even though his own Jewish prophetic literature unproblematically refers to the most intimate ways of relating as knowing, he himself does not do this, but continues the tradition of using "knowing" for rational-noetic cognition. But nothing prevents us from taking his insights and re-naming them with language faithful to Jewish prophetic literature. In deep, open, and intimate relations in which respect for the other and humility toward the self are restored, I am called to hear and see anew what I thought I already knew but did not. Re-cognition takes place. Levinas introduces intimacy in human relationships not as just a *source* of relating (knowing), but as an irreducible *way* of relating (knowing), *leading to* a unique "knowing" (as the prophets say) of what is itself to be respected as unique.[61] This leads to a knowing of other selves and to a self-knowledge which cannot be contained in words or concepts, but is possible only in a relating which surpasses language and understanding.

If this transition from discursive knowing to self-knowledge through being self in relation to others makes sense,[62] we may also appreciate the transition in knowing from discursive, rational, conceptual knowing to poetic knowing. It seems plausible that poetry gives us truth and knowledge not available to discursive conceptual knowing. If we were to translate into premise-like propositions and link syllogistically what the poet is doing poetically, the truth made known in the poem would be irrevocably lost. A similar knowledge-transformation takes place in novels, films, and songs. But in all of these examples I am still in the neighborhood of words and language. Can we also go beyond that to forms of knowing in the absence of words and concepts altogether? I believe we can. Music in all its forms helps us know what is not knowable in other ways. It makes differently knowable what in other ways remains unknown. Music helps us know fundamentally other-wise. "Songs without words" *say* much. They reveal what can only be made manifest "otherwise." So do many of our relationships to one another, our wordless touches, our silent looks, our sighs too deep for words. Those who have known long years of intimacy know a slight movement of the other's body in a way that transcends all discursive understanding.

Polany's tacit knowing is of this sort: it lies silently but revealingly

beyond our explicit focus in words and concepts.[63] It is a knowing that
is integrated into our bodies. We do not have (adequate) concepts of
what we tacitly know. But we do *know* what we so know. And the time-
honored distinction between knowing *that* and knowing *how* (conceptual knowing and instrumental/methodical knowing in doing) does not
go far enough to cover the difference, nor does adding knowing by
acquaintance. My bowels in their pain and my breast in its sobs tell
me I know things that in my head I have sealed off. The feeling touch
of a therapeutic friend can unlock this knowledge, without thereby
transforming it into adequate discourse.

There is not much literature in professional epistemology that lends
support to any notion of "knowing *other*-wise," although in both of
her epistemological studies Lorraine Code from time to time wonders
why we have allowed knowing numbers and things from an objectifying distance in our heads to stand as a model for all knowing. She suggests
that we would likely have a rather different view of knowing if it were
modeled on knowing friends in all the subtle dimensions of subjective
intimacy. It is not surprising, therefore, that one of the main characteristics of knowing that surfaces in her books as perhaps more crucial
than truth or objectivity is responsibility.[64] Responsibility hardly comes
into view, of course, in knowing syllogistic rules, periodic tables, or
the difference between waves and particles. But objectivity or rational-
conceptual truth seem to recede in the background when we consider
knowing friends. Can we tell which knowing is true knowing? Must it
be just one of these? Could it be both? Could they be integrated?

If we were to consider truth in knowing *other*-wise, knowing *other*-
wise needs to be recognized as a knowing that is spiritually open. In
fact, I would argue this for all knowing, conceptual knowing as well.
Conceptual knowing has become unreliable in our culture precisely
because in its development it has closed itself off from relating beyond
its grasp. Instead, we have learned to see the grasping as true in itself
and for its own sake. But knowledge worthy of the name places us into
a relationship with our world in its directionality, in its being taken up
into history, in its movement through time. If we are aware of this in
our knowing we will also be aware that knowing in spiritual openness
makes all our knowing a matter of responsibility. Recently the mail
brought me reports from the Salvation Army and from a metropolitan
food action agency in Toronto, Canada. The former is obviously a
religious agency, the latter is a secular one. The religious agency, not
known for its pro-gay agenda, nevertheless reported that in its World

Services program its single largest budget item was for a cause still largely associated with gay men by most Western religious people, namely, integrated AIDS prevention and treatment.[65] The secular agency recorded the following from a discussion of special diet needs for HIV-positive people: "The feedback on Elisabeth Escobar's talk on spirituality and food was wonderful. A lot of people living with HIV for a long time have developed a spiritual aspect. Preparing food with love is a way of showing people how much they mean to you; this idea really spoke to them."[66] The spiritual dimension of fruitful knowing is evident in both the secular and the religious reports. Both agencies knew *other*-wise than might be expected from general conceptual frameworks operative in their communities. The Salvation Army responsibly reached out where we might have expected a spirituality of closure. The secular agency opened itself up to spirituality when it considered all the dimensions of responsible approaches.

MANY MODES OF KNOWING

What I have thus far called different *kinds* of knowing could perhaps better be referred to as different *modes* or dimensions of knowing. This manner of speaking better preserves a sense of the integrality of knowing. My intent is to present knowing as multidimensional in all of its manifestations, though in any actual instance a specific dimension would set the tone. And given the many dimensions, many different kinds of knowing would be possible, though none would be one-dimensional. Integral knowledge is then present precisely where the intensification of one mode of knowing has not switched off the other modes. Feminist epistemologists often stress that in science as we know it, knowledge has become conceptually reductive and other modes of knowing besides its rational-conceptual dimensions have not been developed as being integral dimensions of science. They frequently point to the example of Barbara McClintock's study of corn, in which intimacy was an activated mode of her study, even though the construction of a theory was her focus.[67]

On this model, the knowledge of conceptual understanding should be conceived of not as pure rationality, but as knowing in which rationality provides the focus without the other dimensions being absent. Similarly, people who are getting to know each other as friends are developing a knowledge focused on the practice of intimacy, but they do not turn off their rational understanding. Examples can be multiplied. People who gather regularly in religious institutions focus their knowledge spiritually, and poets focus their knowledge on symbolic imagination. In religious institutions rational understanding remains present in religious doctrine, even though that doctrine is not pure logic and evidence, but reason following the lead of spiritual knowing. And the symbolic-imaginative dimension of knowing, which dominates in poetic knowing, is found in rituals and songs in religious institutions, be it designed to spiritually lead people to a vision of their hope.

Before I develop a little more the notion of knowing focused in spirituality, I will first touch on the multidimensionality of knowing as present in rational understanding. Examples of trying to reduce rational knowing to pure rationality are Descartes' cogito, Kant's transcendental logical ego, and the verification principle of logical positivism. A significant modern countermove against this logical purification of knowledge is found in Michael Polanyi's *Personal Knowledge*, one among the few existing epistemological accounts of what I call knowing *other*-wise. Polanyi elaborately tried to show the multidimensionality of even the most abstract scientific knowledge. Logical precision and rigor, he argued, are possible only in a setting that is imprecise and loose.[68] No knowledge is possible except as the knowledge of persons, whose whole personhood is present in their knowing in all of its dimensions.[69] Traces of knowing other than rational knowing are undeniably present in rational knowing in Polanyi's analysis. A similar theme can be found in Mary Hesse's theory of the metaphorical character of scientific concepts and in Herman Dooyeweerd's theory of the analogical structure of all concept-formation.[70]

In this context special mention needs to be made of the impressive research of George Lakoff and Mark Johnson, who argue that body-based imagination lies at the root of all concept-formation.[71] Hence the title of Johnson's *The Body in the Mind*. They marshall a vast body of evidence and argument to show that our concepts and categories are idealizations and approximations heavily dependent on factors beyond pure logic or reason. Reason itself is inconceivable except as "impure" in their view.

This presence of other modes of knowing within rationally focused knowing points to a need to develop, respect, and integrate these other modes of knowing even for the sake of a healthy rational understanding. For this to occur, rational understanding needs to be in touch with knowing in which these other modes are in focus and where rational understanding is subsidiary or tacit. Rational understanding cannot purify itself as pure reason, it cannot swallow up other knowing, and it cannot in the long run deny other knowing as real knowing. It can, however, take its own relative place in the integration of all knowing and acknowledge and accept knowing other-wise. In philosophy this could take the form, for example, of developing ontologies in which the world is not encompassed by, contained within, or grounded on rational categorial structures. Such structural ontologies of order are primarily projections of what becomes visible of reality in a predominantly rational approach. But in other knowledges reality appears (validly and truly) otherwise. We can also entertain "grand" stories in which reality is taken seriously as opened up by hope, or in which the future is conceived as more assured when supported by love,[72] or in which evil is approached by reconciliation and forgiveness rather than by attempts at rationally explaining it. Reason would, that is, not create the universe out of its own logical resources, but would accept the world's own fabric as both other and same, as both beckoning and present. The universe of reason would then not be the totality of all that is real, constructed by extending present reasoning, but one way of knowing reality next to many other valid ways. And the universe of reason would be constructed in openness to these otherwise known worlds.

Before I ask what the restoration of spiritual knowing would look like, and how rational knowing would be in touch with it, I wish to remove one misunderstanding. Spiritual knowing is not primarily a matter of religious beliefs or systems of doctrine. The history of how this misunderstanding grew is long and complex, but it is clear that the adaptation of Christianity to the rational climate of Hellenic culture played a major role. The formation of the Christian church was characteristically the labor not of politicians, merchants, artists, or even prophets, but of thinkers. The church fathers were people who set the tone for the development of Western spirituality with philosophy as a model. They were aware of how the authority of reason in the West was at odds with the authority of spiritual traditions from the start. At least as early as John Scotus Eriugena the clash in authority between faith and reason *within* Christian thought surfaces in the literature.[73] By defending their tradition rationally in order to make it respectable in their climate, they shaped a religion of beliefs and doctrines. This development adds to the paradoxical character of reason adopting a spiritual stance against spirituality. The misleading character of reason philosophically developed as the source of all knowledge was further complicated in the church by the parallel paradoxical development of faith as belief, that is, as a form of reason, as assent to propositional understanding. The naturalistic view that science is no more than the perfection of ordinary knowing finds its ecclesiastical counterpart in the view that theology is the sophistication of ordinary faith. Wilfred Cantwell Smith's *Faith and Belief* remains a classic analysis of this process.[74]

THE KNOWLEDGE OF SPIRITUALITY OR KNOWING SPIRITUALLY

Spiritual knowing or knowing spiritually is more authentically approached as knowing focused in hope and trust. Knowing what direction to take in a universe surrounded by mystery, knowing which guidance to accept in the face of life's existential boundary conditions, is not a matter of faith *rather* than knowledge, but a matter of fiduciary knowing rather than rational knowing, even though a rational dimension is not absent.[75] The Enlightenment's adoption of autonomous reason as the road to emancipation was not a choice *against* faith or the authority of revealed religion, but a *religious* choice *for* faith in reason.[76] That much was clear to Karl Popper.[77] Kant's idea of Enlightenment included putting religion within rational boundaries. But neither he nor his followers were aware of the ideological depth of the commitment they were making to autonomous rationality, or of the a-rational trust required to overlook the fact that the idea of a rational foundation for reason was a rationally incoherent notion. Hence the Enlightment's titanic struggle with reason as spirit, that is, with the closure of conceptual control as the openness to mystery.

Knowledge focused rationally and conceptually is inadequate in the face of ultimates, because conceptual understanding *con*-ceives, grasps encompassingly, seeks to enclose. Reason seeks to grasp by conceptual enclosure. Spiritual knowing, however, seeks to embrace an open vision of hope in embodied trust, without domination or totalization. In an embrace we are intimately close and have a "hold" on the other we embrace. But the "hold" receives much of its meaning from our own "letting go" in the embrace and from our letting the other *be other* in it. It is a hold not just by one of the other, but a hold of one another, of *each other*. The hold of an embrace remains open, developing, on the move. It is not a grand narrative in which the universe is comprised, grasped, or enclosed in one hand. It is unfinished. In living hope or lived trust we come to know our future, our comfort, our neighbor in ways that give shape to communal traditions in narratives which direct, edify, and comfort us by keeping us open to a future with hope, by putting us in touch with a past and its wisdom of how to live with the experience of good and evil, life and death, origin and destiny. In those narratives we preserve and nurture our trust in spiritual powers that we remember as hopeful and foster our distrust of spirits that mislead us.

Spiritual knowing thus needs to be restored as knowing focused in faith as trust, in which "belief" is a metaphorical or analogical form of rationality within spirituality. In spiritual knowing, belief is subsidiary to the focus on trust. Belief here loses its grasp character and attains a sense of provisional approach in confessional articulation. If within faith we speak of matters such as God's right hand, we are not articulating beliefs in the originally rational-conceptual sense of the word, but using metaphors to express our trust. All faith-talk is in that way metaphorical. It breaks through the limits of given language to remain open to saying what lies beyond being said. It does not lend itself to closed logical-conceptual relationships. God-as-father is an image of a certain time. No conclusion as to essential divine maleness is possible here. Attuned hearing of that language allows translation into God-as-mother in our time.

To take beliefs of faith in a rational-conceptual way makes them offensively irrational. Both fundamentalism and naturalistic atheism make this mistake. They define spiritual language as straightforwardly propositional and thereby render it incomprehensible. They also miss the character of religious faith as giving us an anchor to *hold on* to and instead see it as a belief system within our intellectual *grasp*. The difference between them is that the fundamentalist defends the faith as rationally respectable, whereas the atheist rejects it as irrational. But spiritual knowing manifest in faith that is trust should not be defended as rational nor rejected as irrational, but be acknowledged as knowing with a different focus from conceptual understanding. What is called "belief" in the context of such spiritual knowing is an imaginative articulation of how trusted forces speak to us as they guide us. Spiritual knowing has its own inner coherence. But that coherence is not one of evidential logic. It is the coherence of lives lived in communities that have been inspired by the narrative traditions through which the trust of faith has been passed on to them. In faith, these narrative traditions make sense. But a rational defense of them apart from the trust they inspire misses their own character.

Properly speaking, beliefs are propositions we have *accepted* as true. Such acceptance, even within the realm of rational understanding, is itself more than rational-conceptual. To conceptually grasp a proposition and to accept it are two different moves within rational understanding. In what we call the acceptance of a proposition, called believing a proposition, we see the evidence of the reach of understanding beyond rational conception. Understanding is rational knowing, that is, is knowing in which the focus is rational. But that knowing also has dimensions besides its rational focus. If our rationally focused knowing did not have a dimension of trust-knowledge to it, we would never be able to *accept* propositions, but only to understand them in the sense of seeing the elements of the proposition as a good rational fit, as logically coherent. *Believing* the proposition, however, takes us beyond that.

As I said earlier, in coming to understand that the verification principle itself cannot be verified rationally, we can see an acknowledgment of our inability to close off rational knowing within merely rational-conceptual or logical bounds, of our inability to have reason provide knowledge from within rationality. In that rejection the Enlightenment's faith in reason was undermined, because it became apparent that even within rational understanding the need became visible for transcending rationality in order to be fully rational. The verification principle was the expression, in faith-language, of a trust and a hope in reason that itself turned out to be rationally incoherent and for that reason undermined the trust it tried to ground.

So what does spiritual knowing amount to in relation to rational knowing? On my account in this paper, our ability to know in trust, to be in touch with what transcends our control, to live in hope creates possibilities for radical openness in rational knowing that is in touch with these other dimensions. Critical theory requires open theory. Open theory requires openings within reason for an awareness of dimensions that transcend rationality, both in the rationally understood and in the rational understanding. French postmodern thought has introduced the term "trace" to name the presence of the transrational within our conceptual awareness. The "proof" for the reliability of knowing these traces does not lie in reasoned argument, but in the fruits of embodying this knowledge in lives that incorporate the hopes inspired by this knowledge.[78] In the final analysis every scientific theory contains an element of trust insofar as it depends on conceptual *belief*. And belief in science means acceptance of conceived realities with less than the rational warranty of verification. Some trust cannot be absent. Thus, even science can in the long run prove itself only in the way it enhances life. When science dictates truth because the scientist is the expert whose knowledge of the truth others must trust, science is turned into religion and the scientist is turned priest.

Philosophy can provide a real service here. If philosophy is practiced as providing the theoretical integration of the largest frameworks of rational-conceptual knowing of which we are capable, then philosophy provides the space par excellence for openness in our rational understanding to what lies beyond reason. For in philosophy we can then stretch our conceptual understanding in the realization that rationality is only the focus, not the whole, of our rational knowing. In philosophy we can make ourselves rationally aware of the other dimensions of rational knowing. In philosophy reason can become open to knowing *other*-wise, can engender trust in what lies beyond reason itself.

NOTES

1. See Charles Taylor, *Sources of the Self: The Making of the Modern Identity* (Cambridge, Mass.: Harvard University Press, 1989).

2. See ibid., p. 3 (emphasis added).

3. See ibid., pp. 520–21 (emphasis added).

4. See ibid., p. 4.

5. Though Richard Rorty's philosophical background is in the analytic tradition, which owes much of its inspiration to the naturalism of W. V. O. Quine, his publications since *Philosophy and the Mirror of Nature* (Princeton: Princeton University Press, 1979) have been much more at ease with spirituality. It is an explicitly discussed theme in that book, for example, in the closing section of chapter 7. On the other hand I have seen a referee's report which evaluated the submission of a paper on this topic recently as "intellectually reprehensible."

6. Taylor, *Sources of the Self*, p. 4, suggests that there has to be an element of the subject-transcending, beyond-our-control character even of this spirituality. He refers to standards which "stand independent of" our own subjectivity.

7. The existential *boundary* situation does not lie at the *periphery* of our lives; it is not superficial. Rather, it is a core issue at the ground and center of

who we are. Its boundary-character has to do with its transcending the boundaries of our thinking. This theme is first masterfully developed by Karl Jaspers.
See for example his 1947 Basel lectures, *Der philosophische Glaube* (Frankfurt: Fischer, 1958) and his later and larger *Der philosophische Glaube ange-
sichts der Offenbarung* (Munich: Piper, 1962).

8. Not only human reality, but all reality whatsoever. Its interconnectedness is dramatically brought to light by chaos theory. If our awareness of this
interconnectedness is itself a factor in this interconnectedness, then our dealing with this interconnectedness in relation to the boundary issues places
every interconnected element in relation to spirituality. In this way all of
reality can potentially participate in spiritual disclosure.

9. This is not the place to make extensive comments on human beings
as selves. A few brief comments, however, may be helpful. I take selfhood as
a designation of the whole person, not as something in a person which one
has in addition to whatever else a person may be. Persons as selves are, to
some degree, persons who are centered-and-grounded-in-relation. This I take
to mean that our being centered is at the same time an ex-centric relation,
i.e., takes its meaning in part from a relationship to what is not-self, at least
not-my-self, such as others, the world, and our origin/destiny.

10. I do not, of course, own English vocabulary. I only indicate here what
I intend some words I use to mean or not to mean. Someone might, for
example, use "ghost" to disapprovingly name what I would call a spirit.

11. See Hendrik Hart, *Understanding Our World* (Lanham, Md.: University Press of America, 1984), pp. 276–80.

12. Kant's three *Critiques* and his *What Is Enlightenment?* are related
projects.

13. Tradition, viewed as embodiment of a culture's or a community's way
to give body and continuity to its spirit, is rightly sensed as exercising spiritual authority.

14. Certainly by the time of John Scotus Eriugena the sense of a conflict
in authority between faith and reason becomes explicit in the literature.

15. Although resistance to religion and spirituality is present before Hegel,
and interest in them continues beyond Comte, between these two thinkers
there is a marked change in the spiritual tendency of philosophy to resist
spirituality. Comte's theory of three stages inspires a mood of having left spirituality behind in an age of positive philosophy. In this volume see James
Olthuis's "Crossing the Threshold: Sojourning Together in the Wild Spaces
of Love."

16. For philosophy as superjudge (called Philosophy by Rorty), see the
"Introduction" to *Philosophy and the Mirror of Nature*.

17. See *Immanuel Kant's Critique of Pure Reason*, trans. Norman Kemp
Smith (London: Macmillan, 1956), p. 9.

18. The designation of theoretical reason as pure did not so much imply
the impurity of practical reason as the incompleteness of reason as theoretical.

19. See in Immanuel Kant, *Werke*, 7 (Darmstadt: Wissenschaftliche Buchgesellschaft, 1968).

20. Alfred Julius Ayer, *Language, Truth and Logic* (New York: Dover, n.d).

21. Rational openness cannot, of course, be absolute openness, because it is bound by the limits of reason.

22. This doctrine would be found, for example, in the work of the Vienna Circle, in positivism, and in forms of naturalism.

23. See Herbert Spencer, *First Principles* (London: Watts, 1937), pp. 14–16.

24. This is a central theme in Hans-Georg Gadamer's *Reason in the Age of Science* (Cambridge, Mass.: MIT Press, 1981).

25. See, for example, Paul Kurtz's assertion that "naturalism is committed to science" and his claim that for such a naturalism it is dubious that there would be realities "over and beyond man's capacity to experience or understand" (in *Philosophical Essays in Pragmatic Naturalism* [Buffalo: Prometheus Books, 1990], p. 14).

26. See Spencer, *First Principles*, pp. 16–17.

27. See Stephen W. Hawking, *A Brief History of Time* (New York: Bantam Books, 1988), p. 175.

28. Charles Taylor's extensive discussion of this (in 19.1–19.2, pp. 321–47) explores a theme running throughout his book, namely, that rationalistic naturalism has an inescapable blindspot in its self-reflection, which makes naturalism blind to the depth of self present in such reflection. See also pp. 401–406.

29. Key figures in the rise of anti-foundationalism were Sir Karl Popper, Imre Lakatos, and Alan Musgrave, around whom a body of literature about the "growth of scientific knowledge" gained considerable prominence in the 1970s.

30. Taylor in this context helpfully uses the expression "self-responsible" reason. He sees it originating in Locke (see chapter 9).

31. "Transcendence" and its cognates have a feeling of being politically incorrect in naturalistic traditions in philosophy. But the meaning of these is first of all simply that of "being more than," "going beyond." What transcends reason is not necessarily and automatically the same as religious transcendence of the experienceable universe. Jürgen Habermas's adoption of transcendental conditions of reason does not, for example, have such religious overtones.

32. Taylor would refer to it as inarticulate, Polanyi as tacit.

33. See Hans-Georg Gadamer, *Truth and Method* (New York: Crossroad, 1984), p. 240.

34. For Rorty and Taylor see above. Alasdair MacIntyre, *Whose Justice? Whose Rationality?* (Notre Dame, Ind.: University of Notre Dame Press, 1988).

35. See Richard Rorty, *Objectivity, Relativism, and Truth* (Cambridge: Cambridge University Press, 1991), pp. 14 and 33.

36. Abstracts for these addresses are printed in *Proceedings and Addresses of the American Philosophical Association*, 68, 1 (September 1994), 75–77.

37. Examples of such technical-philosophical discussions are found in the work of Donald Davidson and Hilary Putnam. Richard Rorty's contributions are much more far-ranging.

38. I am for the moment leaving undiscussed the influence of W. V. O. Quine, which also does much to account for the limited nature of the discussion. A helpful brief account of his influence as well as discussions with those he influenced can be found in Giovanna Borradori, *The American Philosopher: Conversations with Quine, Davidson, Putnam, Nozick, Danto, Rorty, Cavell, MacIntyre, and Kuhn* (Chicago: University of Chicago Press, 1994).

39. See Karl R. Popper, *Conjectures and Refutations: The Growth of Scientific Knowledge* (New York: Harper and Row, 1963) and Thomas S. Kuhn, *The Structure of Scientific Revolutions* (Chicago: University of Chicago Press, 1962).

40. In the opening words of his address to a plenary session of the 1988 World Congress of Philosophy in Brighton, England.

41. See Kuhn, pp. 152, 157ff.

42. Among Anglo-American philosophers Richard Rorty also exposes the oppressive features of the Enlightenment.

43. Philosophy as epistemology, reasoning about the transcendental limits of rational knowing. A feminist epistemologist like Code questions this epistemology-centered philosophy and therefore is ambivalent about a project of feminist epistemology. See Lorraine Code, *What Can She Know? Feminist Theory and the Construction of Knowledge* (Ithaca, N.Y.: Cornell University Press, 1991), the last chapter, "A Feminist Epistemology?" pp. 314ff. Later in this paper I will deal with knowing beyond the bounds of reason.

44. See Genevieve Lloyd, *The Man of Reason: "Male" and "Female" in Western Philosophy* (Minneapolis: University of Minnesota Press, 1984).

45. See Andrea Neye, *Words of Power, A Feminist Reading of the History of Logic* (New York: Routledge, 1990). That even an abstract discipline like logic can be shown not to have been objective and neutral is damaging indeed.

46. See Nancy Tuana, *Feminism and Science* (Bloomington: Indiana University Press, 1989). Especially noteworthy is the essay dealing with the misinformation caused in cell biology by aggressive male-biased language for the articulation of the relation between ovum and sperm (pp. 172–87).

47. Code, for example, integrates her epistemological discussions fully with discussions about the relation of knowing to the larger dimensions of human life.

48. What, for example, are we to make of Levinas's granting the "last

word" to philosophy? See the end of the first chapter of the interview with Philippe Nemo dealing with the relation between philosophy and the Bible, *Ethique et Infini* (Paris: Librarie Arthème Fayard and Radio France, 1982).

49. For example, what will be the "status" in academic philosophy of Richard Rorty, Jacques Derrida, and Michel Foucault?

50. What does it mean, for example, that John Caputo (in *Radical Hermeneutics: Repetition, Deconstruction and the Hermeneutic Project* [Bloomington: Indiana University Press, 1987], chapter 8) chooses for not going beyond reason in knowing, as he sees Heidegger doing, but for expanding and liberating reason? See pp. 222–28 and 234.

51. From a narrowly semantic point of view it would be possible to use "knowing" as referring exclusively to specifically rational-conceptual understanding. The fact alone, however, that science, being the professional and methodical extension of rational-conceptual knowing, would then become knowledge par excellence and the scientist our knowledge expert, is enough to persuade me to stick to more encompassing meanings of "knowing."

52. See Hendrik Hart, "Creation Order in Our Philosophical Tradition: Critique and Refinement," in *An Ethos of Compassion and the Integrity of Creation*, ed. Hendrik Hart, Robert S. VanderVennen, Brian Walsh (Lanham, Md.: University Press of America, 1995).

53. See George Lakoff, *Of Women, Fire, and Dangerous Things: What Categories Reveal About the Mind* (Chicago: University of Chicago Press, 1987) and Barrie Allen, *Truth in Philosophy* (Cambridge, Mass.: Harvard University Press, 1993).

54. See the opening chapter of Alasdair MacIntyre's *Whose Justice? Whose Rationality?*

55. See *Rationality and Relativism*, ed. Martin Hollis and Steven Lukes (Cambridge, Mass.: MIT Press, 1982) and Joseph Margolis, *The Truth About Relativism* (Oxford: Blackwell, 1991).

56. An instructive discussion of this issue has been carried on over a number of years by Jürgen Habermas and Hans-Georg Gadamer.

57. It is seen this way, for example, by Richard Rorty and Lorraine Code.

58. Richard Rorty's denials notwithstanding, even Joseph Margolis, who calls himself a relativist, continues to see danger in Rorty's "arbitrary" (because not "logically" tight) relativism.

59. See Michael Polyani, *Personal Knowledge: Towards a Post-Critical Philosophy* (New York: Harper and Row, 1958). Also see John Dewey, *How We Think* (Boston: Heath, 1933).

60. Please recall that I am using "rational" in a narrow sense: conceptual, logical, inferential, propositional knowing is what I have in view, as well as a focus on order, structure, generality, and regularity.

61. E.g., Hosea. In the Old Testament in general, there is a close conection between knowing and loving. To know is, for example, used for sexual intercourse.

62. For a more extensive discussion see Hendrik Hart, "Self As Question: A Response to Gerrit Glas," in *Christian Philosophy at the Close of the Twentieth Century: Assessment and Perspective*, ed. *Sander Griffioen and Bert Balk (Kampen: Kok, 1995), pp. 79–84.*

63. *See Michael Polanyi, "Tacit Knowing," in The Tacit Dimension* (Garden City, N.Y.: Doubleday, 1966), pp. 3–25.

64. See Lorraine Code, *Epistemic Responsibility* (Hanover, N.H.: University Press of New England, 1987).

65. See the pamphlet *Reach Out and Touch Someone . . . Today* (Toronto: The Salvation Army, Summer 1995).

66. See Phyllis Benson, "Dialogue: Eating Positively With HIV," in *Foodshare's Food Action* (Fall 1995), 3.

67. See the index of books such as Code's *Epistemic Responsibility* and *What Can She Know?*, Tuana's *Feminism and Science*, and Sandra Harding, *The Science Question in Feminism* (Ithaca, N.Y.: Cornell University Press, 1987).

68. See *Personal Knowledge*, pp. 249–68.

69. See ibid., pp. 195–202.

70. See Mary Hesse, *Models and Analogies in Science* (Notre Dame, Ind.: University of Notre Dame Press, 1966) and Herman Dooyeweerd, A *New Critique of Theoretical Thought* (Amsterdam and Philadelphia: H. J. Paris and The Presbyterian and Reformed Publishing Company, 4 vols., 1953–1958). Dooyeweerd develops an elaborate theory of the impossibility of any kind of experience without its being integrally interwoven with all other kinds. Our experience of reasoning, for example, depends on our experience of space (conceptual extension), motion (progress of an argument), feeling (perception), and so on.

71. Besides Lakoff's *Women, Fire, and Dangerous Things* also see Mark Johnson, *The Body in the Mind: The Bodily Basis of Meaning, Imagination and Reason* (Chicago: University of Chicago Press, 1987) and their jointly authored *Metaphors We Live By* (Chicago: University of Chicago Press, 1980).

72. See the closing essay by James Olthuis in this volume.

73. Such a clash had earlier, of course, been signalled between Greek and Christian thought, between Athens and Jerusalem, already alluded to in the writings of St. Paul.

74. See Wilfred Cantwell Smith, *Faith and Belief* (Princeton: Princeton University Press, 1979).

75. If all genuine knowing were purely rational-logical-conceptual, fears of fideism would be well grounded. But if no knowing is possible without a fiduciary dimension, as Polanyi argues (*Personal Knowledge*, pp. 264–68), the fear is only an *irrational* expression of a *commitment* to reason.

76. I use "religious" here as indicating the inescapable human condition

of having to live out of a pervasive and inclusive orientation which requires spiritual commitment. This usage makes it possible to recognize that the Enlightenment's revolt against the authority of tradition and religion was a revolt against strictures on being human which thwarted its infatuation with autonomous freedom. This use of "religious" is consonant with Taylor's notion of the moral and the spiritual and with Rorty's concept of final vocabularies. (See the opening paragraphs of "Private Irony and Liberal Hope" in *Contingency, Irony, and Solidarity* (Cambridge: Cambridge University Press, 1989), p. 73. See also Hendrik Hart, "Faith as Trust and Belief as Intellectual Credulity: A Response to William Sweet," in *Philosophy and Theology*, 8, 3, 251–56.)

77. The opening words of his address to a plenary session of the 1988 World Congress of Philosophy in Brighton, England were: "I want to begin with my confession of faith."

78. Our solidarity with all members of the human race requires us to know our own humanity in a way that cannot exclude some provisional concept of what it is to be human. But it also includes our awareness that the concept cannot possibly grasp all that ever was or will be human. The continuity and inclusiveness we require in our knowing ourselves to be human makes for a connection with all other members of the human community. But this can never take the form of having a concept of a constant universal.

2

Points of Convergence Between Dooyeweerdian and Feminist Views of the Philosophic Self

Janet Catherina Wesselius

RECENTLY IN NORTH AMERICAN PHILOSOPHY, there has been a growing number of challenges to the traditional, Kantian concept of the self, otherwise known as the transcendental logical ego.[1] Many of the challenges come from feminist philosophers who attempt to transform traditional philosophy by proposing a more complex view of self than that offered by traditional philosophy.[2] Feminist philosophy is a recent phenomenon in the history of philosophy, arising as it does out of the contemporary feminist movement.[3] But fifty-five years ago the Christian philosopher Herman Dooyeweerd, working in the continental tradition of philosophy, was already advocating a view of the self that is remarkably similar to the contemporary feminist view in its emphasis on integration.[4] His critique of the transcendental logical ego is rooted in his Christian conviction that philosophy is influenced by religious commitments, whereas many feminist critiques are rooted in the realization that the traditional concept of self is unable to account for the experiences of women.

Dooyeweerd asserts that "philosophical thinking is an actual activity; and only at the expense of this very actuality (and then merely in a theoretic concept) can it be abstracted from the thinking self."[5] Many feminist philosophers also argue that people do philosophy only as aggregate and complex beings. For example, Lorraine Code also asserts that "it is persons who know—not abstracted, isolated intellects, understandings, imaginations, or faculties of reason."[6] Without claiming that Dooyeweerd was a feminist, I argue here that his Christian goal of replacing the transcendental logical ego with the multi-faceted person in philosophic thinking finds resonance in the concerns of many feminists.[7]

I shall examine how feminist and Dooyeweerdian views of the self converge in the insistence that only empirical humans do philosophy. Specifically, I think that Dooyeweerd's argument provides theoretical reasons for rejecting the transcendental logical ego, whereas feminist arguments for new ways of viewing selfhood can concretely unfold the implications of Dooyeweerd's emphasis for integral human being. I shall first examine the traditional concept of self, namely, the transcendental logical ego. In this opening section I shall primarily refer to Kant's concept of a transcendental logical ego because it is against this Kantian conception, which has had so much influence on contemporary philosophic views of the self, that Dooyeweerd, for the most part, argues. Second, I shall discuss feminist arguments against the transcendental logical ego and the new views of self that they oppose to the traditional view. Third, I shall discuss Dooyeweerd's argument against the transcendental logical ego. I shall then explore the convergent implications of Dooyeweerdian and feminist views of the philosophic self.

Kant's Transcendental Logical Ego

The transcendental logical ego is a consequence of Kant's answer to what he sees as the basic question of all epistemology: "What are the necessary conditions for any knowledge whatsoever?" Kant believes that the philosopher cannot start with his particular experience, since experience is contingent and personal and thus will not satisfy the requirement that it provide the conditions of all knowledge whatsoever. Hence, Kant maintains that it is necessary to look away from experience and gaze inward at the thinking self in order to discover its structure.

Kant is looking for an a priori answer to his question because (according to him) only a priori conditions can be necessarily and universally valid.[8] If empirical reality reflects the structure of the mind, and if the structure of the mind is a priori, then empirical reality can be known with complete certainty. In order to discover that which is a priori, we must eliminate all that is empirically based in our thought.[9] When we analyze our activity of thinking, we can distinguish between that which is non-logical (and thus contingent and variable) and that which is purely logical (and thus necessary and universal). Since it is the self *as it thinks* that Kant is examining, it is necessary for him to eliminate all that is non-logical. In addition to abstracting all that is

not rational from a particular self, we must, according to Kant, methodically eliminate all that is individual and unique about a particular
subject in order to arrive at the a priori conditions for knowledge. The
residue of this methodic elimination is the transcendental logical ego,
that is, pure thought.[10] This ego is a transcendental prerequisite for
knowledge because all knowledge is necessarily related to a unified 'I'
which thinks.

By eliminating non-logical aspects and particularities from his
thought, Kant believes that he can get at the a priori structure of his
mind. But the transcendental logical ego is not merely the structure
particular to Kant's mind; it is the necessary structure of all human
minds. No experience is possible without it. Although every thinker's
self has the logical structure of the transcendental logical ego, this ego
cannot be found anywhere *in* empirical reality, since it is the external
condition *for* any empirical experience.[11] We cannot gain any self-
knowledge from a Kantian ego since this ego can never be an object
of human thought; it is always presupposed by any human thought.
According to Kant, pure reason discovers that the transcendental logical ego is a necessary presupposition for all experience whatsoever.
The transcendental logical ego is the bare minimum necessary for
knowledge; it is the consistent factor in all theoretical investigations.
The time and place of the thinker change, the personal experiences of
the thinker change, and the thinker himself changes, but the transcendental logical ego remains the same for all thinkers everywhere at all
times. Consequently, every human who does philosophy will inevitably think in the same manner, since the transcendental logical ego
is universal.

Kant's methodic elimination has a further implication. He thinks
he has eliminated his particular self in his self-reflection. But if his self
is no longer present in his thought, who is doing this thinking? He is
able to limit self-reflection to logical self-reflection only by identifying
his *entire* self with the logical structure of his mind. Thus, he believes
that it is this product of methodic elimination—that is, the transcendental logical ego—that thinks and does philosophy, because it alone
is pure thought.

The transcendental logical ego transcends empirical reality by being
the most basic condition for any possible act of thinking. As an a priori
structure of the self, it also transcends gender, since gender is an empirical aspect of empirical individuals. An ego that is a priori and has
no gender is also impartial because it has no commitments or interests

of any kind. In turn, this means that an a priori, genderless, impartial self is also universal since it is necessarily valid for all thinkers. If the transcendental logical ego is a priori, genderless, impartial and universal, then it is also autonomous because it is not conditioned or determined by anything outside itself—on the contrary, it determines the conditions for all knowledge.

FEMINIST CRITIQUES

Despite the fact that a Kantian view of the purely logical self has no empirical existence, it continues to function as a philosophic ideal.[12] Many feminist philosophers argue that such a self is too abstract to deal with the reality of human life. Moreover, many of their criticisms stem from a growing awareness that women as a group have been excluded from the tradition of philosophy simply because they are women.[13] As a universal ideal of pure reason, the transcendental logical ego should transcend gender, since gender is a contingent attribute of particular and embodied individuals.[14] Genevieve Lloyd asserts that gender is one of the things which truly rational thought purports to transcend: "[T]he aspiration to a Reason common to all, transcending the contingent historical circumstances which differentiate minds from one another, lies at the very heart of our philosophical heritage."[15] Theoretically, then, women should fare just as well as men in the realm of philosophy, but experientially this has not been the case. The tradition of philosophy has been dominated by men and the few women who are philosophers are philosophers "despite, rather than because of, their femaleness."[16] As Lloyd asserts, "the obstacles to female cultivation of Reason spring to a large extent from the fact that our ideals of Reason have historically incorporated an exclusion of the feminine."[17] Lloyd cogently argues that in traditional, philosophic dichotomies, reason has been associated with maleness and thus valorized, whereas the non-rational has been associated with femaleness and thus devalued. The transcendental logical ego, as an ideal of reason, was considered to be gender-neutral. However, if Lloyd and other feminist philosophers are right, this ego is definitely masculine.[18] Since this purportedly genderless ideal excludes one particular gender, it cannot live up to its own claim to be genderless. Whatever else a philosophic self may be able to do, it cannot transcend gender. Hence, to the asexuality of the transcendental logical ego, feminists oppose a self that is always gendered.[19]

If it is true that a transcendental logical ego is a masculine ideal of reason that excludes the feminine, then it follows that it is not impartial, and hence not universal in the sense of being valid for all thinkers. What has been claimed to be a neutral and universal standpoint as seen or constructed in the transcendental logical ego is not a standpoint that women can unproblematically adopt insofar as they are women. Since many female philosophers find that they are excluded by this putatively impartial and universal standpoint, they are continually forced either to question its impartiality and universality or to repudiate their own experiences as women. The transcendental logical ego is supposed to be impartial, but it excludes women; it is supposed to be universal, but it cannot explain the experiences of women. Whatever else a philosophic self may be, it is not impartial and universal. Hence, to the impartiality and universality of the transcendental logical ego, feminist philosophers oppose a situated and particular model of self.[20]

The transcendental logical ego is never based in empirical reality, since it is Kant's ideal to transcend the contingencies of experience, thereby rendering universal knowledge. However, feminists argue that such an a priori notion is unable to account for many women's (and indeed many men's) experience, and as such, it is of little use for philosophic theory.[21] The editors of *Feminist Perspectives* argue that feminist philosophers base their theories on actual humans: "broadly speaking, this [feminist] perspective is based in the *experiences* of feeling, thinking, temporally located human beings. . . . Such an emphasis resists attempts to superimpose theory upon experience. It rejects claims to the effect that theory must transcend experience."[22] Philosophic theories should grow out of, rather than transcend, human experience. In contrast to the a priori character of the transcendental logical ego, feminist philosophers oppose an empirical, experientially based model of self.[23]

The transcendental logical ego is autonomous since pure reason discovers that it alone is a *necessary* presupposition for all knowledge. Once again, feminists charge that the theory of the autonomous self is far too abstract to adequately explain human life and that it in fact contradicts much of human experience. Our experience teaches us that we are never wholly autonomous in any area of our lives and that our intellectual lives are no exception. This interdependence is not to be lamented since mutuality is a large part of being human and it does not exclude choice and responsibility for individuals. As Code pointedly remarks, "philosophical interpretations of the value of autonomy have often tended to result in an autonomy-obsession which serves no one's purposes well."[24] An over-emphasis on autonomy is harmful because humans are not essentially autonomous creatures and any attempt to be autonomous is going to result in less humanness rather than more. To the autonomous transcendental logical ego, feminists oppose a model of self that is connected to other knowers in interdependent relationships.[25]

DOOYEWEERD'S CRITIQUE

A feminist critique is motivated by the exclusion of the feminine from the tradition of philosophy and is often supported by appeals to experience. In contrast, Dooyeweerd's critique is motivated by his conviction that theory is never religiously neutral in the sense of being purely logical and is supported by theoretical arguments. Central to his philosophical system is his belief that "our ego [self] expresses itself as a totality in the coherence of all its functions within all the . . . aspects of cosmic reality."[26] I am always an integrated whole active in all the different aspects of my being. For example, I can never bracket the physical aspect of myself while doing philosophy because I can never do philosophy except as a physically embodied creature. The very possibility of philosophic activity assumes that I must have eyes with which to read, hands with which to write, and a brain with which to think. I may ignore this physical aspect as I do philosophy, but I cannot transcend it, thereby becoming a pure transcendental logical ego. Against the concept of the transcendental logical ego, Dooyeweerd contrasts a holistic, integrated view of the self.

According to Dooyeweerd, reality can be analyzed into different aspects of which the rational is only one.[27] He asserts that in this multi faceted coherence no single aspect stands by itself; every one refers within and beyond itself to all the other aspects.[28] In pre-theoretical experience, there is an indissoluble interrelation between the aspects of reality; in theoretical experience, an entire human being distinguishes reality into its different aspects.[29] Furthermore, in theoretical thought, we oppose the logical aspects of our thinking to the non-logical aspects of reality.[30] The non-logical aspects become the *Gegenstand* or object of an investigation which is characterized by focusing experience logically. For example, in everyday life I am tacitly aware that the novel I read takes up space (its spatial aspect), that it costs money (its economic aspect), that it evokes certain feelings in me (its sensitive aspect); however, if I read it as a literary theorist I bracket all these dimensions of the text and concentrate on its aesthetic aspect. I attempt to isolate its aesthetic aspect and I oppose the logical aspect of my act of thinking to the novel's aesthetic aspect in order to judge it as well or poorly written. But my focus on the text's aesthetic characteristics does not mean that its other aspects do not exist.

Dooyeweerd agrees with Kant that the self is functioning logically when theorizing and that the logical aspect is opposed to the non-logical aspects in theoretical thought. However, he thinks that Kant has made a major error by supposing that the logically objectified self (which is merely the logical aspect of our selfhood) constructs this *Gegenstand* in isolation from the rest of the self.[31] When I theoretically self-reflect, a transcendental logical ego does not oppose my thought to itself. When I reflect on myself as a thinker, I (as a multi-faceted creature) oppose the logical focus of my experience to non-logical aspects. When I critically examine my thinking self, I see that I have opposed my logical function to all my non-logical functions, thereby making my non-logical functions the *Gegenstand* or object of my logical function. Nevertheless, it is *I* who perform this abstraction and set up this *Gegenstand* relation, and I am more than my logical function. I am even more than the sum of my functions.[32] Both theoretical thought and my thinking self are logically focused, but both thought and my self have non-logical aspects that continue to function when I think. The antithetic *Gegenstand* structure is the structure of theoretical thought, but it is not the structure of all of reality. Hence, we need to carefully avoid any tendency to reify this relationship.

As I have already stressed, the transcendental logical ego does not empirically exist. On Dooyeweerd's model we can see it as an absolutization of the logical function of a whole self. My entire self, which transcends the diversity of my functions, and of which the rational is merely one aspect, is always responsible for creating this *Gegenstand* relation. We must always remember that the splitting up of the aspects of reality and the opposition of the logical to the non-logical aspects is the result of theoretical thinking and is empirically artificial: "[T]his theoretical antithesis does not correspond to the structure of empirical reality."[33] The transcendental logical ego is the extreme result of an abstraction from the entire self which functions in all its aspects.[34] But the logical function of thought can never be a self-sufficient activity because it depends upon myself in my entirety.[35] Thought doesn't think; *I* think.

For Dooyeweerd, philosophy is undoubtedly and properly a theoretical activity.[36] Philosophy provides us with a theoretical insight into reality, but there are many more kinds of insights. Friendship and music, for example, provide us with other kinds of knowledge. Philosophy can theoretically analyze social or musical insights but it can never replace them. Hence, a philosophical analysis of them should not be identified with the social or musical insights themselves. Moreover, recognition that philosophy is a rational and theoretical activity does not entail the existence of a transcendental logical ego. On the contrary, the necessary condition for all knowledge is an entire multifaceted self. Only complexly embodied human beings have knowledge.

COMPARISON

On a perfunctory reading, feminist and Dooyeweerdian criticisms of the transcendental logical ego are quite different. There are, however, a number of important points of convergence. Both Dooyeweerd and feminist philosophers agree that the transcendental logical ego is an artificial and harmful creation of the philosophic tradition. Theories that presuppose a transcendental logical ego are distorted because they begin with a premise that isn't realistic; humans are not essentially transcendental logical egos.[37] If philosophy is an activity undertaken by humans only as aggregate and complex beings, then philosophy must deal with the empirical gender specificity, particularity, situatedness, and interdependency denoted by these selves in order to construct adequate theories about humans in our world.

To the a priori nature of the transcendental logical ego, Dooyeweerd and feminists oppose an empirical and embodied self which is, by implication, gendered. Dooyeweerd, being an early twentieth-century European, never discussed gender in his philosophic arguments for an empirical self. However, his assertion that only actual, situated humans do philosophy implies that no one can transcend one's gender. The extent to which women and men, and femininity and masculinity, are inherently different remains an open question.[38] However, insofar as the tradition of philosophy has excluded women, philosophy has failed to adequately theorize about reality, since reality is experienced by both women and men, and rational analysis is both a female and a male activity.

Both Dooyeweerd and feminist philosophers argue that it is not transcendental logical egos but, rather, particular, complex persons who know. And such an argument implies, according to Code, that "particular capacities and inclinations are neither incidental nor transitory. They form an integral part of a human being's nature as an actively knowing organism and are evident in his or her ensuing knowledge."[39] Both Dooyeweerdian and feminist arguments further converge in the insistence that philosophers are not autonomous either in the sense of being free from non-rational influences or in the sense of being free from the influence of others.

In order to construct adequate theories, philosophers must realize that they are first and always human beings. As such, we are not ahistorical and undifferentiated entities; we are situated individuals.[40] We do not come to know our environment through our own unaided efforts; we are nurtured and raised by others.[41] We do not do our thinking in isolation; we belong to a community of knowers; we are taught, criticized, and challenged by our colleagues, students, and teachers; we share our knowledge with one another.[42] We do not acquire knowledge through our rational activities alone; we gain knowledge through every kind of experience (physical, aesthetic, fiduciary, ethical).[43]

We can only be our particular selves, even when doing philosophy, which means that our work will always show our own influences, aspirations, and commitments. We can, however, explore how philosophic problems are reconstituted when seen from our particular standpoints. Moreover, we can theoretically analyze our own standpoint. We all bring more than our rational selves to philosophy. We must therefore theorize as multifaceted selves, rather than pretend that philosophy transcends empirical selves. The convergent insight of both feminist and Dooyeweerdian views is that philosophy is best done when the philosopher acknowledges that she is a situated, complex human being.

NOTES

1. The editors of *After Philosophy: End or Transformation?*, ed. Kenneth Baynes, James Bohman and Thomas McCarthy (Cambridge: MIT Press,

1987), pp. 3–4, claim that many postmodern themes are presented as critiques or variations upon Kantian themes, such as the autonomous rational subject (pp. 3–4). The same is true for feminist themes. See, for example, Lorraine Code's discussion of the knowing subject in *Epistemic Responsibility* (Hanover, N.H.: University Press of New England, 1987); Kathryn Pauly Morgan's reasons for rejecting the standpoint of a detached transcendental knower in "Women and Moral Madness," in *Science, Morality and Feminist Theory*, ed. Marsha Hanen and Kai Nielsen (Calgary: University of Calgary Press, 1987), pp. 201–26; and Ann Ferguson's discussion of the shortcomings of theories of self which fail to take account of the many aspects of human selfhood in "A Feminist Aspect Theory of Self," in *Science, Morality and Feminist Theory*, pp. 339–56.

2. Many feminist philosophers are aware of (and accept) the deconstruction of the unified self of Enlightenment humanism; see, for example, *Feminism/Postmodernism*, ed. Linda J. Nicholson (New York: Routledge, 1990) and Susan J. Hekman, *Gender and Knowledge: Elements of a Postmodern Feminism* (Boston: Northeastern University Press, 1990). Even when postmodern critiques are not wholly accepted, it is arguable that feminist reconstructions of selfhood do not necessarily retain the Enlightenment ideal; for example, Lorraine Code argues that "because of the fluctuations and contradictions of subjectivity, this process [of knowing oneself or others] is ongoing, communicative, and interpretive. It is never fixed or complete; any fixity claimed for 'the self' will be a fixity in flux" ("Taking Subjectivity into Account" *Feminist Epistemologies*, ed. Linda Alcoff and Elizabeth Potter [New York: Routledge, 1993], p. 34).

3. I confine my comments in this paper to the work of North American feminist philosophers; there are important differences between North American feminism and European or third-world feminism, and this project is too short to deal with all of them adequately. I also acknowledge that North American feminist philosophers are not a homogeneous group, although I think there is sufficient commonality in the broad themes of their work to compare it in general with that of Dooyeweerd.

4. Although better known in Europe, Dooyeweerd (1894–1977) and his work are not well known in North America. From 1926 to 1965 he was professor of law and was twice rector of the Free University of Amsterdam. He published more than two hundred articles and books, his chief work being the four-volume A *New Critique of Theoretical Thought*, which was published in 1935. In the course of his career he was also president of the Society of the Philosophy of Law, a member of the Royal Society of Arts and Sciences of the Netherlands, editor of the journal *Philosophia reformata*, and one of the founding members of the Society for Calvinist Philosophy in the Netherlands.

5. A *New Critique of Theoretical Thought*, trans. David H. Freeman and William S. Young (Philadelphia: Presbyterian and Reformed, 1969), I, p. 5.

6. *Epistemic Responsibility*, p. 101.

7. I am in no way claiming that Dooyeweerd was a protofeminist. However, such a realization makes the points of convergence between his work and that of many feminist philosophers all the more intriguing. Although it is beyond the scope of this chapter to examine possible reasons for these convergences, I suggest they are partially due to the marginalization shared by both Dooyeweerdian and feminist thought by mainstream philosophy.

8. "For if we eliminate from our experiences everything which belongs to the senses, there still remain certain original concepts and certain judgments derived from them, which must have arisen completely *a priori*, independently of experience, inasmuch as they enable us to say, or at least lead us to believe that we can say, in regard to the objects which appear to the senses, more than mere experience would teach—giving to assertions true universality and strict necessity, such as mere empirical knowledge cannot supply" (*Critique of Pure Reason*, trans. Norman Kemp Smith [London: Macmillan Education, 1929], A2). Kant is saying that we can discover a priori concepts by eliminating from experience that which belongs to the senses. Experience is identified with the senses and contrasted with the purely a priori.

9. Kant writes that "the subject of the present enquiry is . . . how much we can hope to achieve by reason, when all the material and assistance of experience are taken away" (*Critique of Pure Reason*, Axiv).

10. "A *priori* modes of knowledge are entitled pure when there is no admixture of anything empirical" (*Critique of Pure Reason*, B3).

11. The fact that the transcendental logical ego does not exist in empirical reality but is, nevertheless, the condition for any knowledge whatsoever poignantly shows the problem of trying to imitate it in an effort to do "real philosophy."

12. For example, Code asserts that "autonomous man does enjoy the status of a character ideal in modern society; his mode of being is considered worthy of admiration and emulation" (*Science, Morality and Feminist Theory*, p. 359). Genevieve Lloyd argues that the ideals of reason are "incorporated . . . into our understanding of what it is to be a person at all, of the requirements that must be met to be a good person, and of the proper relations between our status as knowers and the rest of our lives" (*The Man of Reason: "Male" and "Female" in Western Philosophy* [Minneapolis: University of Minneapolis Press, 1984], p. ix). And Morgan claims that "striving to adopt the standpoint of a detached transcendental knower, many philosophers hope to define human nature in a way which is unaffected by the vissicitudes of human history, human culture, and evolutionary variability" ("Women and Moral Madness," p. 203).

13. For example, the two collections of essays in *Feminist Perspectives*, ed. Lorraine Code, Sheila Mullet, Christine Overall (Toronto: University of Toronto Press, 1988) and *Science, Morality and Feminist Theory* demonstrate

the widespread dislike of feminists for the idea of the transcendental logical ego. See the introduction and essays in *After Philosophy* (pp. 3–4) for some critiques of or variations upon the Kantian theme of the autonomous rational subject of contemporary non-feminist philosophers.

14. The belief that pure reason is genderless did not originate with Kant. For example, Augustine believed that the mind (as distinct from the body) had no gender; see Lloyd, *The Man of Reason*, pp. ix, 28–33.

15. Ibid., p. ix.

16. Ibid., p. 108.

17. Ibid., p. x.

18. Views on the capacity of women to reason competently depend not only on the gender-neutrality of the transcendental logical ego but also on the differences (or lack thereof) between men and women. Lloyd argues in *The Man of Reason*, p. 44, that Descartes, for example, thought that there was no difference between women and men insofar as humans are rational creatures, and so he also believed that "even women" could gain knowledge if they followed his method. The *cogito* applied equally to the sexes. In contrast, Kant asserted that women and men usually have very different characteristics and that it is the masculine characteristics that are conducive to rational thought, thereby implying that only men are capable of pure thought. See Jean Grimshaw, *Philosophy and Feminist Thinking* (Minneapolis: University of Minneapolis Press, 1986), pp. 42–45 and Lloyd, *The Man of Reason*, pp. 64–70. In neither case is it admitted that the transcendental logical ego is masculine.

19. There is no simple agreement among feminists as to whether or not reason is ultimately able to transcend gender. Lloyd argues in *The Man of Reason*, p. 107, that "the confident affirmation that Reason 'knows no sex' may likewise be taking for reality something which, if valid at all, is so only as an ideal. . . . Notwithstanding many philosophers' hopes and aspirations to the contrary, our ideals of Reason are in fact male; and if there is a Reason genuinely common to all, it is something to be achieved in the future, not celebrated in the present." What is agreed upon is that the present ideals of reason, including the transcendental logical ego, are male and that empirical subjects (insofar as they are empirical) are gendered.

20. In "Philosophical Methodology and Feminist Methodology: Are They Compatible?", *Feminist Perspectives*, pp. 20–21, Susan Sherwin contrasts feminist and philosophic methodology when she writes: "[F]eminists readily admit to bias in their perspective, while philosophers continue to assume bias should and *can* be avoided" and "feminists have political as well as intellectual aims that they are quite willing to admit to." The editors of *Feminist Perspectives*, p. 6, write that "in feminist philosophy there is a constant awareness of history, process, and change" and Sherwin writes that "while philosophers seek objective truth, defined as valid from any possible viewpoint,

feminists consider it important to look to the actual view of the individual speaking" (p. 19). Furthermore, she accurately remarks that "recognizing that what has been claimed to be objective and universal is in reality the male point of view, feminists concentrate on women's own experience and explicitly avoid any claims of being 'objective, abstract, or universal' " (p. 19). She goes on to assert that "feminists acknowledge that their perspective is not universal or unpremised, recognizing that women's perspectives might in fact be different if the world were different" (p. 19).

21. For example, while Code in *Epistemic Responsibility*, p. 99, credits Kant's epistemology for placing the epistemic subject at the center of the cognitive process, she argues that his model of self "is too poor in its failure to take into account the affective, cultural, and historical aspects of human life."

22. *Feminist Perspectives*, p. 3.

23. In "Women and Moral Madness," p. 203, Morgan expresses the disgust of many women when she writes, "I am inclined to accept the existence of such reflecting transcendental egos about as much as that of the Great Pumpkin. As far as I can determine only empirical egos engage in philosophical reasoning, and empirical egos invariably walk about in gendered garb." Her article "Women and Moral Madness" provides eloquent evidence that the cherished fantasy of the philosophic tradition to be a purely rational ego has been a nightmare of moral (and epistemic) madness for many women.

24. *Science, Morality and Feminist Theory*, p. 358; see also *What Can She Know?*, *Feminist Theory and the Construction of Knowledge* (Ithaca, N.Y.: Cornell University Press, 1991), p. 73.

25. In "Second Persons," *Science Morality and Feminist Theory*, pp. 35782, *Epistemic Responsibility*, and Chapter 3 of *What Can She Know?* Code argues that it is impossible to be an autonomous knower and that all our knowledge is dependent, to varying degrees, on being part of a community.

26. *A New Critique of Theoretical Thought*, I: 4. "Ego" is not a fortunate choice of word since it implies an abstraction from an entire self; rather, "self" is closer to what Dooyeweerd means here. However, we must remember that he was writing in Dutch fifty-five years ago. It becomes clear in the context of his work that by "ego" he means the whole person.

27. According to Dooyeweerd, human "experience displays a great diversity of fundamental modal aspects. . . . These aspects do not, as such, refer to a concrete *what*, i.e., to concrete things or events, but only to the *how*, i.e., the particular and fundamental mode, or manner, in which we experience them. Therefore, we speak of the modal aspects of this experience to underline that they are only the fundamental *modes* of the latter. They should not be identified with the concrete phenomena of empirical reality, which function, in principle, in all of these aspects" (*In the Twilight of Western Thought* [Philadelphia: Presbyterian and Reformed, 1960], p. 6). The fifteen aspects (or modes) of reality are: numerical, spatial, kinematic, physical, bi-

otic, sensitive, logical, historical, lingual, social, economic, aesthetic, juridical, moral, and pistic (A *New Critique of Theoretical Thought*, I, p. 3).

28. Ibid., I, p. 3.

29. Ibid., I, p. 38.

30. Ibid., I, p. 39.

31. "The only, but fundamental, mistake in their [the Kantians'] argument was the identification of the real act [of thought] with a purely psychical temporal event, which in its turn could become a 'Gegenstand' of the ultimate transcendental-logical 'cogito' " (Ibid., I:50).

32. "Our selfhood does not coalesce with the mutual *coherence* among all functions which we have in the cosmos" (Ibid., I, p. 16).

33. Ibid., I, p. 40. Dooyeweerd points out that "the theoretical act in which we perform this analysis is, of course, not identical with the abstracted modal structure of the logical aspect. . . . In its theoretical abstraction this modal structure has only an intentional existence in our act of thought, and can be made into the "Gegenstand" of our actual logical function. It is, consequently, not the latter which can be made a 'Gegenstand', but only the abstracted, purely intentional, modal structure of the logical function" (Ibid., I, p. 40).

34. "It is even isolated to the greatest conceivable degree of abstraction, since it is the product of a methodical process of elimination by which the thinker imagines, he is able, ultimately, to set the logical function of thought apart as a self-sufficient activity" (Ibid., I, p. 6).

35. "Philosophical thought, however, cannot isolate itself in its subjective logical function, because it has no *selfhood* as mere thought, as so-called '*reines Denken*'. All actuality in the act of thinking issues from the ego, which transcends thought" (Ibid., I, p. 7).

36. "Philosophy should furnish us with a theoretical insight into the intermodal coherence of all the aspects of the temporal world" (Ibid., I, p. 4).

37. Code, for example, insists that "the problem is that characterizations of this abstract figure lend themselves to a starkness of interpretation which constrains philosophical inquiry while, at the same time, enlisting philosophical positions in support of constraining social and political policies" and she cites the tendency in medical ethics to emphasize patient autonomy to the exclusion of every other consideration as an example of a constraining social policy that is the result of a stark interpretation of human beings ("Second Persons," *Science, Morality and Feminist Theory*, p. 359).

38. As Grimshaw points out, "conceptions of masculinity and femininity are complex and shifting things; they have varied historically and are not at all monolithic or homogeneous" (*Philosophy and Feminist Thinking*, p. 61). For feminist analyses of the notion of 'women's nature' see Diana Fuss, *Essentially Speaking* (New York: Routledge, 1989); Denise Riley, *Am I That Name? Feminism and the Category of "Women" in History* (Minneapolis:

University of Minneapolis Press, 1988); Elizabeth Spelman, *Inessential Woman* (Boston: Beacon Press, 1988).

39. *Epistemic Responsibility*, p. 101.

40. For example, in "Philosophical Methodology and Feminist Methodology: Are They Compatible?", *Feminist Perspectives*, Sherwin argues for a view of the self that acknowledges our situated particularity, and in "A Feminist Aspect Theory of Self," *Science, Morality and Feminist Theory*, Ferguson argues against thin conceptions of the self and for a theory that takes into account the many facets of the self.

41. See, for example, Code's "Second Persons," in *Science, Morality and Feminist Theory*, where she argues that absolute autonomy is an impossibility for humans.

42. See, for example, Code's *Epistemic Responsibility*, where she argues that a community of interdependent knowers is necessary for all knowledge.

43. See, for example, Sheila Mullett's "Only Connect: The Place of Self-Knowledge in Ethics," in *Science, Morality and Feminst Theory*, pp. 309–338, where she explores the various kinds of self-knowledge and their contribution to the moral life, and also Code's "Credibility: A Double Standard," in *Feminist Perspectives*, where she argues that we gain different kinds of knowledge through different kinds of experience.

3

Taking the Risk of Essence:
A Deweyan Theory in Some
Feminist Conversations

Carroll Guen Hart

A CHARACTERISTIC TERM in postmodern discourse is "essentialism." This term and its opposite, "anti-essentialism," have become so intuitively obvious in certain contexts that they can be used, respectively, to damn or praise something without further argument. The mere suggestion of "essentialism" becomes enough to jettison a position without further scrutiny, as the term "anti-essentialism" becomes enough to recommend another. However, many feminist thinkers are reminding us that the issue is not nearly this simple. Essence appears to be something that we can't live with but can't live without. As Elizabeth Grosz says,

> Feminism is placed in an unenviable position: either it clings to feminist principles, which entail its avoidance of essentialist and universalist categories, in which case its rationale as a political struggle centered around women is problematized; or it accepts the limitations patriarchy imposes on its conceptual schemas and models and abandons the attempt to provide autonomous, self-defined terms in which to describe women and femininity. Are these the only choices available to feminist theory—an adherence to essentialist doctrines, or the dissolution of feminist struggles into localized, regional, specific struggles representing the interests of particular women or groups of women?[1]

Put bluntly, the question is this: Do we need to accept on pragmatic political grounds a position that is intellectually suspect and possibly in bad faith? Is this what it comes to? Either be co-opted philosophically or give up politically?

Some feminist philosophers refuse the choice and instead question the parameters of the choice itself. Both Elizabeth Spelman and Diana

Fuss look at the ambiguities of essence and suggest, in their own ways, that we need a reconstructed theory of essence. In response to this need, I suggest that John Dewey's discussion of "essence" might be a useful starting point for a reworked conception of essence. Rather than proffering Deweyan essence as a final solution (in any case I am suspicious of "final solutions"), I shall try to develop Dewey's position in light of these feminist discussions, as a possible conversation partner. I will conclude by suggesting some of the risks that my modified Deweyan construction of essence may call us to take.

FEMINIST DECONSTRUCTIONS OF ESSENCE

Many feminists begin their discussions of essence by acknowledging that essence in some form is important for feminist organizing. However, they still have questions about essence. I suggest that they are engaged in what Gayatri Spivak calls "deconstruction": "The critique in deconstruction, the most serious critique in deconstruction, is the critique of something that is extremely useful, something without which we cannot do anything."[2] These discussions of essence, I suggest, are deconstructive in this sense when they accept the fact that a shared identity among women is important for feminist politics; their criticisms are intended to discover the hidden agendas in our usual conceptions of essence which systematically obscure some forms of oppression.

The Hidden Agenda of Essence

I pick up the story of essence in contemporary feminist philosophizings with Elizabeth Spelman's analysis in *Inessential Woman*. Spelman argues that, if we think of many different pebbles of different shapes, sizes, colors, and textures, then "essence" would be their common "pebblehood" which cuts across these differences.[3] "Essentialism," then, is the conviction that "pebblehood" is more real than the individual pebbles, such that "The pebbles, in their multiplicity, physicality, and changeability, are significant only insofar as they are instantiations of the single, nonphysical, and unchanging Form of pebblehood."[4] Out of this grows the assumption that *really* knowing something means excluding difference and grasping the essence—that intangible something which pebbles (or women) share, which makes them pebbles (or women), as opposed to being smooth or bumpy (or, in the case of women, being rich or poor, white or black, lesbian or straight).

Spelman goes on to analyze the historical development of this assumption, specifically with respect to our understanding of the essence "woman." The purpose of this essence, then, is to isolate oppression that is directed specifically at women. This tight abstraction is needed in order to provide a specific focus for feminism. If a number of people are oppressed because they are women, then we need an analysis of oppression that focuses on sexism, that form of oppression which is specific to women, as opposed to those forms of oppression which are based on race or class. An essence, once isolated, would enable us to apply the same insights directly to other women, thereby increasing our efficiency in creating a community of solidarity.

Naturally, then, we look at those instances in which "pure" sexism is clearest and least bound up with other issues. It is no coincidence, Spelman suggests, that the paradigmatic instance of sexism is found in the lives of women for whom race and class are not problematic—that is, for women of the dominant race and class. For in the privileged classes, any oppression of women cannot be based on race or class, and therefore must be due to sexism. While this has undeniably been helpful in highlighting previously unnoted forms of oppression, it has also had a variety of unhelpful results. For by focusing on "woman" as distinct from "white" and "privileged class," this essence has obscured the function of race and class in enabling these women to be "just women" and to focus on just women's issues. After all, says Spelman, being white and being privileged are already being celebrated everywhere in our culture, and so are not areas of vulnerability. This provides a level of security for white privileged women to focus on gender issues. In a sense, says Spelman, gender itself may be a mark of privilege.

Spelman points out that this race and class blindness (and therefore privilege) in the notion of "woman" occurs wherever thinkers compare or contrast "women" to other groups such as slaves, blacks, Jews, and so on. Categorizations like this only perpetuate the notion that "woman" has nothing to do with race or class. It blinds us to the hidden agenda of race and class both for those who are present as "just women" and for those who are defined by "slave," "black," or "Jew" but who are also women.

When we try to apply this essence to women of other races and classes, however, we get some curious results. African American women, for example, may be required also to separate "being a woman" from "being African American." Only in doing this would they be accepted as real feminists; to do otherwise is to be a collaborator, to compromise their feminism. It is to fail to maintain solidarity with women. In order to be real feminists, then, women of other races and classes must bracket race and class in order to focus on sexism. Spelman points out that this bracketing acts to preserve the status quo by keeping race and class out of feminist discussions. By definition, then, it becomes impossible to point out that part of sexism against African American women stems from racism on the part of white women (as was the case with Southern slave-owning women, who were particularly hard on female slaves, especially those who might be attractive to white men). It also becomes impossible to see that, for example, maintaining the ideal of Southern Womanhood required the suppression of the womanhood of a great many African American women. In addition, an exclusive focus on women's solidarity may also serve to split the African American community, thereby tacitly preventing it from challenging race privilege. Altogether, bracketing race and class operates to preserve privilege by not calling attention to the social mechanisms of exclusion that sustain it (for if the mechanisms were visible, someone might get the idea that it could be changed).

Rather than accepting this state of affairs, Spelman questions the fundamental assumption behind essence—the assumption that "woman" can be separated from "white" and "middle class" and the related assumption that sexism can be isolated from racism and classism. The assumption that they can be separated is itself a mark of privilege. Moreover, the assumption that "woman" automatically has priority over racial or class identity reflects the situation of the privileged class for whom this is really possible. Spelman's fundamental point is that commonality cannot be arrived at by bracketing difference but only through an acknowledgment of difference. But this in turn challenges the assumption that we could isolate an essence and then simply apply it to women across the board. Commonality then becomes a difficult achievement which can happen not by manipulating concepts but only by holding discussions with women who may not share our priorities. If we take difference seriously, there is no way (aside from the use of force) to determine absolute priority among essences: for some women, "woman" may have priority; for others, "African American" may have priority. All of this complicates the issue, because we then must fight many different forms of oppression all at once, and we can form only shifting and partial alliances. What we gain in inclusion we lose in efficiency.

Spelman acknowledges that the positing of "essence" common to all women has, potentially, a valuable political function. It enables women to find solidarity with each other rather than just caring about the interests of individual women or of women of their own (privileged) class or race. It is particularly valuable in enabling the oppressed women to say, I have this in common with you as a woman, so I should have the same privileges you claim as your own.[5] However, essences become problematic—become, in fact, "essentialism"— when the dominant group uses its power to determine the identities of all women. As Spelman says,

> . . . essentialism invites me to take what I understand to be true of me "as a woman" for some golden nugget of womanness all women have as women, and it makes the participation of other women inessential to the production of the story. How lovely: the many turn out to be one, and the one that they are is me.[6]

This is part of the hidden agenda of essence: assuming that the many are identical to the one who is privileged to tell the story. The other side of the hidden agenda of essence is its implicit somatophobia; it splits off the universal, "woman," from the particular women it is intended to represent. The intangible essence thus becomes more "real" than the particular women, as well as self-sufficient. The essential woman has "no color, no accent, no particular characteristics that require having a body."[7] In fact, all of these characteristics are tacitly assimilated to the practices of the dominant culture, and are not worth remarking because they are familiar and assumed to be "normal."

Spelman concludes her analysis of essence and essentialism on a rather discouraging note. For although it remains important to be able to make useful generalizations about women—generalizations that would enable women of different races and classes to have a common interest—every possible way of doing this turns out to be a concealed form of imperialism. The best she can do is to remind us that whenever we use the term "woman" we mean in fact "women of the dominant race and class." For essence itself is a product of privilege and functions to obscure the mechanisms of privilege, thereby preserving it.

The Preservation of Essence

Diana Fuss begins with the contemporary "binarism" of essence and construction: ". . . while the essentialist holds that the natural is *repressed* by the social, the constructionist maintains that the natural is *produced* by the social."[8] She notes the stranglehold this binarism appears to have on feminist theorizing, in its assumption that essence is always theoretically conservative, whereas construction is always politically radical.[9] This set of assumptions allows feminists to use essentialism as a blanket term of disapproval and constructivism as a blanket term of approval, without looking further. This, insists Fuss, is misleading because it misses many of the subtleties contained in these notions. For when we define "essentialism" in opposition to "difference," we overlook the differences within essentialism.[10] Her own strategy is to "work both sides of the essentialist/constructionist binarism at once, bring each term to its interior breaking point."[11] It then appears that, on the one hand, essence (even naturalized, unchanging essence) is constructed as such for certain purposes, and that construction, where it has a normative purpose, almost always essentializes certain assumptions in order to protect them from scrutiny. Thus whereas essence and construction appeared to be mutually exclusive, they now appear to be "inextricably co-implicated with each other."[12] All essences are constructed, and for some purposes to construct them as, for example, rooted in body, may serve good political ends. The relevant question then becomes not Is there essentialism here? but rather, Who is using it, and "what motivates its deployment?"[13]

Fuss goes on to illustrate different kinds of essentialisms and the ways in which they are constructed to serve different purposes. For my purposes here, I shall focus only on her discussions of French feminists Monique Wittig and Luce Irigaray. First Wittig, whom Fuss chooses because she is a materialist who espouses anti-essentialism in its "strictest and most uncompromising form."[14] Wittig is a constructionist in the sense that not even biology escapes the political at this moment in history, which happens to be that phallocentric discourse which Wittig calls "the straight mind."[15] For Wittig, the lesbian inherently de-essentializes the signifier "woman," because of the fact that, under the dominant phallocratic (straight) schema, lesbians are "not real women."[16] The fact that lesbians remain biologically female but are still categorized as "not real women" reveals that the very category "woman" is socially and politically constructed to serve the interests of men. But because lesbians are constructed into a space which is "not-woman" but also "not-man," this also defines a "free space" where women can love in a way that is free from domination and servitude.[17]

However, Fuss locates some crucial places at which Wittig's anti-essentialism presupposes some form of essentialism. First, she posits "the lesbian" as an "absolute subject" whose "true nature" is to be monogamous, faithful, and mutually loving.[18] When she speaks of "the lesbian" or "the lesbian body" she implicitly erases the political, race, and class differences within the group. Moreover, when she insists that lesbians exist in "a pure space above and beyond the problematics of sexual difference,"[19] she sets up the lesbian subject as a natural agent of subversion, an inherently revolutionary subject.[20] However, maintaining this transcendental privilege also requires the erasure of women's oppression of other women, even within the lesbian community. It must be labelled "false consciousness," a remnant of the dominant culture.

Second, Wittig's need to maintain lesbian privilege causes her to insist that homosexual men, *qua* men, are *accepted* by the phallocentric culture because they prefer men. With lesbians privileged as transformers of culture, no other group, not even those who have been oppressed and excluded in their own ways, can share this privilege. According to Fuss, Wittig accepts the essentialist view of men as "always and everywhere dominating," regardless of their social constructedness. She thus ignores the very real oppression and exclusion suffered by homosexual men, making them into her own "repressed other."[21] Fuss points out that Wittig assumes that there is only one sexual "economy"—the one which devalues woman—and ignores other possible ones which might devalue gay men in different terms.[22] In this way Wittig virtually accepts as permanent a certain construction of all "men" as oppressors, thereby merely "displacing" essence from biology to sociality.[23]

Fuss does not insist that the mere existence of these essentialisms is the problem, for every normative construction takes certain things for granted. Rather, the problem resides in the way in which Wittig's constructions deploy essentialism. It seems problematic to me because on the one hand she constructs lesbians as inherently revolutionary sexual subjects who exist completely outside relations of domination and servitude; but on the other hand she constructs men, whether gay or straight, as essentially and necessarily involved in such relations. By essentializing lesbians she occludes more subtle forms of oppression among women, and by essentializing men she precludes any construction that might allow a subversive role for gay men. This shows that social constructedness may well deploy essentialism in ways that privilege one oppressed group at the expense of another.

Next Fuss looks at Luce Irigaray, a thinker who is typically dismissed as an essentialist but who nevertheless has some very helpful things to say. Irigaray works against the background of Lacanian psychoanalysis, which emphasizes the "phallus" as a representational symbol distinct from the penis as anatomical organ.[24] The phallus determines a whole "Symbolic order" into which we all are socialized. "Woman," for Lacan, is significant because ". . . it is woman who escapes complete subjection to the Symbolic and its formative operations."[25] But by the same token, since the Symbolic order represents our point of entry into "subjectivity, into the realm of speech, law, and sociality," Lacan also insists that woman cannot speak of her own pleasure.[26] Hence in Lacan's "specular economy,"[27] men understand woman's pleasure by looking at statues of women.

In deliberate contrast to all of this, Irigaray uses the female labia to conceptualize woman's pleasure. The labia consists of two "lips," which, in constantly touching and moving against each other, constitute for women a basic form of sexual pleasure that does not require a penis. This movement situates "women's autoeroticism, their pleasure, in a different economy from the phallic, in an economy of ceaseless exchange and constant flux. . . ."[28] Thus Irigaray says that ". . . within herself, she is already two—but not divisible into one(s)— that caress each other."[29] She then expands the notion of "touching" into a "logic of touch" which supplants the phallic "logic of the gaze."[30] Presumably the logic of the gaze, in its larger outlines, signifies not only woman's sexual appeal for men but also the male ideal of detached objectivity; the logic of touch, on the other hand, dissolves the subject–object distinction, for it is impossible to distinguish what is touching from what is being touched.[31] The implication of this change in logic is that "A woman's exchange of herself with herself, without the agency of the literal penis or the Symbolic phallus, is exactly what puts into question the prevailing phallocentric specular economy."[32]

Many feminists assume that Irigaray's acknowledged essentializing of the female body means that "she is more interested in questions of subjectivity, desire and the unconscious than in questions of power, history, and politics."[33] Fuss argues that, while there is truth in this assessment, it is oversimplified, for Irigaray's focus on subjectivity, desire, and the unconscious is part of her political agenda. For Irigaray implicitly expands the notion of the political, including not only "group militancy or open confrontation" but also "psychic resistance."[34] Irigaray says that her proposed "economy of touch" precedes any socialization by men and is women's defense against it. As Fuss says,

> The point, for Irigaray, of defining women from an essentialist standpoint is not to imprison women within their bodies but to rescue them from enculturating definitions by men. An essentialist definition of "woman" implies that there will always remain some part of "woman" which resists masculine imprinting and socialization.[35]

As Irigaray says, we don't have to be "turned into women" by men because "we are women from the start."[36] Irigaray thinks that it is important for women to separate themselves from phallic culture, at least for a time. For we need both a " 'global' politics that seeks to address the problems of women's universal oppression" and a " 'local' politics that will address the specificity and complexity of each woman's particular situation."[37] Since we have no existing model for this, we need to spend time among women in order to conceptualize it for ourselves. However, Irigaray does not seek to make this essentializing moment into a new "cultural Symbolic" that would replace the "phallic economy"; rather, she seeks a "female imaginary" which may find its own "specific symbolization."[38] That is, this is an essentialism which attempts to articulate an identity for women, rather than imposing an identity on everyone else.

Using a motif reminiscent of Irigaray, Diana Fuss as an anti-essentialist wishes to "preserve" essence, in the dual sense of "embalming" and "maintaining" it.[39] In embalming it, she rejects any appeal to essence as a non-conventional Reality which relativizes all cultural expressions to a prior oneness or as an appeal to universality based on exploitation of the "repressed other." Even a supposedly "real" essence is so constructed, and can be constructed differently. However, she preserves essence as a deliberate but limited strategy against oppression—a strategy that requires constant vigilance so that strategic essentialism does not in time become a form of oppression to others.

A DEWEYAN CONCEPTION OF ESSENCE

As I have pointed out, both Spelman and Fuss refuse the automatic assumption that essentialism is bad and anti-essentialism is good. Each is, I believe, struggling with a deconstructionist critique that tries to tease out what may be useful in essence while identifying where it goes wrong or how it may be used improperly. However, the discussions can be so nuanced that it becomes difficult to distinguish between essence and essentialism, and between anti-essentialism and what I might call anti-essence. In an attempt to sort out some of these issues, I turn to John Dewey's theory of essence. This is a natural history of the concept of essence, which asks some fundamental questions: what is essence, and why have we historically been so attached to it? Dewey goes on to define essentialism and the damage it does in human life. He himself suggests a functionalized conception of essence in which logic is situated within the changing meanings that constitute human communal and political life. I will examine this conception of essence to see if it has any resources for the above-mentioned feminist conversations about essence.

The Dynamics of Lived Meaning

I begin my analysis with Dewey's comment that essence is "a pronounced instance of meaning."[40] In order to understand this comment, I first need to look at Dewey's construal of "meaning," which itself emerges out of the biological substrate of human existence. Dewey says that on the organic level we exist as other living organisms exist; in this context the continuity means that we exist in biological associations. Dewey says that "There is no mystery about the fact of association, of an interconnected action which affects the activity of singular elements. There is no sense in asking how individuals come to be associated. They exist and operate in association. If there is any mystery about the matter, it is the mystery that the universe is the kind of universe it is."[41] We live on the whole in groupings for the purpose of raising young, and so on. But there is a further level of association which is distinctively human; that is the level of shared meaning which constitutes a community as opposed to a flock or a clump (PP, 250–51; EN, 133, 144ff.).

Meaning, for Dewey, is not primarily a thing but a relationship between at least two persons and a shared object. Dewey uses the example of person A pointing to a flower (EN, 137ff.). What makes this into a meaning-relationship rather than just an organic one is that the pointing is done for the sake of person B. When B sees A pointing to the flower, he participates in A's intent and brings the flower to A.

Hence the participation in intent also relates to the object. The way of acting with respect to the object has, once acted on, been shown to correlate with a potentiality in the object, what Dewey here names "portability." This tripartite relation is what Dewey calls "meaning." Now, persons have many purposes, and objects as concrete existents have many dimensions. In the situation described above, "portability" may be said to be the objective correlate or means[42] to the fulfillment of a specific shared human intent or purpose in the world.

The concreteness of this little example must not mislead us. What is primary is "the making of something common" between two persons.[43] This "something" which is made common is what Dewey calls an "object." It is external in the general sense that it is a means to "whatever is made common"; it then takes on emergent qualities as a result of partaking as means in this shared human intent. We could also use the example of "home" or "family." Both are conceivably grounded in biological realities but become shared meanings which transform both the persons and the object involved. The persons now become involved in a community of shared intent; they act "from a standpoint that is not strictly personal but is common to them as participants or 'parties' in a conjoint undertaking" (LTI, 52). Individual persons can then act together, with reference to other people, in order to enjoy and preserve meanings which they value jointly. These meaning relations shape us as individuals and provide us with the content of our beliefs and intentions, the goals toward which we strive (PP, 251). We teach them to our children. Likewise "home" and "family" emerge as complex cultural objects shaped with respect to that shared intent.

These meanings are "emergent." On the one hand they emerge out of biological relations and, therefore, exist in continuity with biological life and hence with all other living beings. On the other hand they establish a qualitatively different dimension of life which is not fundamentally determined by the biological. Thus, while our biological structures may be constant, our emergent meanings are not. Dewey insists that while we may decide that it is important for us to take our biology into account, "none of the *distinctive* features of *human* association can be deduced from it" (PP, 357). On the contrary, human meanings react back onto our biological functioning, giving even our biology acquired and emergent meanings. These human meanings are what Dewey calls language, communion, communication. As such, language is final or, in Dewey's terms, "consummatory." It is "a sharing in the objects and arts precious to a community, a sharing whereby meanings are enhanced, deepened and solidified in the sense of communion" (EN, 159). Ultimately, the consummatory function of language is most important, because it is in enjoying and living in community (not in thinking about it) that we find our richest satisfactions. This is the level of what I might call lived meaning.

Here meanings remain implicit; we dwell within them and live them but do not focus on them in themselves. We focus on individual, concrete situations in their qualitative distinctness. Meaning holds onto sameness beneath individuality but remains implicit. Nevertheless, such meanings are potentially generalizable "ways of acting" with others and with things (EN, 147). Though implicit, they have a dynamic character and an unforeseeable reach into the future; in short, having once emerged they retain their emergent character, continually giving rise to new meanings as we live our lives in the world. I turn now to two different forms of emergent meaning: emergent instrumental meanings formed for specialized purposes and emergent political meanings.

Lived Meaning and Instrumental Essence

Primary or lived meanings are predominantly final or consummatory in the sense that they are made to be lived and enjoyed. However, it is clear that they also have an instrumental dimension, and it is primarily this dimension that characterizes the emergent groupings with which I now deal. These are emergent meanings which constitute communities of shared intent, but their explicit purpose is to cultivate and develop the primary groupings, although in a secondary way they are also enjoyable in themselves. Examples of such emergent groupings are economic, aesthetic, and logical meanings.

Emergent meanings like these begin as ways of "thinking" things for various specialized purposes. We may say, for example, that a pair of shoes is worth so many dollars. This statement

> does not say that the article is literally or in its ultimate "reality" so many dollars and cents; it says that for purpose of exchange that is the way to *think* of it, to judge it. It has many other meanings and these others are usually more important inherently. But *with respect to trade*, it *is* what it is worth, what it will sell for, and the price value put upon it expresses the relation it bears to other things in exchange.[44]

Thus, rather than formulating value with respect to trade in barterable equivalents, i.e., that so many potatoes are equivalent to so many pairs of shoes, we come up with an abstract medium of exchange, money, into which we translate these different values. As we see in our own day, this abstraction has rendered money infinitely generative of unanticipated meanings and consequences. But to return to the pair of shoes. The primary or lived meaning of shoes is obviously found in wearing them rather than in selling them, but for specialized purposes of exchange they may be "thought" in terms of abstract monetary value.

Similarly, logic is based on the fundamental human need to control and cultivate the things we value. If we simply look at human events qualitatively, it is evident that goods are limited to a fortunate few, and as long as we view these events as discrete and unconnected, it seems that there is nothing we can do about this. But, as with the islands in the sea, we begin to suspect that they may be connected under the surface, and we realize that if we can discern the connections we may be able to control or modify the visible results. We need to know what reliably "goes with" or connects with something less visible. However, the primary stuff of our direct activities and enjoyments is not, in itself, at all suited to providing such evidence: for "their testimony is almost worthless, they speak so many languages. In their complexity, they point equally in all directions; in their unity, they run in a groove and point to whatever is most customary."[45]

This is why we must "think" such events in a different way; we must "turn away from" and "let go of" the goods we now experience in order to gain more inclusive and accessible goods (EN, 107). We must surrender our own personal claim on goods so that, in becoming more impersonal they may in the end become personal possessions for a great many more people (QC, 174). We must "break up" the complexity and "reduce" or "resolve" it into independent variables which are more manageable. At the same time, we must let go of what *customarily* goes together in order to discover what *reliably* goes together. Dewey says that "The very conception of cognitive meaning, intellectual significance, is that things in their immediacy are subordinated to what they portend and give evidence of" (EN, 105). More specifically, within this larger purpose of control, logic is a functional distinction whose dynamic is twofold: *inference*, which, through careful analysis of past experience, tells us which visible things are reliable evidence of less visible connections; and *analysis*, which finds a stable, delimited variable that can be manipulated more precisely than the whole situation in its complexity.

Hence, logic begins with the shared meanings that constitute a community, but then refines them into a set of meanings designed for reliable inference and reasoning. It arrives at a set of definitions facilitating reliable kind-identification and analytic manipulation, based on relatively regular "sequential bonds" (EN, 101) abstracted from ordinary experience, developed into a specialized form of language characterized by "semantic coherence," the internal organization of a mechanism, and logical equivalence. The result is what Dewey calls "logical kernels" which represent the "net profit" of past experience for gaining understanding of new situations (IEL, 356). We thus "think" events in terms of a continuous mechanism in which we may intervene in order to help more events reach their consummation.

Dewey reserves the technical term "essence" for logically specialized meaning, as is clear when he says that

> Meaning, fixed as essence in a term of discourse, may be imaginatively administered and manipulated, experimented with. Just as we overtly manipulate things, making new separations and combinations, thereby introducing things into new contexts and environments, so we bring together logical universals in discourse, where they copulate and breed new meanings. [EN, 152]

Why is this form of meaning called "essence"? "Essence" is clearly a laudatory term, signifying that which is the most real, the most important. Clearly, within philosophy, which is a form of theoretical thought, sameness is "essential." Neither science nor philosophy could do its work without privileging sameness, for it is our cumulative knowledge of how things can be expected to work. But it is also clear from Dewey's account that this sameness is difficult to get at, partly because as persons we are so attached to individuality, and partly because sameness, unlike qualitative individuality, lies deep under the surface. Dewey's Baconian image is of digging out raw ore and refining it into workable metal. Another image, implicit above, is that of extracting a "kernel" from within a tough husk. Still another image comes from the perfume trade: the "distilled essence" of many individual things concentrated for human purposes (EN, 144). In another way, if we think of essence as the successful result of a "search for common ground," we can understand why it is held onto and valued. The labor required to achieve this essence is immense and the refined product extremely valuable. In logical terms, sameness is also grasped with great difficulty and, once grasped, is worth holding onto.

Emergent Political Meaning

The universality and fecundity of Deweyan shared meanings ensure that meaning and community are continually emergent. However, there is an implied distinction here between meanings and communities that are relatively settled and those that are in the process of emerging. This is not an absolute distinction, for in any given situation different relations may be either settled or emergent. Rather, it is a functional or relative distinction. This emergent community is particularly constitutive of the political dimension.

Dewey begins with existing communities that carry on their activities. Now, all human interactions have consequences, and not all of them can be anticipated. Nor are they necessarily limited to the persons actually involved in the interaction. On the one hand, since cultural meaning is open-ended, new groups keep forming. It is not uncommon that such minority groups are squashed by existing groups which have an interest in maintaining existing institutions and power structures. This is clearly the case in Dewey's example of the new industrial interests that arose in England and challenged entrenched traditional associations. On the other hand, existing interactions normally have unanticipated, harmful consequences for innocent third parties; this can also be true of the logical or scientific essences that grow out of those primary communities. In any case, it is important that the persons thus affected organize themselves in order to isolate and regulate such consequences or to further their own shared interests. Dewey calls these groupings "emergent" because they were not there (as such) before. This is because third-party consequences need not limit themselves to existing social groups, but may cut across them in unanticipated ways. Because of this, such a group may, to begin with, have no common interest at all except a negative one. The task of "organizing" is to articulate a common interest and common meanings which will enable these persons to coalesce for a certain purpose. Such groups will need to formulate new and emergent meanings or essences. I suggest that the category "women" is exactly this sort of emergent essence. It is inherently political, and is not intended to replace ethnic groupings but to deal with consequences that go beyond the boundaries of relatively more primary groupings. It seems plausible to me that at a certain point a group of women realized, as Spelman notes, that there were forms of oppression specifically linked to gender. And once they had begun to formulate shared meanings among them-

selves, those meanings were immediately, and normally, extended beyond the group to other sorts of women who then also wanted to join
the group.

On Dewey's account, then, the ongoing task for a heterogeneous
group like this, with no inherent common interest, is to *create* such
interests. Since an emergent grouping has at first only a negative common object—the fact that all are affected by actions outside their control—no already-existing "object" or participative intent, it must create
out of this a positive set of shared meanings around a common object.
And since meanings and objects alike belong to participative action,
they are created in the context of action. First, they are created by that
face-to-face working and talking which we call community-building.
Second, they are created when women engage in political action, that
is, when they begin to try to identify and regulate the consequences
which affect them. The idea seems to be that (to take our own example) as women begin to try to articulate a common interest and to
deal with the consequences which affect us, we continue to create our
common interest in ways that include all. For Dewey, as a liberal
"socialized" democrat, the idea is a community whose members voluntarily serve a common good which all have shared in creating and
which furthers their individual flourishing. In this way Dewey would
agree with Diana Fuss that politics creates affinity, not the other way
around.[46] Eventually, of course, since members of these emergent
communities continue to belong to more primary groupings, they desire to incorporate the new meanings into the shared life of the larger
communities. The political structure needs ways in which the new
meanings may gain a hearing and conceivably, in time, grow from
minority to majority status.

Dewey's own example is that of the emerging industrial interests in
nineteenth-century England. In order to further their interests, such
groups formulated the notion of the "individual" who possessed natural rights and abilities, chief among them economic rights and abilities. This meaning had definite rhetorical advantages in challenging
entrenched and stifling interests. On the other hand, an example of
damaging third-party consequences would be a chemical plant which,
in the course of producing its product, pollutes water and farmland
beyond its own bounds. In both cases, established groupings are shown
to be open-ended and, for good or ill, productive of further groupings
which then organize themselves and bring new awarenesses to the original groupings.

Uses and Misuses of Essence

In his analysis of essence, Dewey makes a fundamental distinction between lived meaning and essence. Lived meaning is, as it were, the genus, and essence the species of meaning which is abstracted and manipulated in order to enable us to make lived meanings more generally available to all in a community. Lived meaning and logical essence, then, are not ontologically different but, rather, occur on a continuum. One might say that both are real and both are constructed, but that the nuances are different for each. In primary lived meaning, the "realness" is uppermost (in the sense that these meanings are our ways of being in the world) and the constructedness remains implicit; in emergent lived meaning, however, while the realness is very present, the constructedness is far more visible. And in logical essence the realness is indirectly present while the constructedness is scrutinized and deliberately refined. In all of this, Dewey's primary ontological commitments are visible: though logical essence is extremely important, lived human meaning has existential primacy because it defines the ways in which we live in the world, enjoying, avoiding, doing, making in response to the qualitative individuality of concrete situations. This is the realm of what exists in the fullest and most actualized way; it also remains fundamentally open to changes in ourselves and in our world. Logical essence has value only insofar as it retains its connections to lived human meanings within a given community.

"Essence," then, is a term signifying something's importance in a given situation. Dewey's general principle here is that "Anything is 'essential' which is indispensable in a given inquiry and anything is 'accidental' which is superfluous" (LTI, 141). I have pointed out that "essence" is the traditional philosophical name for the structural sameness which constitutes logical concepts. And I have said that, for a scientific or philosophical community, such sameness is really the essence of human experience. However, following Dewey's principle of relativity, surely this could be expanded to all other communities of meaning. By definition, any set of shared human meanings constitutes the identity of a community, and is therefore of fundamental importance to that community. It is understandable that, within that community, when we are engaged in those particular activities, we find ourselves biased toward those particular meanings. A settled community values the shared meanings that have shaped it and that have provided a communal life which it can celebrate. An emergent community values the shared meanings that are even now bringing it into being and giving it an identity which it can celebrate. In general, then, "Essence . . . is but a pronounced instance of meaning; to be partial, and to assign *a* meaning to a thing as *the* meaning is but to evince human subjection to bias" (EN, 144). In a broader sense, then, any set of meanings that is germane to a particular purpose or to a particular community is in that situation "essential."

Moreover, it is understandable that when we are particularly devoted to the possibilities of a particular set of meanings, when they are essential to us, we think of them as important for all people in all times and places. We like to think of them as the essence of reality in a wider sense. All of our meanings are distillations of experience which are particularly valuable to us. Nevertheless, however important any particular distillation might be, it remains only one possible distillation; it never "[contains] existence as the perfect includes the imperfect" (EN, 144), thereby defining the one real meaning or purpose of existence. Although any distillation is ontological in the general sense of constituting a real human community, it is never ontological in a privileged or exclusive sense (EN, 151); it does not define the really real, either of ourselves or of the cultural objects to which we relate.

However, it remains tempting for us to ontologize and absolutize any particular set of shared meanings, and this is what Dewey calls "essentialism." The central meaning of this, of course, revolves around the specialized logical sense of "essence" and hence concerns the absolutizing of logic and conceptuality.[47] When this happens, we use a set of functional meanings, fitted to a specific human purpose, as the ultimate measure of reality, making all else either unreal or inadequate. As Dewey says,

> This capacity of essences to enter readily into any number of new combinations, and thereby generate further meanings more profound and far reaching than those from which they sprang, gives them a semblance of independent life and career, a semblance which is responsible for their elevation by some thinkers into a realm separate from that of existence and superior to it. [EN, 152–53]

When the economic way of "thinking" things is ontologized in this way, things become valuable simply with respect to their possibilities for trade; exchange becomes the privileged "essence" of human existence. Similarly, when the logical way of "thinking" things is given ontological privilege, it promotes the notion that existence itself is a mechanism, thereby marginalizing all in human life which is not mechanical, or indeed leading us to think that we can "reduce human beings to the plane of inanimate things mechanically manipulated from without" (PP, 359). Or ontologized logical meanings lead us to think that we could just manipulate ideas or meanings as a substitute for working with existential situations and people. When split off from the situations and contexts to which they apply and made into *things* in their own right, they constitute a "logic of rigid universals" (RP, 189) that forces real persons and situations into the mould set by universal concepts. In general, ontologizing instrumental essences of any kind results in contempt for the complexity of ordinary life, in its messiness but also in its richness.

But, working again with the aforesaid principle that essence is whatever meanings are most important in a given situation, it is clear that lived human meanings, whether primary or emergent, may also be made into essentialisms. First, primary lived meanings legitimately define distinctively human communities in contrast to organic associations. However, they remain anchored in our human "participation in intent," which is irreducible to biology. When the importance of these meanings is challenged, perhaps by emergent groupings or by attempts to understand the production of goods so as to increase their availability, such human relations are often collapsed into biological existence in a mistaken attempt to "naturalize" these human associations. Implicitly, such naturalization is a way of foreclosing the formation of new groups that potentially destabilize existing groups and power structures, and also of foreclosing the attempt to share valued things more broadly, which threatens existing interests. Naturalizing primary human lived meaning in this way makes existing associations look fixed and permanent and unchanging, just part of the landscape, thereby limiting the threat of emergent human choice and the possibility of change. It also hides the mechanisms of choice and construction behind an imaginary "naturalness," thereby foreclosing critique. In Dewey's example of nineteenth-century liberalism, traditional associations like church and aristocracy tried to do this in order to protect their interests from the rising middle classes.

Emergent meanings may also be turned into essentialisms. Such meanings are extremely vulnerable and very much aware of their minority status with respect to primary associations and scientific communities of meaning. Thus they often try to anchor themselves in the "natural" biological sphere in order to gain leverage, rhetorically portraying themselves as "real human nature" smothered by tradition and established power. To use Dewey's example, individualism was constructed as "natural" in order to strengthen its rhetorical force against a variety of well-established cultural groupings. However, as Dewey points out, this strategy of naturalizing or exclusively ontologizing an emergent essence ultimately plays on the same field as conservative movements. Too often it smothers the ability of the new movement to continue constructing itself in new ways, thereby limiting its ability to create significant structural change. Moreover, in hiding the mechanism of construction it sets up yet another hierarchy of privileged knowledge.

Specifically, then, essentialism is an attempt to absolutize concepts, making ordinary reality fit the concepts and dismissing as not really real what doesn't fit. In more general terms, however, it represents any attempt to absolutize any form of human meaning so as to close off others or to close down change. A time-honored way of doing this is, of course, to identify any one of them with "nature," taking advantage of our deep privileging of the natural (as the really real) over the merely cultural. In Dewey's terms, this remains an unwise option, and its evils are not mitigated by using it in different situations—for example, emergent rather than primary groupings. For wherever it is used, essentialism is a way of trying to compel an exclusive loyalty to one community or one set of issues, to render one description of ourselves invulnerable to change or criticism, to find a shortcut to agreement or unity.

However, Dewey argues that we should be anti-essentialists without needing to be anti-essence, because essence properly used and within proper limits is a great gift to human life. In a similar way, in Bosnia we see that group meanings, when construed in a certain way, can become a source of violence and death, but this need not mean that we should abjure group meanings. Logical essence for Dewey finds its proper place when it is firmly instrumentalized and used to enhance our shared life in community. Although logical essences are clearly limited by the meanings (including the biases and blind spots) of its larger community, it also needs to be open to changed meanings within that community; that is, when a community becomes aware that a certain group is clearly to be understood anew as subjects, they must also be included in the scientific process so that one group in the community does not use logical meanings to control other members of the community. Moreover, the mechanisms of logical essence must be open to all so that anyone could repeat the operation and scrutinize the choices made. Similar things, of course, can be said of lived human meanings themselves. We struggle to keep our primary communities open to emergent meanings, just as we struggle to keep our emergent meanings open to further developments and to more primary meanings. It is the part of wisdom to know what is "essential" in any given situation, to be able to determine when it is appropriate to engage in analysis using logical concepts and when it is appropriate simply to celebrate a situation or to engage in that participation in intent which builds human community.

On my reading, Dewey has tried to articulate a theory of essences which highlights both the root meaning of essence as shared human meaning and a number of different ways in which that human meaning can be developed. The theory is designed to wean us off the traditional understanding of essences as fixed, universal, and unchanging. Nevertheless, it attempts to show how essences rightly come by that honorific title—why, in fact, they are so important to us and why we do not easily let them go. But whereas traditional essences focused on their character when they are finished and firmly entrenched, Dewey's theory attempts to provide a natural history of such things, so that we can see that they are human constructions and that they can be changed. It also emphasizes a plurality of communities and hence a plurality of essential meanings; this is an attempt to do justice to the complexity of life, in contrast to the artificial simplicity imposed by traditional essences. So the theory is designed to foster a community that is open to the creation of new essences and the challenging of old ones.

DEWEYAN ESSENCE IN FEMINIST CONVERSATIONS

The time has come for me to try to make good on my claim that Dewey's conception of essences helps me sort out some of the important issues raised by Elizabeth Spelman and Diana Fuss. This is only a tentative beginning to the sort of conversation I have in mind, but will sketch some possible directions which I think such a conversation could usefully take.

To return to Spelman's analysis of essence, on my reading she is right that essence privileges sameness. Dewey points out that sameness is particularly important if we wish to cultivate certain virtues in our children, or if we wish to ensure that the goods we take for granted are available to all in our community. Such cultivation requires a sound knowledge of underlying structures and processes so that we have a reasonably good idea of how the things we value come to be. In short, there are excellent human reasons for valuing sameness. But Spelman is saying more: that sameness is given ontological privilege, to the exclusion of difference. In Deweyan terms, this is logical essentialism, and it would mean that what Spelman takes to be essence is already essentialism.

She goes on to point out that the concept of sexism is based on situations in which no other form of oppression is operative, that is, situations of privilege. Now, on Deweyan terms I think this is quite normal, for surely it is just this sort of situation which would open our eyes to the existence of further forms of oppression. It is also normal that a concept of sexism would optimally have a clear, crystalline structure, purified of extraneous elements such as aspects of oppression that would be due to other factors. That simply is due to the definition of sexism as gender-related oppression. I think feminists properly highlight this specific form of oppression. However, although a concept of sexism has this crystalline structure, there is no reason to assume that all situations involving sexism must look exactly like the concept in order to be real sexism. That assumption, too, seems to be a residue of essentialism from the philosophical tradition. An instrumentalized Deweyan conception would insist, first of all, that any concept of sexism be linked with other related concepts, and that all the possibilities be taken into account. When Spelman highlights the sexism experienced by African American women, she properly notes a blind spot which requires changes in the system of logical essences and the possibilities they engender. Second, a Deweyan conception would insist that any concept is only a guide which brings our cumulative experience to bear in helping us to ask questions we may not have thought of otherwise. It also reminds us of possibilities we need to consider. But it is not a substitute for individuals; rather, it is an instrument that needs to be used wisely in coming to understand any given individual situation.

If Spelman's analysis of essence is essentialist, this is understandable, given that nearly all of the philosophical tradition has been essentialist. But I think it also gives her analysis a despairing tone which it need not have. She seems to hear all of these challenges as challenges to essence itself, as if we have to choose between philosophy and feminism. Indeed we do if we view essence as fixed and unchanging, and as definitive of the really real. But if we distinguish between essence proper (that is, instrumentalized) and essentialism, then in order for essence to work properly, on a Deweyan account, we would be required to make the adjustments she asks us to make. Moreover, I wonder if she has unnecessary essentialist guilt-feelings which make her ashamed that feminists haven't immediately come up with the perfect, all-inclusive concept. On a Deweyan view, the challenges she describes, though tortuous and occasionally embarrassing, are normal to the development of finite communities of meaning; rather than being ashamed of it, perhaps we could enter into the process more wholeheartedly if we could accept it as normal. I think, however, that her text can be read very profitably as an exposé of the human dangers of essentialism. She is particularly effective in her description of the way in which an (absolutized) essence necessarily hides the mechanisms of privilege in order to maintain that privilege.

The situation is somewhat different for Fuss. I return to her basic definitions: ". . . while the essentialist holds that the natural is *repressed* by the social, the constructionist maintains that the natural is *produced* by the social." Here she is identifying two extremes that are mutually exclusive and that fight over the same turf. I think her instincts are exactly right when she pushes each extreme to its internal breaking point, so that its repressed other appears. Thus, she points out that Irigaray the essentialist is actually constructing the female imaginary for definite political purposes, whereas Wittig the constructionist uses very absolutist and exclusive essentialist categories in her construction of lesbianism. She also breaks down the bad/good dualism conventionally assigned to these extremes. Quite correctly, she asks us to look not at the labels but at the way in which things are deployed. For on a Deweyan analysis it is precisely the manner of deployment which distinguishes essence proper from essentialism.

The question I want to raise here is Fuss's identification of essentialism with the body. My questions here are difficult to articulate, but I shall try. Surely it is important for women to construct meanings that value the female body, particularly in the context of traditions that have in various ways denigrated the female body. On a Deweyan account, this would be quite normal because, in this particular situation, it is likely to be our identification as female bodies that is the source of our marginalization. We could also choose to ignore the source of our marginalization, but surely one option is to re-imagine it in a positive

way. To my mind, that is quite different from collapsing human meaning into biology; that would be a mistaken attempt to render a certain
description, as they say, untouched by human constructions and therefore more real. It would also be an attempt to compel agreement or
commitment to a single exclusive understanding of the female body.
But not all descriptions try to do that, or at least they need not be taken
that way. A Deweyan analysis of essence tries to maintain both the
continuity and the distinction between organic body and shared meaning. This would enable us to acknowledge that body is less malleable
than human meaning, but is, by the same token, more deeply
grounded in the ecology of life. One could say that, in different ways,
both mutually influence each other: body provides material constraints
and possibilities for meaning, while meaning, in constructing body in
terms of human community, leaves traces on the body. Witness a
shame of the body which can become virtually second nature. I worry
that any reference to the materiality or enduring quality of the female
body is construed as essentialism, and on this basis we are frightened
away from the body altogether.

I must say that these feminists' analyses of essence have also helped
me to identify flaws in Dewey's analysis which represent further possibilities for conversation. Feminist analyses reveal, I think, that Dewey's notion of unintended third-party consequences does not quite do
justice to our endless capability for self-interest and self-deception. I
think we must acknowledge that not all third-party consequences are
unintended; it is all too possible that we deliberately construct things
so that, indeed, certain identifiable groups of people are deliberately
left out. This also complicates the process of forming emergent meanings, because people who have been consistently marginalized have
often been psychically damaged and lack the confidence to create new
shared meanings. That said, however, I think Dewey properly reminds
us that some bad things are the unintended by-product of pursuing
very good intentions.

In pushing the conversation further, a Deweyan account of essence
also helps us see what a thoroughgoing anti-essentialism might look
like. First, it involves a fundamental commitment to the enjoyment
and celebration of lived meaning in primary communities. Theory,
though it is important, is never the whole of life, not even for feminists. We all come out of primary communities which have shaped us,
and we should be free to acknowledge this. I myself have been deeply
formed by the Christian tradition and by the meanings that we cele-

brate. Among the most important: our understanding of baptism, which initiates us into a community under the sign of suffering love, of death and resurrection; our understanding of eucharist, which is the practice of ongoing community-building among a disparate group including the outcasts of society; the doctrine of creation, in which all of us have a privileged and immediate openness to the ongoing creative and transformative activity of our creator. All of these things are shared human meanings constitutive of my identity, meanings which I am happy to celebrate and to act upon in the world.

Implicit in Dewey's theory, however, is an acknowledgment of plurality within these communities of meaning. There are always majority as well as minority voices within a given tradition. In part this is because shared meanings continue to develop over time and in response to those "objects" which are also part of Dewey's theory of meaning. I believe that the meanings I have identified above are constitutive of the Christian tradition; but I also admit that too often this is a minority voice. More dominant, for the most part, is an authoritarian church long ruled by powerful men and in collaboration with oppressive regimes in the larger society. Spurred on by my own reading of the Christian tradition, I have joined a number of emergent communities—feminist, gay and lesbian advocacy, non-profit housing—which also challenge things in the church I think need challenging. In the process, I am coming to realize that the church is also deeply implicated with patriarchy. I am indebted to a host of other women who have pointed out that my own community, as it has developed in the Western cultural and philosophical tradition primarily by men, has privileged mind, rationality, form. These meanings have constructed "woman" as matter, body, or nature. As Spelman, Irigaray, and many others have pointed out, this locates "woman" in the realm of non-being; being essentially beneath culture she is not able to occupy the "subject-position" in human culture; possessing no inherent form or subjectivity of her own, she needs to be shaped or to have (male) form or culture imposed on her. My gay and lesbian friends have pointed out to me that most Christians are deeply implicated with heterosexism, and my friends in non-profit housing show me how deeply middle-class I still am. In fact, it is these emergent communities which have shown me that I belong to a great many communities, and that, whether or not I realize it, I am deeply involved in maintaining and celebrating meanings which privilege me in different ways. Following Elizabeth Spelman, I would acknowledge that the most secure meanings are the least visible to me, and that the meanings which seem the most precarious are the ones most central in my consciousness. In contrast with traditional essence, which would provide a very clear view of who I fundamentally am, as opposed to what I am only at certain times, a more emergent theory helps me to see that *who I am* is also in process and is defined not only by our shared meanings within the group but by who or what is excluded. Knowing this about my own tradition, it is important for me to remember that this is also likely to be true of other traditions.

Dewey's anti-essentialist taxonomy of meaning also makes it clear that belonging to an emergent community need not mean that one does not still belong to other emergent communities, and to a variety of primary communities. It then becomes evident that human existence has a richness and multiplicity that cannot be contained in any one set of meanings or purposes. For it is all of them, and the number is always capable of expansion. Each is "essential" to the identity of some community of purpose within existential life, but no one has absolute privilege; no one encompasses the whole of life. This multiplicity of essences leaves us with multiple (possibly conflicting) identities, and with multiple (possibly conflicting) loyalties. In such a situation decisions regarding the allocation of time and resources are enduring practical problems. Because these emergent processes are conditioned by the multiple specifics of local situations, rather than by the magisterial unfolding of logical implications, constitutive meanings are entirely likely to differ from group to group, and there is, a priori, nothing to guarantee that "woman" will have a constant meaning or that it will take automatic priority in the thinking of a group or an individual.

It seems to me that one thread of continuity among multiple identities and loyalties is the individual person, the concrete existent, in whom they reside. Exclusive ontological privilege is not granted to any of these identities or loyalties; thus, they have no set, predetermined pattern. But they do all constitute me in some way. And in telling my own story, I struggle to articulate a coherent, enduring identity in the midst of the varied meanings that constitute me. I then struggle to harmonize them to some degree, at least to avoid being ripped apart by them, or to prevent my having to live separate lives in self-enclosed compartments. But when I open these multiple and conflicting essences to each other in trying to tell a coherent story, I enter new and risky territory, not only for myself but also for those shared meanings I

have come to value. To paraphrase Dewey, the meanings from different parts of my life come into contact with each other and spawn new
meanings, with the result that I put what seemed settled at risk once
again, and I do not know where I will end up. In telling the story I
modify some meanings, retrieve others, and often allow the conflict to
work itself out more fully. At any rate, it seems to me that the distinctive way in which each of us comes to terms with this provides the
individual novelty that can then enrich all of our communal vocabularies. But this is why I continue to insist, with Fuss, that it is important
to listen, though not uncritically, to individuals' experiences.

On this view, historical development is piecemeal and partial rather
than unified. Emergent groups form, not as part of the logical and
orderly unfolding of ideas, but as a result of various contingent pres-
sures and situations. This results in an enormous variety of groups and
interests. Emergent groups may find that, in order to increase their
leverage for change, they need to try to get together and create shared
meanings among themselves. At any rate, although this is possible it
is not automatic. The creation of such shared meanings involves, on
Dewey's account, the slow processes of working together on potentially
common issues. This is what is happening with those pro-choice and
pro-life women's groups that are currently involved in a "search for
common ground." Logic cannot be a shortcut here, because logic
takes place only where there are already relatively stable shared meanings and purposes. Perhaps this is why the essence "woman" will never
automatically do what we might wish it would do. Where there are not
such shared meanings, only the ordinary, laborious human activities of
community-building will do. As Spelman points out, solidarity can be
achieved not by bracketing difference, but by acknowledging it and
working through it.

In this struggle for coherence and continuity, whether within the
individual or among different communities, it is understandable that
we use any means at our disposal to simplify things. And essentialism—granting absolute ontological privilege to one essence or meaning—will remain tempting because it is part of what Dewey calls the
"quest for certainty." It is a way of trying to set absolute priorities for
all individuals in advance. For example, if we could determine that
"human" (understood even as "male human") takes automatic or natural precedence over "woman," we could in effect limit the challenge
of feminism to the body politic. Or if we could determine that, for
biological females, "woman" understood in a certain way must auto-

matically take precedence over all other meanings (like "human," or "race," or "class"), we could make all women speak as one, thus increasing our leverage for change. In addition, granting exclusive ontological privilege to one set of meanings would enable us, in principle, to have access to a logical, clean way of manipulating agreement among people. In theory, if "woman" in general has an essence fully and universally determined by Reason or Nature, we can invoke agreement by insisting that to disagree is to be unnatural or unreasonable. This too, Dewey might say, is the illusion put forward by essentialism.

If we wish to avoid the temptations of essentialism, I see two things we can do. First, it will be increasingly important for us to struggle within our communities for an openness, on our community's own terms, to engage with others in the formation of shared human meanings. In my own Christian community, I am working to retrieve the implications of God as Creator and of "creature" as a term which includes more than just Christians. I am also exploring our traditional understanding of the church as sacrament, as a community made separate for the purpose of training itself to be inclusive. For if we can understand that God cares about all creatures, and that the church is called to be continually opening itself beyond its own boundaries, then perhaps Christians can begin to see that we ought to be outside the bounds, creating new communities of meaning in order to find new common ground and speak to new situations. Many other communities are struggling with themselves to make room for this sort of awareness. This is of the utmost importance, especially for those of us who belong to large and influential communities. For if we can build openness toward others into the meanings which we celebrate for ourselves, we can harness the good energy of essence in the struggle against the evils of essentialism.

Second, I think it will be important for emergent communities like feminism to learn that members often need to work within their own primary communities, and that this does not necessarily mean that they compromise their identity as feminists. It may mean that they resist any attempt by others to coerce them into believing that a certain definition of feminism or of feminist issues should be given priority always and in all situations. This applies to scholars with loyalties to Derrida or Hume, just as it does to Christians or to African American women. There are times when it will be important for us to work with men in those communities, and to speak a language internal to that community, in order to promote feminist issues within those communities. I would like to see the feminist community be flexible enough to support feminists who are working on feminist issues within their own primary communities, even when they are not using explicitly feminist language or working on overtly feminist issues. In my own community, for example, it is important for me to work at the background notion of creation as part of my feminist project within the church. Similarly, an African woman might need to speak her tribe's language and work at local background issues in order to provide alternatives to clitoridectomy. Or a Kant scholar may need to use detailed Kantian language to work at a feminist issue in her own area. A thoroughgoing anti-essentialism should promote the flexibility for feminists to work at a range of problems in a range of different ways and languages.

TAKING THE RISK OF MEANING

Many feminist thinkers, including the ones I've looked at here, speak of essence as a "risk." They acknowledge that, since essence is crucial to sustained political resistance and the creation of alternative communities, we cannot afford to do without it. At the same time, they remind us that it is a dangerous implement that can easily do as much harm as good. A Deweyan account can, I have argued, further this line of argument by providing a clear distinction between properly functionalized essence and that distortion we call essentialism. In this sense, positing essence is a risk we must take, because it can give us a degree of wisdom in dealing with the affairs of life; but, just as easily, it can produce a contempt for the untidiness of ordinary human life. For Deweyan essence is clearly *daimon* or *pharmakon*. Essence as constitutive of community is to be celebrated as an ultimate human good of shared life, but in the process it marginalizes and damages other people. The human meanings celebrated, respectively, by the Serbs and Muslims are also used as reasons for genocide. Moreover, essence as instrument—whether economic, logical, or other meanings—can be used by communities to expand the scope of human goods to all their members, or they can be used by an elite to control other people. Deweyan essences as shared human meanings bring us right into the tangle of life as it is lived, in which the possibilities of good and evil are inextricably entwined, and asks us not to opt for an artificial purity or certainty.

Thus, to functionalize essence in a Deweyan way opens us to risk in a larger way. Working off of Derrida's question, "Is not strategy itself the real risk?"[48] I would go further and ask, Is not shared action the real risk? For the activity of creating shared meaning is irreducible to something which is already there; it is fundamentally new and is sustained by our mutual commitment. Shared meanings are dependent on ongoing human commitment to sustain, celebrate, and develop them. Fundamentally, then, to live within a community of shared meaning is to live on the edge of human existence, in a fragile network that remains vulnerable to history and to the fluctuations of human commitment.

Shared human meaning is also risky because, having itself reached into the future, it *continues* to reach into the future. When we really commit ourselves to the creation of shared meanings and purposes with other people, we have embarked on an open-ended process that leads into the future in unpredictable ways. As we explore the potentially universalizable scope of our shared meanings, they will provoke resistance. Other groups will come into being to resist our meanings or to change them. We ourselves may be part of those groups. It is always tempting for us to batten down the hatches, to preserve what is comfortable and what sustains and nourishes us. Indeed, often it is important for us to maintain our own meanings, even when they are challenged. But it is also important for us to struggle to find the resources within our own communities of meaning to deal with new situations, or even to change our meanings when the pressure of other communities has given us an awareness of our shortcomings. But Dewey would also ask us to embrace the risk, to reach across ideological gulfs and begin the search for common ground, for shared meanings and objects.

This open-ended understanding of human meaning implies that any actions we take, any shared meanings we form, are going to be partial and contingent. They will create conflict within our society and within ourselves. Yet this open-endedness of essence, its continual spawning of unanticipated consequences, does not call us to fatalism. For often there are situations, whether of damaging polarization or of hurtful third-party consequences or of communities that exclude certain kinds of people, when we must begin to act in concert with others. If we really believe that the situation is oppressive and damaging, we have an ethical obligation to do something, to move forward into an unknown future, with the very real risk that we may be wrong. It is very natural for us to fear and to avoid risk; but I believe that authentic ethical and political action takes place in the arena of risk. And I think our ethical culpability comes not in our initial (perhaps unwitting) exclusion or marginalization of some people, but in our response to them once we hear their cries of hurt, rage, and oppression. If we batten down the hatches and look for rationalizations, or if we penitently welcome them as partners in reformulating the categories (or even if we simply allow them to tell us where we have gone wrong), this is the moment of truth. And it is knowing that this will happen—knowing that we will be taken to task as oppressors and have our imperialism exposed to the gazes of others—that also defines the risk of meaning.

The intellectual side of ourselves would always prefer to anticipate problems and wait until we get our concepts straight before we act. This means that we would like to formulate the perfect, unoppressive, politically correct notion of essence before we try to act on it. The fear, I think, is this very fear of exposing our own exclusions and blind spots. However, if we take a more functionalized, Deweyan view of essence, we realize that such things cannot be done prior to action. For if essence fundamentally *is* a way of acting with respect to a specific purpose, then we can define and re-define our meanings only in the course of action. Although I do not by any means denigrate the value of thought or theory, I also believe that the process does not really begin until we choose a course of action and act on it. To use my own language as a Christian, I believe that it can be an act of sacrificial love to take the risk of essence, knowing full well that our own blind spots will be held up to criticism. For it is only as we are willing to commit ourselves to political action and confront the multiple faces of oppression within ourselves, and intentionally engage in the creation of redemptive and liberating shared human meanings, that we contribute to a culture that nurtures the best of human possibility.

NOTES

1. Elizabeth Grosz, "Sexual Difference and the Problem of Essentialism," in *The Essential Difference*, ed. Naomi Schor and Elizabeth Weed (Bloomington and Indianapolis: Indiana University Press, 1994), p. 93.

2. Gayatri Chakravorty Spivak, "In a Word: Interview with Ellen Rooney," in *The Essential Difference*, p. 156.

3. Elizabeth V. Spelman, *Inessential Woman: Problems of Exclusion in Feminist Thought* (Boston: Beacon Press, 1988), pp. 1–2.

4. Ibid., p. 2.
5. Ibid., p. 140.
6. Ibid., p. 159.
7. Ibid., p. 128.
8. Diana Fuss, *Essentially Speaking* (New York: Routledge, 1989), p. 3.
9. Ibid., p. xiii.
10. Ibid., p. xii.
11. Ibid., p. xiii.
12. Ibid., p. xii.
13. Ibid., p. xi.
14. Ibid., p. 40.
15. Ibid., p. 42.
16. Ibid., p. 42.
17. Ibid., p. 42.
18. Ibid., pp. 43, 47.
19. Ibid., p. 45.
20. Ibid., pp. 43, 46.
21. Ibid., p. 46.
22. Ibid., p. 49.
23. Ibid., p. 6.
24. Ibid., p. 8.
25. Ibid., p. 12.
26. Ibid., p. 59.
27. Ibid., p. 60.
28. Ibid., p. 58.
29. Ibid., p. 58.
30. Ibid., p. 60.
31. Ibid., p. 60.
32. Ibid., p. 60.
33. Ibid., p. 66.
34. Ibid., pp. 68, 69.
35. Ibid., p. 61.
36. Ibid., p. 61.
37. Ibid., p. 69.
38. Ibid., p. 60.
39. Ibid., p. xiv.
40. John Dewey, *Experience and Nature*, The Later Works, 1925–1953, Vol. 1: 1925, ed. Jo Ann Boydston (Carbondale: Southern Illinois University Press, 1981), pp. 137ff. Hereafter in text as EN.
41. John Dewey, *The Public and Its Problems*, The Later Works: 1925–1953, Vol. 2: 1925–1927, ed. Jo Ann Boydston (Carbondale: Southern Illinois University Press, 1984), p. 250. Hereafter in text as PP.
42. I take this to be more or less what Dooyeweerd means by "object func-

tions." See Herman Dooyeweerd, A *New Critique of Theoretical Thought*, trans. David H. Freeman and William S. Young (Philadelphia: Presbyterian and Reformed, 1953–1958), III, pp. 57–58. Both posit some real cooperation of objects and human purposes, though Dewey's theory is tripartite, necessarily involving at least two persons in relation to a common object.

43. John Dewey, *Logic: Theory of Inquiry*. The Later Works: 1925–1953, Vol. 12: 1938, ed. Jo Ann Boydston (Carbondale: Southern Illinois University Press, 1986), p. 52. Hereafter in text as LTI.

44. John Dewey, *The Quest for Certainty*. The Later Works: 1925–1953, Vol. 4: 1929, ed. Jo Ann Boydston (Carbondale: Southern Illinois University Press, 1988), p. 108. Hereafter in text as QC.

45. John Dewey, "Introduction to *Essays in Experimental Logic*." The Middle Works: 1899–1924, Vol. 10: 1916–1917, ed. Jo Ann Boydston (Carbondale: Southern Illinois University Press, 1980), p. 342. Hereafter in text as IEL.

46. Fuss says that "Whereas Haraway posits a coalition of women as the basis of a possible feminist socialist politics, I see politics as the basis of a possible coalition of women. For Haraway, it is affinity which grounds politics; for me, it is politics which grounds affinity" (Fuss, *Essentially Speaking*, p. 36). Perhaps it is possible to split the difference here. Perhaps we could say that common oppression (perhaps even on the basis of an *attributed* essence), not a common essence or natural affinity, is what grounds political action of any kind. But for there to be a specifically "feminist" politics, those women who identify oppression need to develop a shared culture and a shared set of meanings. On this level, various articulated affinities determine specific issues and strategies, as well as various levels of identification and cooperation.

47. Gilson also makes this point when he says that, for medieval essentialists, ". . . all that which is real is essence; existence is not an essence; hence existence is nothing. And, since each and every essence is an object of both concept and definition, the very fact that there is no concept of existence as such is to them a sure sign that existence itself is nothing" (176). As Dewey says, essentialism forces existence to live up to the requirements of concepts, rather than the other way around. He says that absolutized Essences may be used to "throw the glamor and prestige, the meaning and value attached to the general notion, over the concrete situation," thereby enabling us to "cover up the defects of the latter and disguise the need of serious reforms" (*Reconstruction in Philosophy*. The Middle Works: 1899–1924, Vol. 12: 1920, ed. Jo Ann Boydston [Carbondale: Southern Illinois University Press, 1982], p. 189). Hereafter in text as RP.

48. Jacques Derrida, "Women in the Beehive," in *Men in Feminism*, ed. Alice Jardine and Paul Smith (New York: Methuen, 1987), p. 192.

ETHICS AND/OF THE OTHER

4

Singular Interruptions: Rortian Liberalism and the Ethics of Deconstruction

Ronald A. Kuipers

> . . . in breaking into my own body of speech, opening up the gaps and listening to the silences in my own inheritance, I perhaps learn to tread lightly along the limits of where I am speaking from. I begin to comprehend that where there are limits there also exist other voices, bodies, worlds, on the other side, beyond my particular boundaries.[1]

INTRODUCTION: CULTURAL CRITICISM IN A POST-PHILOSOPHICAL AGE

As GLOBE-SHRINKING TECHNOLOGIES and the mass movement of the earth's peoples continue to increase at an ever-accelerating rate, we in the West are becoming more and more aware of the many diverse and incommensurate perspectives that exist both inside and outside the confines of Western culture. This acute awareness of cultural plurality in the West also happens to coincide with a growing loss of faith in the promises of the Enlightenment. Many of us now no longer believe that human reason can supply us with permanent, neutral criteria with which to assess the legitimacy or illegitimacy of any of the many different perspectives that exist in the world today. The loss of such a guiding meta-narrative has left only a multiplicity of narratives in its wake, and no overarching method by which we may assess the legitimacy of these narratives with any absolute intellectual certainty.

Many thinkers consider such uncertainty as symptomatic of an unfortunate loss of coherence, a loss of a common vision of the world and of what we should be striving for in that world. Other thinkers, however, consider this incredulity toward meta-narratives (joined with an awareness of cultural plurality) as a liberating return to a particularly human world in which we no longer strive for a "God's eye view."[2]

In North America, a good example of the latter sort of thought is Richard Rorty's post-philosophical neopragmatism. On the Continent, Jacques Derrida's deconstruction of Western logocentrism provides an infamous example. While Rorty and Derrida share similar criticisms of the Western philosophical tradition's totalizing pretensions, their respective criticisms have different flavors, and this affects each thinker's vision for life in a post-philosophical culture.[3]

Rorty places much hope in the potential of a culture that would no longer feel the need for any sort of necessary, transcendental guidance. We see this sanguinity emerge when he unproblematically divides human discourse along the lines of the public and the private. According to him, our public selves and our private selves speak two different languages. The public self operates on the level of the universal, speaks a shared, argumentative language, and concerns itself with matters of social justice and cultural legitimation. The private self, on the other hand, operates on the level of the singular, speaks an idiosyncratic language, and concerns itself with matters of poetic self-redescription and imaginative self-making. Rorty wants to give both kinds of discourse equal weight and then put them to different purposes. They are, he says, "as little in need of synthesis as are paintbrushes and crowbars."[4]

Derrida envisages the role of post-philosophical cultural criticism somewhat differently than Rorty does. For him, the public and private aspects of the self are more inextricably interlaced. Derrida shows this interlacement by demonstrating how thoroughly the singular is implicated in the universal. Derrida's thought calls attention to the singularities, the marginal traces, that resist containment by any theoretical system and that thereby serve to interrupt unremittingly the universalizing tendencies of human thought.[5] Following Levinas, Derrida exhibits a vigilant, ethical concern for these singularities.[6] Although theory necessarily works on the level of the universal and the total, Derrida argues, it is always already opened upon the singular, which is at the same time its limit and condition.

Broadly stated, the difference between Rorty and Derrida is that Rorty refuses to admit that the ethical call of the singular comes to us in the form of a quasi-transcendental 'imperative.' There may be a call, but we will hear and respond to such a call only when someone who speaks our language can interpret it in such a way that we will be able to make sense of it and thereby include it in our cultural conversation. We are not called to justice by anything exterior, transcendental, or trace-like. Even so, says Rorty, we can still pursue the liberal goals of diminishing cruelty and of gathering more and more different perspectives while we cut these goals free from arguments of transcendental necessity.[7] Our own "connoisseurs of diversity" (sociologists, anthropologists, literary critics, novelists, and poets) will keep the public aware of those who suffer on the margins of this society.[8]

Therefore, it is not fair to say that Rorty is simply unconcerned about the ethical direction of a post-philosophical culture; he is, rather, more sanguine about the potential of a culture that no longer requires outside guidance and instead relies only upon that which it distills from its own immanent conversations. I wonder, however, whether Rorty's liberal desire for inclusion would extend beyond the "bazaar" and enter the "gentlemen's club."[9] A failure to extend the operation of difference all the way down could prevent us from reforming our private clubs, or from hearing the call of the other person who is not a good "haggler," or the person who does not even get as far as the bazaar in the first place.

For thinkers like Derrida and Levinas, a merely public incorporation of the marginalized would betray the very exteriority and singularity of the call they place on us. The question such thinkers would put to Rorty, I think, is whether or not he thinks that the liberal desire to include difference extends all the way down from the public to the private. Rorty is very much aware of the fact that his theoretical separation of the private and the public creates problems in these areas, and his complex and nuanced defense of this position does take such ethical objections into account. But is his defense adequate?

Two Motivations?
Rorty's and Derrida's Critique of Western Logocentrism

Before exploring these criticisms of Rorty's private/public split, I would first like to situate the argument in philosophical space by examining the general intellectual terrain that Rorty and Derrida share. Derrida's work has had a tremendous influence on Rorty. Not only does he think of Derrida as an ally of his own philosophical project, but he also thinks of Derrida as one of its heroes. According to Rorty, Derrida has helped demythologize philosophy by describing it as one kind of writing among many. [10] As well, Derrida has criticized the philosophical idea of truth as adequation to, or representation of, the mind-independent objects of human experience. Such a criticism of the Western conception of truth sits close to the heart of Rorty's project in *Philosophy and the Mirror of Nature.*

For his part, Rorty looks forward to life in a 'post-philosophical' culture. In such a culture, people will no longer consider 'truth' as the discovery of a direct relationship between our words and a world independent of those words. In such a culture, says Rorty, we will no longer search for that set of permanent, antecedent criteria that would secure a direct relationship between our words and the mind-independent objects those words are said to represent. In this culture, there will be no theoretical discipline to tell us when we are in touch with reality and when we are not. For this reason, we shall no longer consider that discipline as the one that undergirds all the others. Instead, says Rorty, we will happily play the many vocabularies around us one against the other, continually redescribing ourselves in the process. Rorty wonders whether the day will come when we will be able to "see ourselves as never encountering reality *except under a chosen description.*"[11]

A salient yearning for something "after philosophy"[12] can also be found in the work of Derrida. Something like (but not entirely the same as) Rorty's rejection of a correspondence theory of truth lies behind Derrida's infamous claim that "there is nothing outside of the text (*il n'y a pas de hors-texte*)."[13] By this phrase, Derrida tells us that the independently real, as such, is inaccessible to us. He goes on to say that

> there has never been anything but writing; there have never been anything but supplements, substitutive significations which could only come forth in a chain of differential references, the "real" supervening, and being added only while taking on meaning from a trace and from an invocation of the supplement, etc. And thus to infinity, for we have read, *in the text,* that the absolute present, Nature, that which words like "real mother" name, have always already escaped, have never existed; that what opens meaning and language is writing as the disappearance of natural presence.[14]

The antecedently real, says Derrida, has "never existed." But if it never existed, how could it have "always already escaped" or disappear? We should read Derrida here not as giving up on the independence of the antecedently real, but as emphasizing its complete exteriority. The moment we thematize it, it has already disappeared, for then it becomes interior to the theoretical system.

An aporia emerges in Derrida's desire to respect this exteriority that cannot be said. Whatever we name by the word 'real' is already a thematization and not this independent exteriority. More so than Rorty, Derrida emphasizes the fact that there is always a residue, or excess, to our thematizations—one that we must respect. For the moment, however, we may read Derrida with Rorty as affirming that we never encounter reality except under a chosen description.[15]

Far too often, we read thinkers like Rorty and Derrida as giving up on 'truth' or the 'world' and affirming an arbitrary "anything goes" attitude toward theory. Our realist intuitions run strong and deep. Yet both thinkers are out to do more than nihilistically trifle with our most cherished assumptions. Each has a vision of something "better,"[16] a more edifying picture of human theoretical activity than the one we now have. In order to appreciate their vision, we must drop our fear that either thinker gives up on the independence of reality. Neither thinker believes that we make the world by describing it, although both thinkers believe that it is fair to say that we do not have a world apart from our descriptions.[17] This distinction is crucial. Both thinkers mean to assess the impact that the linguistic, historical, and cultural contingency of our various descriptions has on our understanding of the world.

In a helpful move, Drucilla Cornell has (for her purposes) renamed Derridean deconstruction as the "philosophy of the limit."[18] Such a description also fits Rorty. Both thinkers urge us to become vigilantly aware of the limits in which human thought always takes place. Rorty emphasizes the various contingencies that situate our thought in time and place, and the inaccessibility of any neutral vantage point from which to judge among different perspectives. For his part, Derrida emphasizes the historico-cultural situatedness of the human subject within a chain of linguistic signifiers, and hopes thereby to expose the universalizing tendencies of philosophy to its limit, to have it open upon the singular other.

Such affinities notwithstanding, one finds certain exigencies in Rorty's overall project that conflict with the underlying motivation behind

Derrida's demonstration of the deconstruction of Western logocentrism. While Rorty wants to expose the limits within which human thought proceeds, he is less concerned than is Derrida to show the deconstructive operation of an exterior, excluded, singular other upon any particular theoretical system. One of his major concerns is to protect, as far as possible, the liberal value of an individual's freedom to pursue private projects of self-making. Argues Rorty: "J. S. Mill's suggestion that governments devote themselves to optimizing the balance between leaving people's private lives alone and preventing suffering seems to me pretty much the last word."[19] The question we must ask ourselves is whether or not Rorty considers preventing suffering as important a goal as leaving people's private lives alone and which, if the two were to conflict, would assume priority. That is, does Rorty's negative ethical injunction that we "prevent suffering" go far enough in the direction of promoting justice in an oppressively stratified world?

Rorty would probably say that the goals of protecting privacy and preventing suffering and cruelty are too different for us to make the question of priority a decidable one. Yet, as Levinas convincingly argues, an ethical concern for the singular Other (*autrui*) interrupts my individual freedom and enjoyment, and calls my 'I' into question:

> The subject is "for itself"—it represents itself and knows itself as long as it is. But in knowing or representing itself it possesses itself, dominates itself, extends its identity to what of itself comes to refute this identity. This imperialism of the same is the whole essence of freedom. . . . But if freedom situates me effrontedly before the non-me, before the Other it retreats. The relationship with the Other does not move (as does cognition) into enjoyment and possession, into freedom; the Other imposes himself as an exigency that dominates this freedom, and hence as more primordial than everything that takes place in me.[20]

Here, Levinas extends the call of the Other all the way down to my private freedom. The Other interrupts the back-slapping enjoyment that we have in our private clubs. Would such an irruption of personal freedom, the retreat of one's "imperialism of the same," sit well with Rorty?

One possible reading of Rorty is as follows: In order to protect individual freedom as far as possible, Rorty drives a deep wedge between the public and the private aspects of human life. Public concerns for justice should intrude as little as possible into private pursuits. From a Levinasian or a Derridean standpoint, such a radical separation of the private and the public is dangerous. If we restrict the demands of justice to the public realm, we will betray the singularity of the ethical call that manifests itself in the "face-to-face." For these thinkers, ethics is as much a private affair as it is a public one. On this reading, Rorty's liberal leanings sit in tension with Derrida's and Levinas's emphasis on the anteriority of the singular to the universal. Therefore, we should look more closely at the ethical consequences of Rorty's private/public split.

RORTY'S TOOLBOX:
SEPARATING PRIVATE AND PUBLIC DISCOURSE

Many consider Rorty's radical separation of the public and the private to be the most problematic aspect of his thought. How does such a radical thinker mean to get away with such a tired old move? In answering such a question, we must not let our initial distaste for Rorty's argument prejudice our reading of him. It may just turn out that, because of the very radicalness of his thought (and of its articulation in unsettling, "naughty" metaphors), we might have quite a different animal by the tail from the one we now think we have.

The first thing we must notice is that Rorty posits this private/public split because of what he sees as the prior failure of universalizing theoretical discourse to unite the two aspects of human life under the aegis of a common human nature, one mind-independent reality, original metaphysical language, or what-have-you:

> Metaphysics hoped to bring together our private and our public lives by showing us that self-discovery and political utility could be united. It hoped to provide a final vocabulary which would not break apart into a private and a public portion. It hoped to be both beautiful on a small private scale and sublime on a large public one. Ironist theory ran its course in the attempt to achieve this same synthesis through narrative rather than system. But the attempt was hopeless.[21]

Notice that the failure of these very different attempts to unite the public and the private belongs to *theory*. For Rorty there is no theory, language, or vocabulary that can unite the public and the private. *In theory*, the split is total. The best we can hope for, Rorty says, is that we make many vocabularies of both kinds available for the various purposes to which we want them put.

The wedge, however, does not go all the way down. Following the passage cited above, Rorty quickly points out that in his ironist culture "such opposites *can be combined in a life* but not synchronized in a theory," and that "ironists should reconcile themselves to a private/ public split within their final vocabularies, to the fact that resolution of doubts about one's final vocabulary has nothing in particular to do with attempts to save other people from pain and humiliation"[22] (emphasis added). We must all, of course, reconcile the various conflicts that occur in life between private desires and shared, public interests. The two will not always coincide. Theory can provide strategies for coping with one or the other, but we have no grand theory or master language by means of which we may reconcile the two.

While Rorty does mark a stark division between two kinds of discourse, that does not mean he is unconcerned with matters of public justice. It is just that he sees such justice as having a better chance if we can pursue it merely because we value it, not because there is something transcendental and necessary backing it up. Since there is no meta-discipline or vocabulary to guarantee the advent of justice, we must proceed ad hoc and case by case.

Rorty's account, then, is radically contextual. Yet he insists it is important that 'liberal ironists' look up from their private concerns and notice difference: "[T]he liberal ironist needs as much imaginative acquaintance with alternative final vocabularies as possible, not just for her own edification, but in order to understand the actual and possible humiliation of the people who use these alternative final vocabularies."[23]

Rorty sees literature playing a key role in helping us reconcile the private and the public, in helping us look up from our private concerns and notice others:

> Within a liberal metaphysical culture the disciplines which were charged with penetrating behind the many private appearances to the one general common reality—theology, science, philosophy—were the ones which were expected to bind human beings together, and thus to help eliminate cruelty. Within an ironist culture, by contrast, it is the disciplines which specialize in thick description of the private and idiosyncratic which are assigned this job. In particular, novels and ethnographies which sensitize one to the pain of those who do not speak our language must do the job which demonstrations of a common human nature were once supposed to do. Solidarity has to be constructed out of little pieces, rather than found already waiting, in the form of an ur-language which all of us recognize when we hear it.[24]

While Rorty does not think there is anything, including literature, that can provide a metaphysical guarantee that we will all get it together and "do the right thing," one reads here a certain gravity surrounding his thoughts on ethical matters: the liberal ironist *"needs"* acquaintance with alternative final vocabularies; novels and ethnographies *"must* do the job" which were once expected from demonstrations of a common human nature; and solidarity *"has to* be constructed" out of little pieces, etc.[25] It seems that, for Rorty, the very fact that there is nothing "out there" to guarantee the advent of justice increases both the fragility and the urgency of the pursuit of justice in the public square.

Rorty's description of how literary texts, by providing thick descriptions of the particular, interrupt our activity and help us become attuned to suffering is quite powerful. Unfortunately, however, there is no guarantee that everyone is going to read Nabokov or Orwell (two of Rorty's favorite examples) and learn the lessons embodied within their great stories.[26] But the fact that we have no such guarantee is not something to be mourned. If we would realize this fact, Rorty seems to suggest, we might finally awaken from our metaphysical slumber and focus our cultural energy on solving the particular injustices of our own time and place.

So it is clear that, for Rorty, reconciling the liberal ironist's private irony with public hope is an important cultural project. Different writers give us different vocabularies to help us do this. One sort of writer helps us answer questions like "What shall I be?" "What can I become?" "What have I been?" The other sort of writer helps answer the question "What sorts of things about what sorts of people do I need to notice?" The person that Rorty calls the "liberal ironist" needs the empowerment that both sorts of vocabularies provide, but he adds an interesting clarification: "For a few such people—Christians (and others) for whom the search for private perfection coincides with the project of living for others—the two sorts of questions come together. For most such, they do not."[27] Rorty paints a somewhat tragic picture of an atheist society here, I think, a society whose individual members are so selfish in their private pursuits that reconciling them with shared public concerns becomes the job of two different vocabularies. Surely, however, many atheists would be unhappy with this picture.

Notice that when Rorty is concerned with protecting the private sphere and maintaining its distinction from the public, he suddenly drops the sense of gravity that pervades his earlier description of our urgent cultural need to pursue justice and notice the suffering of others in its thick particularity. When he concerns himself specifically with protecting the private sphere, one gets the feeling that the terrain has shifted. His previous noble sentiment seems to evaporate. Given his distinction between the private and the public, however, this is just what one would expect to happen. A public vocabulary concerned with justice is out of place when we are talking about our private desires. At an ethical level, however, this state of affairs does more to indict Rorty's radical distinction than it does to recommend it.

RORTY'S SCALES:
BALANCING PRIVATE AND PUBLIC DISCOURSE

It is to be hoped that this exploration of Rorty's peculiar way of distinguishing the private and the public has helped bring out its subtlety and nuance. His distinction is much more than a utilitarian liberal move. Rorty prizes individual freedom so heavily that at first one takes this to be the motive behind his making the split. But on closer examination it is not clear which side Rorty comes down on. In fact, he probably does not privilege either. His work continually mentions our need to step back from our private projects in order to listen for and notice the suffering and humiliation of others—suffering and humiliation that our preoccupation with our private lives abets.

Simply put, Rorty is trying to describe a kind of society where public and private pursuits no longer conflict, not because they find synthesis under a common metaphysical rubric, but simply because they can operate side by side, like two tools for different purposes.[28] Rorty puts as much stock in what liberal democracies have been able to achieve for individual freedom as he does in how they have helped maximize human solidarity and minimize public cruelty. It is by no means evident that he values one more highly than the other.

I raised the criticism earlier that Rorty splits the private and the public in order to salvage individual freedom as much as possible. He does want to preserve this freedom, it is true, but whether or not he values it more than he does human solidarity, public justice, and the diminution of individual suffering really is an open question. Lacking the critical resources to metaphysically guarantee the inevitability of his liberal utopia, Rorty can only fall back on the beliefs and desires that liberals have come to cherish. Individual autonomy is one of those, but it shares the floor with human solidarity and the diminution of marginalization and cruelty.

To put the point more strongly: one could even say that Rorty cherishes whatever human solidarity we have been able to achieve as a valuable, yet fragile, cultural construct—one with a "merely poetic" foundation. I am concerned, however, that, if we follow Rorty's advice and radically distinguish our private projects from our public ones, we will become so consumed with our private lives that we will fail to tend to the maintenance of the public solidarity that makes such private life possible. In the end, such neglect would destroy the flourishing of both private and public life. While I think it is clear that Rorty does not intend to prioritize the private at the expense of the public, his overweening concern to protect the private sphere harbors its own dangerous consequences. In times like ours, we need a greater willingness to tear ourselves away from our private concerns than is present in the sort of willingness Rorty describes.

Another concern I raised in the previous section is whether or not such a private/public split would enable us to reform our private projects once we opened them on the exigencies of the singular and particular. I raise this question because, while Rorty does see the need for our "we" to include more and more "theys,"[29] such inclusion might also be violent if it does not lead us to an auto-critique of what we understand by the word "we." "We" might end up robbing the excluded of the last shred of dignity they have left by making them become one of us.

As far as I can tell, Rorty does not take this possibility seriously enough, although he would prize the excluded's "privacy" as individuals. There is textual evidence, however, that shows he is aware of the problem. Including the marginalized, he says, is a process that we should try to keep going: "We should stay on the lookout for marginalized people—people whom we still instinctively think of as 'they' rather than 'us.' We should try to notice our similarities with them. The right way to construe the slogan is as urging us to *create* a more expansive sense of solidarity than we presently have."[30]

It is the idea of our ability to create a more expansive sense of solidarity that shows that Rorty is aware that inclusion of the marginalized will also change how we think about ourselves. Rorty's ethical desire to include more and more "theys" is not akin to a kind of cultural imperialism. What takes the "curse" off Rorty's ethnocentrism, he explains, is that "it is the ethnocentrism of a 'we' ('we liberals') which is dedicated to enlarging itself, to creating an ever larger and more *variegated ethnos*."[31] It is, he says, an ethnocentrism that is suspicious of ethnocentrism. Unfortunately, however, Rorty concerns himself more with the inclusion, the accretion of more and more cultural perspectives, than with the self-reform that such inclusion generates. He does not examine this call for self-reform, leaving it as a dangling by-product of his liberal anti-ethnocentric ethnocentrism.[32]

There is no question, however, that Rorty's ethical concern for the excluded is deeply felt. But he gives such concern quite a different spin from that of the deconstructionists, who trace such concern back to Levinas. One might say that, for them, inclusion results as a by-product of self-reform, rather than the other way around. Ongoing self-reform is called for because the cry of the Other can be heard within the fissures and openings that this singular Other exerts on any "totality" that is presumed closed. That is, the inclusion of the marginalized other can and should occur because the *ethnos* (and its public sphere) is already fractured.

I think that Rorty's misses the ethical pulse of Derrida's thought because he reads Derrida as a purely private writer (one who helps us with our private projects of self-redescription). Such a reading is curious,[33] for, as Simon Critchley points out, "insofar as deconstruction is ethical—that is, in so far as it is a certain opening on to the Other—Derrida's work has an irreducibly public function by Rorty's own definition."[34] I would like therefore now to turn this examination over to deconstructive philosophy. If such philosophy is meant, even in part, to be the sort of discourse that Rorty describes as public, then perhaps deconstructive philosophy can help us find a way out of some of the ambivalences that emerge from Rorty's private/public split.

DECONSTRUCTION AS PUBLIC PHILOSOPHY, AS JUSTICE

Many thinkers are just recently coming to grips with the ethical implications of deconstruction and the debt that Derrida owes to Levinas. In the context of this discussion, as Critchley points out, ethical concerns receive a different spin than Rorty gives them. Deconstruction seeks to demonstrate the openness, the ruptures and the fissures, that any presumed closed totality (text, society, institution) has with respect to the Other. Deconstruction also seeks to base an ethics on this confrontation of the totality with its Other: "The basis of ethics is not *identification with* those whom we recognize as like ourselves, instead the ethical relation inheres in the encounter with the Other, the stranger, whose face beckons us to heed the call to responsibility."[35]

Rorty's ethics, on the other hand, seems to be based on just such a recognition. We have to make the face of the stranger look like one of us. One must bear in mind, however, that, at an ethical level, Rorty's definition of "one of us" is as thin as possible. That is, the other need not throw off all her difference in order for "one of us" to welcome her. Rather, urges Rorty, it is incumbent upon us to see her difference from us as not mattering so much as her similarity with us—her ability to experience pain and humiliation. Rorty uses quite peculiar language here to make a very Levinasian point: The other is "one of us" because she is human too. She, like us, has a face.

It is still true to say, however, that for Rorty the very strangeness of the stranger is not enough to elicit our responsibility; we must first shepherd that stranger into the light.[36] To his credit, Rorty does stress the cultural importance of keeping a team of "connoisseurs of diversity" on hand to draw our attention to the suffering of others when it occurs. But surely our connoisseurs of diversity do more than point out the suffering of others, suffering that Rorty himself says is so obvious that it needs no pointing out. Surely such connoisseurs also bring to light the complicity of our Western modes of living with the cause of the oppressed's suffering and marginalization. The suffering other may not need a light shed on her. She sheds her own light on our darkness.

Cornell describes Levinas's face-to-face relation with the Other as the subject's experience of "the resistance to encapsulation" of the beyond. It is the very resistance of the Other to inclusion or encapsulation that calls for our ethical response. The singular exteriority of the Other irrupts not just my "I" but also our "we." "The beyond . . . is within totality as its very disruption, but not just its negation."[37] For public deconstructionists like Cornell, such a disruption places ethical demands on us. Our totalities are always already disrupted; the Other always already calls.

To reiterate: Derrida shows how our texts and theories deconstruct themselves by pointing to something outside of our thematizations, something that we neglect at our own peril. Derrida himself describes this moment of nonclosure as harboring an "unconditional appeal."[38] It may be that Rorty's refusal to admit the operation of anything non-immanent makes him suspicious of this 'Kantian' side of Derrida. But Derrida does not go Kantian all the way:

> [W]hat remains is to articulate this unconditionality with the determinate . . . conditions of this or that context; and this is the moment of

strategies, of rhetorics, of ethics, and of politics. The structure thus described supposes both that there are only contexts, that nothing *exists* outside context . . . but also that the limit of the frame or the border of the context always entails a clause of nonclosure. The outside penetrates and thus determines the inside.[39]

Here Derrida skates between a Kantian transcendentalism and a strict Rortian empiricism. As John Caputo makes clear, the "unconditional appeal" in Derrida issues from the ineffability of the singular, not from the universalizability of pure reason. The appeal is "full of *pathos* and very empirical."[40]

Rorty, however, would have a problem with something being both empirical and ineffable at the same time. He would most probably consider such talk about deconstruction's "openness upon the Other" as just one more vain attempt to "eff the ineffable," one more vain attempt to provide some transcendental or metaphysical guarantee that we humans will act ethically and responsibly. There is something to be said for Rorty's argument here. Is the strangeness of the stranger enough to elicit a response? Is it not just so much nonsense to say that the Other always already calls? In our day-to-day dealings with others, do we not first need to make such a call intelligible by building a framework in which such a call can put on a recognizable voice?

Derrida, for his part, is aware that the universal is necessarily implicated in order to make the call of the Other intelligible:

> The third party is always witness for a law that comes along to interrupt the vertigo of singularity. . . . Does not my relation to the singularity of the Other as Other pass through the law? Does not the law command me to recognize the transcendent alterity of the Other who can only ever be heterogeneous and singular, hence resistant to the very generality of the law? But this co-implication, far from dissolving the antagonism and breaking through the aporia, aggravates them instead. . . .[41]

Like Rorty, Derrida sees our need to "interrupt the vertigo of singularity" and make the Other's call intelligible through such universal discourses as jurisprudence. But Derrida differs from Rorty in that, in this process, he sees a certain aporetic betrayal of the singularity and exteriority of the Other as Other. All this talk of "aporia" and "betrayal" would mystify Rorty, I suspect.

Rorty simply wants us to work from out of the networks that we are. Such networks, he says, include the beliefs that suffering does not belong and that cruelty is the worst thing we do. He thinks that de-

creasing such suffering is an important and crucial activity, but he
wants us to pursue such activity of our own will; he wants us to make
the diminution of cruelty our own desire. He is not hopeful for the
prospects of a justice that depends upon some quasi-transcendental
"Other" commanding us to respond.

So we can, I think, see Rorty's point. But do we need to concede it?
I must admit that I find the idea of an 'Other' that perdures beyond all
attempts at totalization, closure, dialectical synthesis, or what-have-
you quite attractive. This idea goes far to explain why the liberal culture that Rorty so cherishes has as one of its most important desires the
diminution of cruelty. But is the idea of a perduring, transcendent
Other merely a ladder that one may throw away once one has attained
the heights that Rorty has? Can a "freeloading atheist" (ORT, 202) like
himself invoke such a particularly Judeo-Christian notion of justice
without assuming all the transcendental baggage that goes along with it?

I do not know that there are simple answers to such questions. Minimally, however, I am willing to say with John Caputo that "obligation
happens." Caputo is right to say that "the ethical does not wait and
does not need to have a space prepared for it."[42] He goes on to say:

> The being obliged does not depend on the principle. The principle is a
> distillation, after the fact, of the being obliged. We do not judge the
> singular in virtue of the principle, but we draft the principle after the
> fact by excavating the singularity and erecting a relatively hollow
> schema—or "principle"—whose cash value is solely the singularities on
> which it is drawn.[43]

Here, Caputo emphasizes that the laws we draft, the societies we construct, all the things we do that Rorty's public discourse is designed to
help us engineer, is a distillation from the fact that "obligation
happens."

Still, these public principles are all drawn upon an anterior singularity that calls. But this state of affairs itself provides no principle. Here
we may read the public deconstructionists like Caputo and Cornell
with Rorty. The call itself is abyssal, without ground.[44] We are seized
from without. The command, says Caputo, "remains wholly on the
level of an imperative coming to us from the singular experience and
on my telling it lacks any deeper grounding."[45]

Rorty would probably say: What more grounding do we need? For
Rorty, we are surely lost if just turning our faces toward the oppressed is
not enough to stir our compassion. Borrowing Orwell's term "generous

anger," Rorty tells us that "the generosity of Dickens's, Stowe's, and King's anger comes out in their assumption that people merely need to turn their eyes toward people who are getting hurt, notice the *details* of the pain being suffered, rather than needing to have their cognitive apparatus restructured."[46] Rorty also claims (again putting his sentiment in the mouth of another) that he neither knows nor cares whether our ability to feel compassion is inherent in human nature or merely a contingent historical development. Such a question, for him, is "without interest or point."[47]

But one cannot help asking whether Rorty is in good faith here, or whether he is setting up a false dichotomy. For Rorty our choices are: (1) accept the contingency of our society and ourselves, realize that there is nothing deep down within us to be true to, and therefore be happy that liberal societies cherish justice and be confident that everything will come out in the wash; or (2) continue to pursue the metaphysical realist's dream of finding something ontologically permanent deep within us and others that commands us to treat people justly. Are these our only two choices? Is there no site from which one might criticize a liberal notion of society and self that is not already occupied by Rorty's metaphysical realist?[48]

I take this dilemma to be Rorty's particular form of religious zeal for his own, avowedly liberal, cultural commitment. "If you are not for me, you are against me," Rorty seems to be saying. So if we do not like Rorty's particular commitment we may either get all metaphysically hot and bothered, or we can simply say, "I don't share your liberal faith." Since I think the world has had its fill of hot and bothered metaphysicians, I am tempted to say the latter. But in fairness to Rorty, we should hear the rest of his sermon.

RORTY'S CHALLENGE:
EMPOWERMENT AND AGENCY AMIDST THE CALL OF THE OTHER

We now have the nuances of Rorty's private/public division in view, as well as some warnings concerning the possible consequences of that view from the camp of Derridean deconstruction. To summarize: both Rorty and Derrida are concerned to hear, include, and do justice to the marginalized other. As well, both thinkers are acutely aware of the limited role critical theory plays in this practical process. There are, however, important differences in their positions.

For Derrida, the totalizing tendencies of human reason betray the singularity of the other, but that singularity perdures and operates deconstructively on the margins of theory. Deconstruction thus seeks to make theory sensitive, pliable, and open to this disruptive singularity.

In an interview with Richard Kearney, Derrida confirms many of our suspicions regarding deconstruction. For him, deconstruction presupposes the affirmation of a call, an ethical call that issues from a singular alterity:

> Deconstruction always presupposes affirmation, as I have frequently attempted to point out, sometimes employing a Nietzschean terminology. I do not mean that the deconstructing *subject* or *self* affirms. I mean that deconstruction is, in itself, a positive response to an alterity which necessarily calls, summons, or motivates it. Deconstruction is therefore vocation—a response to a call. The other, as the other than self, the other that opposes self-identity, is not something that can be detected and disclosed within a philosophical space and with the aid of a philosophical lamp. The other precedes philosophy and necessarily invokes and provokes the subject before any genuine questioning can begin. It is in this rapport with the other that affirmation expresses itself.[49]

Here Derrida describes an ethical rapport that is prior to philosophy, one that cannot be disclosed in philosophical space, and to which philosophy must be responsible.[50] Derrida has placed the ethical rapport with the other outside of theory, while at the same time striving to make theory sensitive to the uncontainability of this prior ethical rapport.

We must take care to notice in the above passage, however, that Derrida is careful to delimit the agency that the self has in this ethical rapport. The deconstructing *subject* itself does not affirm, he says, while deconstruction itself mysteriously constitutes a positive response to the call of the other. Here we catch a glimpse of the major difference between Rorty and Derrida, I think. Rorty has a stronger sense of the self as agent than Derrida does. Many read Rorty to say that we can pick and choose among various vocabularies for different purposes. For Derrida, on the other hand, it is truer to say that we are at the mercy of the differential play of language than to say that language is at our disposal.

Rorty also wants to describe the limits of our ability to manipulate theory, but in a more pragmatic way. It is true that he often describes theory as a kind of tool.[51] For Rorty, we develop and use languages and vocabularies as tools. The way in which such vocabularies evolve depends on the uses to which we need them put, needs which are themselves historically contingent. Rorty appears to be painting a picture of a strong autonomous agent, but we must remember that the metaphor of tool is, primarily, Rorty's reaction to the Enlightenment's pretending to have discovered *the* Tool to end all tools. From a pragmatic point of view, the idea of a tool that could perform any existing or yet-to-be-anticipated task is silly. Seen from this angle, Rorty's tool metaphor may also be read as a delimitation of the totalizing pretensions of human theorizing.

The tool metaphor does, however, make switching vocabularies sound as easy as putting down the hammer once the chair is built and picking up the paintbrush once we decide on a color. The kind of agency that Rorty here ascribes to the individual sits in tension with his description of the self as "a centerless web of beliefs and desires" and the human as an animal that is socialization all the way down.[52] This is not a damning tension, however, as I hope to show.

Rorty has often been criticized for retaining a strong sense of private liberal autonomy. One easily understands such criticism, given the extent to which such an image has desensitized liberal societies to marginalization, cruelty, difference, and exclusion. The autonomous Enlightenment subject was not a neutral human but a wealthy, white, European man. Anything else was, implicitly or explicitly, considered less than human.[53] But Rorty challenges us to think of autonomy and agency without insisting that such traits inhere in a particular kind of pre-defined subject. He may want to empower those once regarded as less-than-human.

Once we understand Rorty's desire to empower the society in which he lives, we may read the tool metaphor differently from the way it is often read. The metaphor has its positive connotations. It evokes the idea of creativity and cooperation. It also suggests that we have a difficult task before us: that we still need to figure out which tools are the best for which job by actually *using* them. Rorty is an impatient fellow and he wants us to get to work. He retains that delicious, experimentalist, "get up and go" spirit of American pragmatism. The result is that his philosophy contains a certain gumption that is hard to come by on the Continent.

We can read Rorty's talk of vocabularies as tools, then, otherwise than as a continuation of the violent tendencies of the Enlightenment. By describing vocabularies as tools and emphasizing the human ability to use them for various purposes, Rorty should not be read as describing what is factually the case for individual members of liberal societies—or any other society, for that matter. We should read him, instead, as proffering an empowering metaphor. Given his talk of the contingency of the self, I think it is disingenuous to claim that, despite such talk, Rorty nonetheless exalts the freedom of the autonomous subject to interpret any way he or she would like,[54] or that Rorty here resurrects a tired, old piece of seventeenth-century metaphysics.[55]

One should, instead, read Rorty as a preacher challenging his congregation. I once heard a sermon in which a preacher advised that, to experience the blessings of the spirit, one had to go up to the fountain and drink. Rorty can be read as offering similar advice. If we do not like the direction of the conversation, he urges us to change the subject. If we come to find another task more important, he urges us to develop different tools. The only way we can make use of something, says Rorty, is to try it on and see if it fits. But for goodness sake, let's get going![56]

Rorty does seem to evoke a certain facility here, it is true. And the voice of the other does sometimes get drowned out amidst all this talk of tools and social engineering. Still, Rorty would seem to recognize the usefulness of deconstructionists, among others, because they help us (including Rorty) notice the possible suffering of the singular other. While Rorty is hopeful, nowhere does he suggest that the task before us is an easy one. The task of building a just society which maximizes freedom and minimizes suffering will take many different kinds of people, with many different motivations and talents, working together. Rorty does not want us to neglect the profound effect that a communal redescription can have on this process, but neither does he say that such redescription is an easy purchase.[57]

If we understand Rorty in this way, as a proselytizer for a liberal cultural ethos, then I think we may forgive him for not "getting Derrida right." He perhaps overdetermines that side of Derrida which he finds useful for his purposes. In doing so, he may neglect the extent to which Derrida himself wishes to be both an "agent of love" and an "agent of justice" and not just a "work of art." But in the end, we cannot fail to notice how Rorty and Derrida come to the same point from different angles. When it comes down to ethical matters, Rorty shows the same deep concern as Derrida does. Both thinkers also emphasize that our theoretical abilities reach their outer limit in our ethical rapport with the singular other. The real question is whether or not

we share Rorty's sanguinity concerning the relationship between liberal democracies and the world's suffering multitudes.

CONCLUSION:
CAUTION AND EXPERIMENT IN A PLURALISTIC WORLD

Perhaps, then, we may read Rorty and Derrida as correcting and balancing each other. In a pluralistic world that lacks necessary, transcendental guidance, we need the empowerment that Rorty's talk of agency
and the ability to experiment gives us. His writing also lends a certain
urgency and impetus to the task before us. Deconstruction, on the
other hand, balances such fervor by urging us to be open and cautious,
to respect the demands of the excluded singularities that call from the
margins of our system-building activity.

Deconstruction has done much to make us aware of the risk (or, as
Kierkegaard would say, the madness) inherent in any decision. Rorty
(madly?) urges us to take that risk. Rorty asks us to risk the dream of a
liberal utopia. While his words are tempting, we have reason for skep-
ticism. This is because Rorty's desire to shelter one's pursuit of private
bliss causes him to neglect the ways in which Western democracies
have contributed to the world's misery, from global pollution and the
international debt crisis to worker alienation and selfish consumerism.

Our times call for a more robust ethics than merely the contingent
desire to alleviate suffering when it is brought to our attention. It is
ironic that, for all the connoisseurs of diversity that we liberal societies
keep stocked in our universities, we still remain so profoundly deaf—
tuned in, yet turned off. While I by no means wish to impugn Rorty's
authentic, heartfelt, ethical concern, I must conclude that I do not
share his sanguine liberal faith.

NOTES

1. Iain Chambers, *Migrancy, Culture, Identity* (London and New York:
Routledge, 1994), p. 5.

2. I am describing this new cultural attitude by combining a Lyotardian
vocabulary with Hilary Putnam's repudiation of any theories of truth that
pretend to access, in a privileged way, a "God's Eye View." See Lyotard's
The Postmodern Condition: A Report on Knowledge (Minnesota: University of

Minnesota Press, 1984) and Putnam's *Realism with a Human Face* (Cambridge, Mass.: Harvard University Press, 1990).

3. On the idea of a "post-philosophical culture," see Richard Rorty's *Consequences of Pragmatism* (New York: Harvester Wheatsheaf, 1982), pp. xxxvii–xliv, hereafter cited as COP. I should also warn the reader that both Derrida and Rorty are critical of any talk about the "end" of philosophy. See Derrida's essay "Of an Apocalyptic Tone Newly Adopted in Philosophy," in *Derrida and Negative Theology*, ed. Harold Coward and Toby Foshay (Albany: SUNY Press, 1992), pp. 25–71. See also Rorty's essay "Putnam and the Relativist Menace," *The Journal of Philosophy*, 90, No. 9 (September 1993), 443–461. In a footnote, Rorty says: "There is a difference between hoping for the end of 'Philosophy 101' and hoping for the end of philosophy. . . . I hope that we never stop reading, e.g., Plato, Aristotle, Kant, Hegel, Dewey, and Heidegger, but also that we may, sooner or later, stop trying to sucker the freshmen into taking an interest in 'the problem of the external world' and 'the problem of other minds.'" Rorty here echoes his concluding reflections in *Philosophy and the Mirror of Nature* (Princeton: Princeton University Press, 1979), hereafter cited as PMN.

4. See Richard Rorty's introduction to *Contingency, Irony, and Solidarity* (Cambridge: Cambridge University Press, 1989), pp. xiii–xvi, hereafter cited as CIS.

5. Derrida has described such a demonstration as the "deconstruction" of Western "logocentrism," and his driving motivation is to demonstrate the ubiquity of this deconstruction at work. This approach is found throughout his writings, but a particularly concise example of the co-implication of singularity and universality can be found in his article "The Politics of Friendship," *The Journal of Philosophy*, 85 (1988), 632–44.

6. See Simon Critchley, *The Ethics of Deconstruction: Derrida and Levinas* (Oxford: Blackwell, 1992) and Drucilla Cornell, *The Philosophy of the Limit* (New York: Routledge, 1992) for particularly convincing demonstrations of Derrida's debt to Levinas and the resulting ethical motivation at work in Derrida's thought.

7. Rorty's claim that a postmodern, bourgeois, liberal culture would contain, as one of its immanent desires, a desire to include difference is his way of countering the criticism that his brand of ethnocentrism results in an inability to recognize the suffering and marginalized other. The fact that such human goals are ungrounded and contingent, he says, does not make them any less worth fighting for. See "On Ethnocentrism: A Reply to Clifford Geertz," in *Objectivity, Relativism, and Truth* (Cambridge: Cambridge University Press, 1991), p. 208, hereafter cited as ORT.

8. See COP, p. 202: "What we hope for from social scientists is that they will act as interpreters for those with whom we are not sure how to talk. This is the same thing we hope for from our poets and dramatists and novelists."

See also ORT, p. 206: "[C]onnoisseurs of diversity . . . insist that there are people out there whom society has failed to notice. They make these candidates for admission visible by showing how to explain their odd behaviour in terms of a coherent, if unfamiliar, set of beliefs and desires. . . ." On the same page, Rorty describes these "connoisseurs of diversity" as "agents of love" and juxtaposes them with "guardians of universality," whom he also describes as "agents of social justice." Does Rorty really intend such a barren notion of justice, one that is so distinct from love?

9. The "Bazaar" and the "Gentlemen's Club" are metaphors that Rorty borrows from Clifford Geertz to connote, respectively, the public and private aspects of human activity. See ORT, pp. 203–210. Nancy Fraser, in her essay "Rethinking the Public Sphere: A Contribution to the Critique of Actually Existing Democracy" (in *Postmodernism and the Re-Reading of Modernity*, ed. Barker et al. [Manchester: Manchester University Press, 1992]), does an excellent job of arguing for the public, discursive recognition of minority concerns that have been banished to the private sphere. She argues for the nurturance of a public space in which marginalized "subaltern counterpublics" can find an authentic voice with which to question the dominant, often oppressive, public vocabulary. She also warns that the Western usage of the words 'private' and 'public' is far from innocent. See p. 117: "In general, critical theory needs to take a harder, more critical look at the terms 'private' and 'public'. These terms, after all, are not simply straightforward designations of societal spheres; they are cultural classifications and rhetorical labels. In political discourse, they are powerful terms that are frequently deployed to delegitimate some interests, views, and topics and to valorise others." While Fraser here refers primarily to the critical theory of Jürgen Habermas, I think her warning applies equally well to Rorty, whose usage of these terms, while carrying its own complex nuance, at times seems rather uncritical. This preliminary criticism, however, should be considered in the light of Rorty's delimitation of the cultural role of the "Philosopher" in general. See PMN, p. 392: "To drop the notion of the philosopher as knowing something about knowing which nobody else knows so well would be to drop the notion that his voice always has an overriding claim on the attention of the other participants in the conversation." Delimiting the cultural importance of philosophy, for Rorty, automatically lets in more voices and levels the playing field. Rorty will not promise—but he makes room for the possibility—that philosophy understood as a contingent conversation could take a turn away from its obsession with universality toward the interruption of singularity.

10. See Rorty's "Philosophy as a Kind of Writing: An Essay on Derrida" (COP, pp. 90–109).

11. COP, p. xxxix.

12. See note 3, above.

13. Jacques Derrida, *Of Grammatology*, trans. G. Spivak (Baltimore: The Johns Hopkins University Press, 1974), p. 158.

14. Ibid., p. 159.

15. As I will discuss later, however, Rorty and Derrida differ on the issue of subjective agency. Derrida questions our individual ability to individuate and benignly choose among the various contexts, vocabularies, and languages that we find about us. For Derrida, the self is more an effect of the differential play of language than a master of language. Our language games play us as much as we play them. This point is summarized by Rick Roderick in his essay "Reading Derrida Politically (Contra Rorty)," *Praxis International*, 6 (1987), 444, and by John D. Caputo in his essay "On Not Circumventing the Quasi-Transcendental: The Case of Rorty and Derrida," in *Working Through Derrida*, ed. Gary Madison (Evanston: Northwestern University Press, 1992), pp. 161ff.

16. See COP, p. xxxviii.

17. See ibid., p. 199.

18. See Drucilla Cornell, *The Philosophy of the Limit* (New York: Routledge, 1992), pp. 1–12. In *Against Ethics* (Bloomington: Indiana University Press, 1993), John Caputo warns that " 'Limit' is a better word for Gadamer's Heideggerianized version of Hegel than for Derrida." See p. 264n8. However, for the purpose of tracing a general philosophical space that both Rorty and Derrida share, it is not inappropriate to point to the fact that both philosophers emphasize human finitude in contrast to the absolute claims made on behalf of a Universal Reason.

19. CIS, p. 63. On the priority of private freedom (achieved through disenchantment with universal religious or philosophical views) over those same universal views, see ORT, pp. 193–94.

20. Emmanuel Levinas, *Totality and Infinity: An Essay on Exteriority* (Pittsburgh: Duquesne University Press, 1969), p. 87.

21. CIS, p. 120.

22. Ibid., p. 120.

23. Ibid., p. 92.

24. Ibid., p. 94.

25. My emphases.

26. See CIS, p. 164, where Rorty offers the following reading of Nabokov's *Lolita*: "But the moral is not to keep one's hands off little girls but to notice what one is doing, and in particular to notice what people are saying. For it might turn out, it very often does turn out, that people are trying to tell you that they are suffering. Just insofar as one is preoccupied with building up to one's private kind of sexual bliss, like Humbert, or one's private aesthetic bliss, like the reader of *Lolita* who missed that sentence about the barber the first time around, people are likely to suffer still more."

27. CIS, p. 143.

28. See CIS, p. 67: "I want to replace [Habermasian universalism] with a story of increasing willingness to live with plurality and to stop asking for

universal validity. I want to see freely arrived at agreement as agreement on how to accomplish common purposes (e.g., prediction and control of the behavior of atoms or people, equalizing life-chances, decreasing cruelty), but I want to see these common purposes against the background of an increasing sense of the radical diversity of private purposes, of the radically poetic character of individual lives, and of the merely poetic foundations of the 'we-consciousness' which lies behind our social institutions."

29. See CIS, p. 192: "[S]olidarity is not thought of as recognition of a core self, the human essence, in all human beings. Rather, it is thought of as the ability to see more and more traditional differences (of tribe, religion, race, customs, and the like) as unimportant when compared with similarities with respect to pain and humiliation—the ability to think of people wildly different from ourselves as included in the range of 'us.' "

30. CIS, p. 196.

31. CIS, p. 198. I have emphasized "variegated" to show how inclusion into the ethnos also changes the shape of the ethnos.

32. Again, this criticism loses much of its sting once one understands how thoroughly Rorty divests the "Philosopher" of his juridical cultural role. An open, attentive society should be a liberal goal, Rorty says, but philosophical criticisms of the traditional metaphysical-cum-epistemological picture are only "nudges" in the right direction. A critique of something as big as a culture's final vocabulary is the task of many different participants in the conversation. And in such a debate, philosophers find themselves playing the role of reporter more often than they find themselves playing the role of judge. See his "Putnam and the Relativist Menace," 457. It is simply not philosophy's job to let people into the conversation, or to adjudicate what legitimate conversation-partners will look like. It is therefore difficult to force Rorty, a philosopher, into such a position.

33. I say "curious" because deconstruction's ethical side has undeniable public consequences. Rorty reads Derrida as a "private" thinker mainly in reaction to such philosophers as Rodolphe Gasché and Christopher Norris, who, Rorty feels, overemphasize the extent to which Derrida can be read as a systematic philosopher concerned with traditional philosophical problems. See Rorty's essay "Is Derrida a Transcendental Philosopher?" in *Essays on Heidegger and Others* (Cambridge: Cambridge University Press, 1991), hereafter cited as EHO. The question remains whether or not Rorty overdetermines Derrida the other way, given Derrida's concern in the last decade to assess deconstruction's impact on social justice issues.

34. Critchley, *Ethics of Deconstruction*, p. 242.

35. Cornell, *Philosophy of the Limit*, p. 66.

36. See ORT, p. 206: "[T]he guardians of universality make sure that once these people are admitted as citizens, once they have been shepherded into the light by the connoisseurs of diversity, they are treated just like all the rest of us."

37. Cornell, *Philosophy of the Limit*, p. 66.

38. See Derrida's "Afterword" to *Limited Inc.*, ed. G. Graff (Chicago: The University of Chicago Press, 1988).

39. Ibid., pp. 152–53.

40. John Caputo, *Demythologizing Heidegger* (Bloomington: Indiana University Press, 1993), p. 197.

41. Derrida, "Politics of Friendship," 641.

42. Caputo, *Demythologizing Heidegger*, p. 198.

43. Caputo, *Against Ethics*, p. 37.

44. Rorty says that we should "substitute a 'merely' ethical foundation for our sense of community—or, *better, that we think of our sense of community as having no foundation except shared hope and the trust created by such sharing . . .*" (ORT, p. 33; emphasis added).

45. Caputo, *Against Ethics*, p. 37.

46. EHO, p. 80.

47. Ibid., p. 78n22.

48. Rebecca Comay makes a similar criticism in "Interrupting the Conversation: Notes on Rorty," *Telos*, 69 (Fall 1986), 124. Here she refers to Rorty's imposed dichotomy as a kind of "gentle blackmail." See also D. Vaden House, *Without God or His Doubles* (Leiden: E. J. Brill, 1994), p. 119.

49. Richard Kearney, *Dialogues with Contemporary Continental Thinkers: The Phenomenological Heritage* (Manchester: Manchester University Press, 1984), p. 118.

50. Rorty offers a similar understanding in ORT, p. 33.

51. Rorty is aware of the limitations of this metaphor: "The Deweyan notion of language as tool rather than picture is right as far as it goes. But we must be careful *not* to phrase this analogy so as to suggest that one can separate the tool, Language, from its users and inquire as to its 'adequacy' to achieve our purposes. The latter suggestion presupposes that there is some way of breaking out of language in order to compare it with something else. But there is no way to think about either the world or our purposes except by using a language" (COP, p. xix). See also COP, p. 100.

52. See CIS, chap. 2, "The Contingency of the Self," pp. 23ff.

53. Obviously, postmodernist philosophers of Rorty's and Derrida's type have feminist criticism to thank for such observations. I think that one of the most exciting areas of theory today is this crossing of feminism and postmodernism. I also think that feminist theory, by calling attention to a sort of oppression that cuts across cultural boundaries, may hold a key to understanding how criticism can be global (or non-local) without going metaphysical. See *Feminism/Postmodernism*, ed. Linda J. Nicholson (New York: Routledge, 1990). For particularly trenchant demonstrations of the androcentric biases of the presumedly neutral philosophical tradition, see Andrea Nye's *Words of Power: A Feminist Reading of the History of Logic* (New York: Routledge,

1990) and Lorraine Code's *What Can She Know? Feminist Theory and the Construction of Knowledge* (Ithaca, N.Y.: Cornell University Press, 1991).

54. See Roderick's "Reading Derrida Politically (Contra Rorty)," 449.

55. See ORT, p. 33*n*16, where Rorty agrees with Hans Blumenberg that "the 'historicist' criticism of the optimism of the Enlightenment, criticism which began with the Romantics' turn back to the Middle Ages, undermines self-foundation but not self-assertion."

56. On Rorty's impatience, see his "Putnam and the Relativist Menace," 447*n*8.

57. I offer this reading of Rorty's talk of autonomy and agency as an alternative to that offered by John D. Caputo in his essay "On Not Circumventing the Quasi-Transcendental: The Case of Rorty and Derrida." But I cannot stress strongly enough how valid, important, and insightful Caputo's reading is, and the crucial role it plays in correcting the potential dangerous excesses of my reading. I refer the reader specifically to pages 164–65, where Caputo lowers the canon on liberal autonomy and begins firing: "[Rorty] would do much better to drop the idea of autonomy, to celebrate more forthrightly the plurality of possible non-Western and non-European language games, to suspect more deeply the vested interests which have their way in the Great American Way, to analyze more carefully the sociopolitical factors which are deeply embedded within any socialization process and which make changing vocabularies harder than it looks. He needs to give more play to the notion of an other whom we cannot bring into our conversation, who doesn't belong to NATO, and who cannot keep up with the fast clip of Rorty's highly sophisticated Euro-American conversation."

5

Face-to-Face: Ethical Asymmetry or the Symmetry of Mutuality?

James H. Olthuis

IN ITS HEART, postmodernism is a spiritual movement which resists the totalizing power of reason. It is that resistance, and the concomitant celebration of difference and diversity, that marks a wide array of disparate discourses as postmodern. Ethically, postmodern discourses share an alertness to plurality and a vigilance on behalf of the other. Modernist rational ethics, in its Enlightenment dream of a world increasingly controlled by a pure rationality, has shown itself not only blind and indifferent to those who are other and different, those who fall outside the dominant discourse, but violent and oppressive to them. For many, the marginalized and voiceless, the dream has been an unrelenting nightmare. And it continues unabated. In the words of Jacques Derrida, "never before, in absolute figures, never have so many men, women, and children been subjugated, starved, or exterminated on the earth."[1] Not only is our time "'out of joint,'" he exclaims, conjuring up the ghost of Hamlet, "but space, space in time, spacing."[2] What now? The foundations are trembling; there is an incommensurability of voices, a pluralism of discourses, communities of the groundless, enclaves of the homeless.

As Emmanuel Levinas says, "The essential problem is: can we speak of an absolute command after Auschwitz? Can we speak of morality after the failure of morality?"[3] What now after the reign of reason? What if we don't have a morality or a religion within the bounds of reason? How do we negotiate civic covenants sensitive to differences of gender, race, creed, age, sexual orientation, socioeconomic class? How are we to envision and give shape to a postmodern ethics of justice and compassion that includes the other, the disadvantaged, the marginalized, "the widow, orphan, and stranger"?[4]

After noting the impasse of modernist ethics, I want, in this essay, to pay particular attention to Emmanuel Levinas's plea for a different ethics, an ethics as "first philosophy"[5] which begins with responsibility rather than freedom, which finds moral focus in corporeality rather than in arguments, in pain rather than in concepts.[6] Of special concern will be the asymmetrical ethical relation in Levinas in which the other has priority over myself, a view that parallels closely the tendency in much Christian ethics to champion selfless *agape* over so-called selfish *eros*. The question will be raised whether in (rightly) challenging narcissistic self-interest, Levinas doesn't (inadvisedly) bring into ethical disrepute all concern for self-interest because, in his view, an individual subjective agent is not only a locus of enjoyment and self-interest, but also, inevitably, unavoidably, and irrevocably, an agent pitted against other agents. This seems to valorize the often adversarial quality of interpersonal relations as the inexorable human condition (which we then need to transcend to be ethical), rather than to envision such opposition itself as the breakdown of relations of mutuality in which my self-interest and the self-interest of the other may interface with each other to the harmonious enjoyment and enrichment of both parties. That is, I want to suggest an ethics of mutuality[7] in which self-sacrifice is seen not as the heart of ethics, but as an emergency compromise[8] ethic because of the breakdown of mutuality.

In other words, the question is whether self-sacrifice is a compromise ethic due to the breakdown of mutuality (my position), or whether self-sacrifice is the only avenue to mutuality (Levinas's position). The discussion is complicated because the self-sacrifice Levinas calls for is not the sacrifice of the deepest self (*le soi*), for that self is *always already* sacrificed before it has itself to sacrifice—and has itself to sacrifice or not to sacrifice only on that basis. At bottom, the heart of the discussion is whether our common ethical concern is better served by describing the self as "substitution," "hostage," or "dis-interestedness," or by portraying the ethical self as "power-with," "responsibility-with," "suffering-with." Instead of conceiving the I (*le moi*) as necessarily, ontologically, and exclusively only a self-interested agent over against other agents, which then needs to be transcended in an ethical awakening to my true self (*le soi*) as substitution for the other, I want to suggest the ethico-ontological possibility of an agent self as power-with, responsibility-with, all the while retaining a realistic awareness of the propensity to power-over violence which constantly lurks within us, to which we so often capitulate, and in which we are so frequently implicated. Instead of an "other-wise than being,"[9] as substitution, as responsibility for, I'm suggesting a being-otherwise, not as mastering, but as connecting-with.

MODERN ETHICAL THEORY

Modern ethical theory in the spirit of the Enlightenment has striven to construct a rational foundation for morality. The benchmark of such theory, whether in utilitarian or Kantian dress, has been the effort to move ethical judgments beyond the contingency and time-bound contexts of moral actors. Inspired by the scientific ideal of objectivity, ethical theory attempted to secure so-called objective moral judgments free from the subjective desires, beliefs, and narratives of the agents who make them. A justified moral judgment needs to take a form that can and must be made from anyone's point of view, independent of time, place, and historical circumstance. Problems emerge and are solved only within the comprehensive framework of a unified "encyclopaedic rationality," as MacIntyre names it. Along these lines, for example, there is Kant's categorical imperative, Hare's universalizability, Baier's God's eye-point of view, and Rawls's original position. As Stanley Hauerwas and David Burrell put it: "What I am morally obligated to do is not what derives from being a father, or a son, or an American, or a teacher, or a doctor, or a Christian, but what follows from my being a person constituted by reason."[10] Moreover, the transcendental turn to the subject, especially in Descartes, Kant, and Husserl, led to an emphasis on a timeless, omniscient, disinterested observer and the loss of attention to the pain and suffering of bodies.

Modernist ethics assumed that reasonable debate should be able to settle our basic life questions. The intent was to arrive at rational agreement without having to resort to violence.[11] But the result has often been a tangle of conflicting positions, a quagmire of unresolved issues. There has been no easy line from moral theories to moral actions. Indeed, the increasing complexity of life has made the arguments even more complex and the disputes even more intractable. The transformation of moral life through rigorous application of moral theory has failed.

Ironically, not only has rational agreement remained out of reach, but the result has been indifference to the real life situations of many people, particularly women, children, and the otherwise marginalized. In general, the abstraction of the full flesh-and-blood person from an ethical case, and the case from its full historical and developmental context, has made the whole exercise of Enlightenment ethics artificial, futile, and alienating. When moral decisions are to be based on rationally grounded principles that are not relative to the character, motives, history, context, interests, gender, body, and worldview of the agents, moral agents are separated not only from all that makes them unique, but from the very corporeality and embeddedness that makes them human persons. There is no other word for such depersonalization than violence. In effect, the "personal" is considered morally significant *only* to the extent that it can be bracketed and translated into the "impersonal." Indeed, complete disembodiment and complete disinterest is regarded as the only appropriate starting point for moral reasoning in the modernist schema.

Anthropologically, in these modernist constructions, the human self is generally understood as some combination of mind and body in which mind has the primary role of controlling corporeal desire. Feelings and emotions are typically considered morally negligible because they merely happen to pre-existing, true, rational selves and are thus held to be transitory and capricious. Universal rules of conduct as our moral duties are contrasted with contingent pleasures of our individual passions. Thus, in the Kantian tradition, sympathy, compassion, and concern—the altruistic emotions—cannot play a substantial role in morality and moral motivation because they are not products of human agency, but in fact easily divert us from the autonomy and freedom needed for moral judgment. [12]

Today, by virtually every account, this approach to persons has failed. And the failure of reason is especially obvious in the area of moral philosophy. It has become increasingly clearer that the scientific model of rationality and neutrality, with its pretense to universality and necessity, has, in fact, been unaware of its own particularity and contingency. Modernism's conviction that we can isolate impartial moral principles from our particular worldviews, loyalties, identities, histories, and communities has been revealed as its own particular faith. "There is no theoretically neutral, pretheoretical ground from which the adjudication of competing claims can proceed." [13] In effect, the culturally and morally particular was elevated to the status of the rationally universal, to the detriment and oppression of anyone and anything that is different, that is, who did not find her/himself within the discourse of universal reason. Thus, to take a classic example,

Carol Gilligan has demonstrated that Lawrence Kohlberg's stages of moral reasoning champion a typical 'masculine' ethics of duty and abstraction as the most highly developed, in contrast to an ethics of connection and responsibility more typical of women.[14] No wonder that women tended to rate much lower than men in "maturity" of moral reasoning!

We have now discovered, under the impetus of the masters of suspicion—Freud, Marx, and Nietzsche—that what was touted as the autonomous human self was in fact an illusion. The encyclopedist's appeal to timeless rational principles does not discard the burden of the past as they intended. Rather their appeal to a unitary conception of reason provides unwarranted privileged status to those who identify their own assertions and arguments with the deliverances of reason. Encyclopedic, impartial reason is exposed by the postmodern genealogist as the unwitting pawn of particular interests which mask their drive for power by false pretensions to neutrality, universality, and disinterestedness.[15]

Critics of modern ethics are unanimous that all our ideas and views are narrative-dependent, including, they emphasize, our view of rationality. There is no narrative-free judgment, and pretending that there is does violence to all, particularly to those who do not hold to the accepted view. While MacIntyre believes, in Gadamerian fashion, that commitment to some or other theoretical or doctrinal standpoint may be the requisite for—rather than the barrier to—genuine moral enquiry, he continues to believe that reason can move toward being authentically universal and impersonal. Such an alternative, which MacIntyre traces back to Plato and, for him, is best represented by Thomism, remains, from a postmodern perspective, unacceptable and even naïve. Postmoderns insist that theory itself has failed. Picking up on Heidegger's critique of the institutionalization of reason whereby everything, in nature as well as in culture, is to be put under the sway of the desire to master and control, postmodernist thinkers such as Derrida, Foucault, and Levinas assail the logocentrism of Western thought.

ETHICS BEFORE ONTOLOGY: THE PRIORITY OF THE OTHER

For Levinas, reason is the instrument by which an ego or society of egos makes same that which is different, possessing and domesticating it. Reason reduces the other, appropriates, disempowers, totalizes. The particular is placed under the general category. What is foreign, what is different, is subsumed within my system. It is made the same to remove its threat. All surprises prove to be just parts of the process, that is, not surprises at all. This is ontology.

Before ontology, however, exclaims Levinas, there is ethics, the relationship of responsibility to the other.[16] The other can never be present within my discourse, my theory, my thought, my ontology. Unless I allow myself to be instructed by the face of the other, I do not "relate" at all, but only dominate in terms of my paradigms and ontologies. The face of the other commands me: Thou shalt not kill. For Levinas the face is not a presence, but a trace, a trace which marks the escape of the other who cannot be contained, who has escaped the reduction to Being.

The face is the epiphany of the nakedness of the other, a visitation, a coming, a saying which comes in the passivity of the face, not threatening, but obligating. I encounter a face, my world is ruptured, my contentment interrupted; I am already obligated. Here is an appeal from which there is no escape, a responsibility, a state of being hostage. It is looking into the face of the other that reveals the call to responsibility as an-archic, that is, before any beginning, decision, or initiative on my part.

For Levinas the other is not another me, awaiting dialogue and reciprocity, as in Buber and Ricoeur. For Levinas my relation to the other is always asymmetrical. The other has ethical priority over the sameness of the I.

> I must always demand more of myself than of the other; and this is why I disagree with Buber's description of the I–Thou ethical relation as a symmetrical copresence. . . . This essential asymmetry is the very basis of ethics: not only am I more responsible than the other but I am even responsible for everyone else's responsibility.[17]

The existence of the other, rather than a conception of the good, is the touchstone of moral existence. The face-to-face relation fissures being. Flesh-and-blood bodies, rather than arguments and concepts, give moral bearings.

The implications of this shift are only now beginning to surface and take shape. In the Cartesian view of the body as external object in space over against the subject as inner consciousness, the body as subject of experience was lost. Similarly, in the Kantian view in which the hav-

ing of feelings is morally indifferent, non-rational ways of knowing
are devalued. Generally speaking, in the rationality tradition, sensory
knowledge is useful, but it is never in itself knowledge of the human
as human.[18] Since reason is that part of being human that is most
human, only reason can know the properties of being, goodness,
beauty, and unity. Thus, for Thomas Aquinas, touch is the lowest and
least worthy of all senses because it is most unlike reason. Since the
pleasures of eating, drinking, and having sex are pleasures of touch, it
is a sin to engage in them solely for the pleasure of eating, drinking,
and having sex.

In the rationality tradition there has been a conceptual neutraliza-
tion of sensation. Spinoza gives voice to the dominant tradition: "Pain
is the transition of a man from a greater to a lesser perfection."[19] Both
pain and enjoyment have been rationalized and their sensory truth
decimated. Even Heidegger, the archcritic of the metaphysics of subjectivity which he traces back to Plato and Aristotle, in the end still
remains captive of this feature of the tradition. He takes the suffering
out of pain by insisting that the essence of pain cannot be pain in a
feeling sense.[20]

In contrast, in the postmodern picture, I myself am my body. The
body as a whole functions as a sensorium, a senser, a knower, a per-
ceiver, a digester. Human knowledge is multidimensional. Sensing
and feeling are as human as thinking. The human self includes per-
ceptions, feelings, emotions, dispositions, attitudes, as well as thinkings. Others present themselves not simply as subjects of discourse,
but, on a more fundamental level, as persons who eat, enjoy, lack, and
so forth. For Levinas, alterity must communicate itself fundamentally
otherwise than predicatively. In *Otherwise than Being* Levinas describes ethical obligation in terms of the subject's corporeal sensibility
and proximity, vulnerability, and passivity toward the other. The ethical subject is subject to the other as "sensibility on the surface of the
skin, at the edge of the nerves" (OB, 15). Since the human person is
susceptible to wounding and pain, ethics is a lived, bodily relation to
the other. "Only a subject that eats can be-for-the-other" (OB, 74).[21]

"Ethics is the spiritual optics" (TI, 78). "To recognize the Other is
to recognize a hunger. To recognize the Other is to give" (TI, 75).[22]
The ethical "[f]ace to face remains an ultimate situation" (TI, 81) and
"in it things figure not as what one builds but as what one gives" (TI,
77). This allows human sensitivity to pain, wounding, and suffering
to be immediately ethically relevant. Ethics in this view is grounded

in corporeality, in creatureliness, with a special marking because of pain, suffering, lapse, delay, and fissure. It is sensitive bodies in proximity that are the space of ethics, the fields of meeting.[23] In my very hearing of the child's cries I am ethically claimed.[24] Face-to-face, flesh-to-flesh, I am wounded by the other's wounding—and responsible for it. Responsibility is prior to freedom. "This responsibility appears as a plot without a beginning, anarchic . . . outside of all finality and every system"(OB, 135). There is no need for a reasoning process to discover or erect a rational reason to provide the moral force.

The other is experienced as an appeal, an absence, in that it creates in me a restlessness for contact that I don't have.[25] And the other is experienced as an excess in that the trace of Transcendence is inscribed in the face. "The Other is not the incarnation of God, but precisely by his face, in which he is disincarnate, is the manifestation of the height in which God is revealed" (TI, 79). "Strictly speaking, the other is the end; I am a hostage, a responsibility and a substitution supporting the world in the passivity of assignation, even in an accusing persecution, which is undeclinable" (OB, 128).

In *Against Ethics* John Caputo describes such views as "responsible" postmodernism because they answer a call from beyond our laws and principles, so that we can attend to the particulars, the lost, the different, the exceptions. This kind of ethic is not against laws, but is aware that laws and rules do not have authority in themselves. As Caputo puts it, with an allusion to Christ healing on the sabbath, we need "to keep the law honest, to keep the eye of the law on the withered hand."[26] Indeed, to simply do what the law dictates is to fall short of doing justice. The law needs to be under justice, not justice under law. Such responsibility demands an exceeding of the demands of the law, incarnating a response to which laws intend to point the direction, but sometimes, in fact, obscure. Likewise, Wyschogrod makes a plea for "excessive desire, a desire on behalf of the other that seeks the cessation of another's suffering and the birth of another's joy."[27] Similarly, although in his typically more dialectical fashion, Paul Ricoeur attempts to establish the primacy of the ethical aim (goodness) over morality by "granting rightful place to moral rules, without letting them have the last word."[28]

ASYMMETRY AND SELF-SACRIFICE

All of this—the morality of corporeality, the spirituality of morality—finds deep resonance in my soul. Along with Levinas I see ethics not as something later, to be fitted in, but as the nature of life itself. Indeed, for me it is of the highest import that life be seen as *conatus amandi* (evocation to love) rather than as *conatus essendi*. In this way, ethics—in the sense of responsibility to love—is as old as creation itself. Love is the quickening, the quivering[29] which evokes life and permeates life. The call to justice and love belong to the very fabric of everyday life, giving it shape and texture. In a world of violence, this call often arises most poignantly in the need of the neighbor and likewise is often discovered most acutely in the cry of suffering. Then the call comes as a summons: heal the wounds, bind up the brokenhearted. Being ethical is a primordial movement in the beckoning force of life itself. As gift and call, love is both the description of life and the prescription for life.

At the same time, I admit to a fluttering, sometimes throbbing, but always bothersome disquiet. For as much as I join with Levinas in his call to responsibility for the other, I am concerned that his emphasis on the priority of the other not give birth—albeit contrary to intention—to a guilting moralism calling for self-forgetfulness and self-forfeiture. For all its importance as a countermove to narcissism, calling for the ethical priority of the other not only has the feel of utopian impossibility about it,[30] but, more ominously, may inadvertently proliferate the very violence it sets out to counteract.[31]

And even though for Levinas the feminine is the other par excellence,[32] what are we, in a time when women are emerging from patriarchy with agency and voice, to make of a view that sees subjectivity as dispossession and subjection? What, indeed, are we to make of Levinas's subsequent depiction of maternity as the paradigm of the behavior of a human subject toward the other?[33]

In his claim that being-responsible-for-the-other is the constitution of true selfhood, Levinas is calling—certainly first and last[34]—for disinterest in, if not repudiation of, all self-interest. For Levinas, I am expiation for the other, held hostage by the other, to whom I must give preference over myself. "The self, the persecuted one," is, in fact, says Levinas, not "in the state of original sin; it is, on the contrary, the original goodness of creation" (OB, 121).[35]

For Levinas an ethical relation is non-symmetrical because "I am responsible for the other without waiting for reciprocity, were I to die for it. Reciprocity is his affair."[36] "The face of a neighbor signifies for me an unexceptional responsibility, preceding every free consent, every pact, every contract" (OB, 88). The face is both my superior which demands my attention and my subordinate, because in his/her vulnerablity s/he cannot compel me to give it.

In recognizing the dance of intersubjectivity as the crucial process in which the moral self is constituted, Levinas is, I believe, rightly claiming that my responsibility for my neighbor is not a function of or derivable from anything else than that s/he is my neighbor. But does this necessarily mean, on an ethical level, the indiscriminate acceptance of others regardless of their motives, an ethical "disinterestedness" (OB, 126) in my own welfare even "were I to die for it"?[37]

There can be no question about the need to avoid reducing the other to another self similar to me. The mystery of each unique identity means that there can be no question of having another person's experience. To the extent that I am a unique self no one else can replace me in my responsibility. In that sense human experience is always asymmetrical.

Human uniqueness—and asymmetry—comes to the fore especially in the intimate ethical relationships of friendship, marriage, and family. In an economy of reciprocity and exchange, things and people have instrumental value in promoting one's interests and are thus replaceable or may be substituted by things or people who meet the need(s) equally well. However, in ethical relations of mutuality persons are unique particulars and the beloved is different, incomparable, and irreplaceable (never a mere instrument). Each relation of mutual love is its own non-interchangeable relation. As opposed to a quantitative hierarchical scale of loves, we have a qualitative array of incommensurate loves in which "we love them all differently because they are incomparably different."[38] Thus, I express the "same" love to my children by loving them all "differently" because they are all unique individuals. You are my friend because you are you. That relation is incomparable with my relationship with anyone else, because nobody else is you.

The question is whether this asymmetry of experience calls for an ethical asymmetry in which the other normatively always has priority over me. Indeed, it seems to me that Derrida makes a good point when he asserts that "dissymmetry itself would be impossible without this symmetry" in which "I know myself to be other for the other. Without this, 'I' (in general: egoity), unable to be the other's other, would never be a victim of violence."[39] That is to say, human intersubjectivity as mutual responsibility is an ethical symmetry of empirical asymmetries. Fom his side, Levinas is afraid of ethical symmetry-talk, not because he does not accept intersubjectivity, but because he is convinced that such talk willy nilly involves a generalizing (i.e., totalizing) insistence that the other be responsible in the same way that I am. That is—and remains, no doubt—a clear and present danger. But is it inevitably the case? Is the only alternative to egoism altruism? Is my ethical insistence on human co-responsibility for justice, for example, necessarily an imposition of my views on others? If I (we) take seriously the situatedness of our freedom and fallibility, my (our) insistence on justice will recognize that there will be differences of response to the common call. More importantly—as I will consider in more detail below—if we begin with ethical symmetry, another possibility opens up in which self and other are not irrevocably and inevitably locked in an economy of war, but in which there is a nonviolent economy of mutuality and love in which justice and care for the neighboring other is of one piece with justice and care of and for myself.

For his part, in insisting on ethical asymmetry, Levinas emphasizes the movement of the other to self (no responding self without an other summoning) at the cost of minimizing the corresponding movement of self to the other (no summoning other without responding self).[40] The result is that, ethically, instead of a two-directional interplay of mutuality, there is uni-directionality. For Levinas, prior to the ethical interruption of the other, the I (le moi) is fundamentally ignorant of, separate from, and closed off to the other. The other must storm the defenses of the self. There seems to be no room, ontologically, for the possibility of a self, of its own initiative, to reach out, attentive and open to the other. And when the ethical self is born ("awakened"), and is "hospitable," the self is, first and foremost, hostage to, and expiation for, the other. In Levinas's ethical asymmetry there is a necessary disinterest in self-concern and a corresponding complete non-indifference to others. "Subjectivity is not for itself; it is, once again, initially for another. . . . the other . . . approaches me essentially insofar as I myself—insofar as I am—responsible for him."[41]

It is true that in recognizing the other as higher (and lower) than myself, as an other for whom I am infinitely responsible, I avoid approaching the other as a rival whose power needs to be nullified. Granted, that is an enormous ethical advance over the modernist power-over mentality. However, one gets the idea that the only alternative to such imperialism is to recognize the other as higher than myself, one to whom I am hostage. Love of self seems to come down to forgetfulness of self and divestiture of all rights and interests. Aside from the impossibility of such divesting (which Levinas understands and accepts as the reality on the non-ethical level of ontology), that seems to be a dangerous message to pass on as the voice from on high. For the many who already struggle to believe that they have any right to have their own needs met and have little sense of their own power, this may encourage a further discounting of self and even self-efface-ment. On the other hand, for the many dedicated to the service of others who find such self-divestiture an impossibility, this may easily feed self-guilt or occasion escape into numbing diversions.

When we hear the paradoxical language ("obsession," "hostage," "substitution," even "occupation") which is descriptive of self for Levi-nas,[42] the questions multiply. What can it possibly mean that I *am* substitution for her/him? Does it mean that in being concerned with myself I am violently denying my true self? Doesn't being hostage to the other suggest a wholesale capitulation to the other? If so, is this not another version of the call to self-less agapic love in contrast to the self-interested love of *eros*? Moreover, what, on a practical level, does it mean to be totally responsible-for-the-other? How does one practice "substitution" for someone who has AIDS, or is unemployed, or is in an unhealthy relation? Suffering-with is one thing, but suffering-for? In general, it seems that the championing of the ethical priority of the other may in everyday life boomerang into a virtuous way of endorsing a demeaning submissiveness with the self-injury that inflicts and the potential backlash against others that it often invites. Don't such de-scriptions of self-extolling passivity, particularly from the viewpoint of women, risk being understood as the glorification of victimization?[43]

Now, this is clearly not what Levinas intends or envisions. He wants to move beyond a self-as-power-over to a self-as-service. With Levinas I agree (in distinction from any modernist, rationally based ethic) that "it is not a matter of thinking the ego and the other together, but to be facing. The true union or true togetherness is not the togetherness of synthesis, but a togetherness of face to face."[44] Consequently, Levinas wants to move beyond the confining and totalizing categories of being as power-against by a discourse of a morality "otherwise than being" which comes "before" ontology.[45]

Insofar as Levinas wants us to face up to the unconditionality of moral responsibility for love of neighbor, his call can scarcely be gain-said. He would then be describing the metaphysical or normative conditions for ethical activity, without describing a concrete ethical agenda. The difficulty is that, for Levinas, proximity, the ethical site, is "before," "beyond," "otherwise" than a place of power: the true self (*le soi*) is called prior to power relationships. The implication is that an activity is not ethical unless there is a complete lack of self-interest and self-concern, a complete passivity without power. Indeed, such concern for self is, in his view, the non-ethical ontological self inevitably closed in on its own self-interest. Disinterest, expiation, total subjection to the other regardless of his/her motivations is what it means to be ethical.

POWER-OVER OR POWER-WITH

Here is where the rumblings become louder. Is the exercise of agentic power always power-against neighbor, and thus unethical? Does non-indifference to the other need to mean disinterest in self? In contrast, I want to suggest the possibility of an ethical exercise of power as power-with.

Levinas insists that one cannot escape the perspective of one's own self. I could not agree more. What I disagree with is his contention that one's perspective inevitably and irrevocably can only totalize the other because that is what it means to have power. Power *qua* power is power-over, and that means war. For Levinas the "invincible persistence," the *conatus essendi*, is interest.[46] "Being's interest takes dramatic form . . . in the multiplicity of allergic egoisms which are at war with one another." Through "calculation, mediation and politics" a "rational peace" of "reciprocal limitation and determination" is established (OB, 4). Nevertheless, "interest remains" and "nothing is gratuitous" (OB, 5). Interest, enjoyment, calculation, and possessions make up an economy of reciprocal exchange in the domain of being which is ontologically non-ethical. Symmetry, interest, and reciprocity cannot avoid being egoistic, imperialistic, selfish. Consequently, to move beyond this means that for Levinas ethics must be "otherwise than being," a "total gratuity, breaking with interest" (OB, 96). Indeed, the breakup of essence is ethics.

It is Levinas's view of power as inherently power-over that I see as highly problematic. Accepting that domination is indigenous to power and at the same time decrying such power-egoism leaves Levinas only one alternative: the ethical priority of the other.

Levinas is, in fact, accepting the long tradition[47] of envisioning power as fundamentally power-over.[48] He outlines his project in *Totality and Infinity* as developing discourse as a "non-allergic relation with alterity . . . where *power, by essence murderous of the other*, becomes, faced with the other and 'against all good sense,' the impossibility of murder, the consideration of the other, or justice"(TI, 47; italics added). Again, in *Otherwise than Being*, Levinas asks "[w]hy should the other concern me? . . . Am I my brother's keeper? These questions have meaning only if one has already supposed that the ego is concerned only with itself, is only a concern for itself" (OB, 117). Thus, although Levinas is very critical of this ontology of power, calling it in fact "a philosophy of injustice" (TI, 46), his move beyond into an ethical metaphysics of alterity consciously builds on and is dependent on a recognition of an ontology of being-as-power-over. His insistence on the necessity of an ethics of deference to the other (because egoism is wrong) is concomitant with the recognition that it is ontologically impossible (because egoism is unavoidable).

Such thinking seems to take the basic opposition between closed selves with all the ambiguity this involves for personal interaction as a fundamental characteristic of human nature.[49] In this paradigm, given in modern times classic formulation in the work of Freud, Hegel, and Sartre, there are only two possibilities: dominate or be dominated. In this paradigm of violence, one either exercises power and becomes dominant and independent—that is, selfish—or one surrenders and becomes submissive and dependent—that is, other-directed.

In this model we have a world of ceaseless conflict and endless competition until one proves him/herself superior. But in such a world, when neither is able to surrender voluntarily, striving eventually becomes empty and meaningless because each person remains alone, disconnected, incapable of change and development. On the other hand, if we choose not to exercise our desire for power and subordinate our needs and interests, we have a relation with another person but at the cost of stifling our own needs and interests.

Within the confines of this paradigm, the route of self-sacrificial *agape* clearly has it all over the wiles of self-interested *eros*. *Agape*, as Nygren classically distinguished it in the Christian tradition, is supposed to be pure and disinterested love over against the egotistical and interested love of *eros*.[50] There is power without surrender (*eros*) or surrender without power (*agape*). Thus, for Reinhold Niebuhr, to take a modern Christian example, self-sacrifice is the end, goal, or ideal of history, and mutuality is a compromise ethic to accommodate fallen existence. "Sacrifical love (*agape*) completes the incompleteness of mutual love (*eros*)."[51]

My fundamental query is: how different, despite the details and complexities, is the position of Levinas? Levinas, it is true, does not ask us to deny or stifle our needs. Rather, acknowledging the needs and interests of the ego, we are then to interrupt them and put them out of play in accord with our higher ethical self. The questions return: Is there no legitimate ethical call to care of self and the needs of self? Is power of agency always self-interested, and therefore below the ethical plane?

Levinas is not unaware of the dangers. He exclaims, "But it is I, I and no one else, who am hostage for others." The "no one else" is important, for "to say that the other has to sacrifice himself to the others would be to preach human sacrifice!" (OB, 126–27). Indeed, he admits that the responsibility for the other "is troubled and becomes a problem when a third party enters" (OB, 157). Significantly, he even admits that "the relationship with the third party is an *incessant* correction of the asymmetry of proximity" (OB, 158 italics added). Faced with unlimited responsibility, the self can, because my neighbor is also a third party with respect to another, "be called upon to concern itself also with itself" (OB, 128). I am also another for the other and a third one. Thank God. Which is exactly what Levinas exclaims: "'Thanks to God' I am another for the others" (OB, 158). In this way, "there is also justice for me" (OB, 159). But, even then, he cautions that the "forgetting" of the "unlimited initial responsibility" is "pure egoism" (OB, 128). Nevertheless, in this way violence and evil may be resisted "when the evil he does to me touches also a third party, one who is likewise my neighbor."[52] Thus, Levinas does allow being for oneself, but always on the basis of a prior being for the other, and only as a function of this being for the other.

A basic question that emerges is whether in Levinas's thought, for all its hallowing of the other, there is the historical possiblity of meeting an other, a neighbor, without distance or without fusion as Levinas desires. Not only is, ethically, the other always transcendent to me, but in "a history and politics," the assymetrical ethical relation takes on "the aspect of a symmetrical relation" (TI, 225). "Separation is embedded in an order in which the asymmetry of the interpersonal relation is effaced, where I and the other become interchangeable in commerce, and where the particular man, an individual of the genus man, appearing in history, is substituted for the I and for the other" (TI, 226). In history, by means of the third party, the ethical priority of the other is transformed into a relation of equals. In history, it seems, we at best have the balanced exchange of reciprocity as welcome respite from the economy of war. But the exchange of "interchangeable" I's sounds more like a trading in sameness, rather than the meeting of unique, irrreplaceable I's in difference. In the end, it appears that we have a chastened or corrected asymmetry in which equality and reciprocity[53] are possible, but not genuine mutuality.[54]

MUTUALITY AS POWER-WITH

As an alternative to Levinas's model in which agency is inevitably and inescapably egoistic, I suggest a model of non-oppositional difference—an economy of love. Such an intersubjective model of mutual recognition, attunement, and empowerment, I believe, honors Levinas's intentions without some of the dangers which seem to haunt his position.[55] Here the movement of the other to myself is coincident with a simultaneous and voluntary movement of myself to the other. The desire of each evokes the desire of the other: mutual recognition, mutual yielding/receiving, mutual delighting, mutual empowering. There is the oscillating rhythm of giving and receiving, the dance of identity and intimacy called love. In giving to the other, I, paradoxically, in being received, am enlarged and enhanced—receiving, in the words of Levinas, "inspiration." In receiving the other, I expand, and paradoxically, through my receiving, give. Instead of power-over (with its corollary of power-under), or power-held-in-abeyance (to avoid domination), there is power-with and the dance of mutual empowerment.

The self is always intersubjective, either a connected (or a disconnected) self. Insofar as a human self is never an autonomous agent in splendid isolation, but always a connective self, the intra-psychic and the inter-psychic need not always be in opposition to each other. Indeed, the formation and nurturing of self-identity is possible only in an intersubjective matrix. It is in being seen (or not seen) that I, as an infant, come to see (or not see) myself. It is in being loved (or not loved) that I come to love (or not love) myself—and others. Since my identity is a gift I receive from and with others, my connection with others is constitutive of my identity. Community is not the sameness of fusion, but the coming-into-connection of diverse identities. We live together, in genuine community, or we strive together, in the violence of war; but in any case there is no I without a We. In other words, otherness and difference are never wholly inside or wholly outside myself. I, or, at least aspects of me, come alive and grow, or retreat and eventually die as I move in and out of relation with other selves. Mutuality assumes we cannot talk about response to and for others over and against response for and to self. In an intersubjective context of mutuality self-desires are not fundamentally desires against the other. In fear and disappointment they often become fixated in that way—and mutuality is ruptured into hostility.

Mutuality is attunement of expression, recognition, and desire, a dance in which simultaneously the differing gifts and needs of each person are honored, recognized, and often met. From our places of irreducible otherness, each of us seeks a rhythm in the other without hierarchy and without abasement—beyond considerations of duty, balance, or advantage. We recognize each other, seek each other's good, identify-with each other—in the process loving the other as we love ourselves. In this interfacing, the giving over or yielding to the other is a voluntary move in which one retains his/her own individuality and difference. The dance between staying with one's self and reaching out is the interplay of difference that is life itself. The aim is not to eradicate, accommodate, suppress, or repress difference, but to allow contact with difference to move, enhance, and change us as we become ourselves more fully. Empowered through the giving/receiving experience, a positive spiral of mutuality begins to take shape in which we are inspired to recognize, reach out, and yield more often and in deepening ways. When it happens (the difficulties and fears are many, and there are no guarantees!), we meet—graced with mutual recognition, mutual pleasure, and mutual empowerment—the fundamental ingredients of love. "The psyche is one open system connected to another, and only under those conditions is it renewable. If it lives, your psyche is in love. If it is not in love, it is dead."[56]

The dance of mutuality is always drenched in vulnerability and risk because it is a non-coerced meeting of two free subjects in the wild spaces of love.[57] Timing and spacing are of the essence. Reaching out does not guarantee being met. The timing may be off; the partner may be otherwise occupied, not-at-home, angry, depressed, in a different space. Venturing out, but not meeting, leads to impasse, and brings with it hurt, grieving—suffering. When people learn to accept that the vulnerablity of mutuality always includes moments of distance, pain, and suffering, impasses may be avoided or broken, and the suffering-from such non-meetings can even turn into suffering-with experiences of empathy, non-blame, and shared disappointment.

Opening to others may lead to indifference, negativity, rebuff, re-buke, assault—who knows? Indeed, it is that unknowing that makes us fearful, incessantly tempting us to try to guarantee the outcome or at least minimize the hazards through subtle or not so subtle means of control and manipulation. It is the fear of non-affirmation and disinte-gration, feeding the urge to take advantage of the other hidden in the recesses of every human heart, which closes our hearts, sets up de-fenses, and makes genuine meeting so difficult. The giving in such encounters is easily (if not consciously) counterfeit, a bribe, a come-on; the "giver" actually a taker. The receiving too becomes contami-nated. Feeling a deep unworthiness, but, at the same time, being des-perate for a gift can lead to a feigned indifference, cloying "thankfulness," a guilt-ridden discomfort. Whether we are giving or receiving, insofar we are deficient in self-esteem, our fears tend to get the best of us and opportunities for meeting degenerate into more or less calculated maneuvers of offense and defense, tugs-of-war of com-petition and resistance.

Since at every turn and in every moment the give-and-receive of mutuality threatens to degenerate into such strategies of manipulation, people often see no choice but to turn ethical relations into economic exchange relations with set demands for return and remuneration. That such degeneration is rampant in our skewed lives, however, need not mean, as is so often assumed, that all human relations are inevita-bly and finally only to be explained in terms of an economy of violence and sacrifice where giving necessarily implies taking from another.[58] The mutuality model calls into question the assumption that appropri-ation (and the fear of expropriation) is intrinsic to human agency. Such an economy of love is not necessarily always already (although it often deteriorates into this) a zero sum game in which giving to one is always a taking from the other. There is, instead, the possibility of a giving as an overflowing to the other which invites and often evokes (but neither demands nor coerces) a return. There is a return to the self (which would bother Levinas), but since it is not at the cost of the other, it does meet Levinas's basic concern. In neither demanding response nor being conditional upon them, mutual relations are not to be confused with or reduced to the reciprocities of market relations of exhange and contract. And there always remains the risk of violence. But in this model, as distinct from the Hegelian model of opposition, there is room for a genuine meeting of self and the other in a middle space, room for a giving in excess, without a why, which increases in its being given, transcending the economy of reciprocity and exchange. Love is the excessive gift that keeps on giving. The very possibility of betrayal and rejection—the risk of violence—is part and parcel of its "without-why"ness, making it a "beautiful risk" (Levinas), a risk worth taking. For when, in spite of the risk, a gift is given and received, both giver and receiver experience a miracle of unmerited grace, the kind that makes all the difference in life.

In genuine mutuality it is not that the other fills up or augments myself; nor do I lose myself in the other. In both these cases, it would seem, there is no alterity, only sameness—with its suspension of genuine risk! In the first case, I ingest or dominate the other into my sameness. In the second, my otherness is assumed or subsumed into the sameness of the other.

In maintaining that ethically I can make no demand on the other, but rather that I give full priority to the other, Levinas seems to come dangerously close to this second situation despite his protestations to the contrary.[59] The problem seems to be that Levinas believes that expecting or seeking a response from the other necessarily means a tit-for-tat reciprocity, at best a contracted exchange of rights, duties, and goods, and at worst a manipulation. It is true, as I have just noted, that the risk and vulnerability of mutuality are often too much for us, so we try to regain control either through covert manipulation or overt reciprocal contract.[60] In both cases, ethical relations take on an instrumental quality. But is an ethical asymmetry (with priority of the other person) the only alternative to either manipulative relationships (with the other as object) or the balanced exchange of economic transactions (with interchangeable selves)? If it is (as Levinas seems to assume), his approach would be my approach. However, as I have attempted to describe, the genuine mutuality of the ethical bears its own distinct mark, neither to be confused with or turned into the balanced exchange of reciprocal economies, nor confused with the priority of the other. Moreover, genuine mutual relations need to be clearly distinguished from their counterfeit, i.e., manipulative relations.

Genuine mutuality is not the calculation of reciprocal advantages in which I determine whether a neighbor treats me with equal regard, and then, if the conclusion is negative, I am absolved of my obligations. Levinas is right, I believe, to refuse to accept such calculation as the mark of the authentically ethical, even if, as we have observed, the difficulty of the ethical venture means that such exchange is often passed off as mutuality. In genuine mutuality both manipulation with its premium on control and reciprocity with its premium on balanced exchange are replaced with an ethics of being-with.[61] Genuine mutuality includes a self-love which is not self-aggrandizment or selfishness. It involves regard for self's own integrity, esteem for one's own worth, commitment to one's own convictions, and trust in one's own intuitions. Without such self-love, I fear, all relations with others, despite all protestations or pretenses to the contrary, will be efforts to gain a sense of belonging and worth at the expense of the other—and thereby violent. Genuine love of other is as fundamentally impossible without love of self as love of self is fundamentally impossible without love of the other. That, indeed, is the great commandment: to love my neighbor as I love myself.

This model of mutuality also calls for a revisioning of the typical selfish *eros*/altruistic *agape* contrast. *Eros* is no longer the drive to unite, dominate, or fuse, returning everything to the Same which needs to be countermanded by an agapic drive sacrificially to give up self. *Eros* is *agape*, the intersubjective desire to connect in difference, the agapic power to interconnection (power-with) which is the meaning of life. *Eros* as be(com)ing-with is a mutual connecting which is neither indifferent nor disinterested, neither invasive nor domineering. Being-with is a power-with which respects, receives, and honors the other, and in so doing there is the mutual enrichment, mutual empowerment, and mutual pleasure of love. Without a self–other opposition, there is no longer a need to oppose *eros* and *agape*.

SUFFERING-WITH

However, as we all know too well, the mutuality of shared power—love—is too rare. *Eros* too often degenerates into selfish imperialism and defensive aggression. In fear the power of love is warped into power-over: violence, hate, evil. The wild spaces of love are turned into the killing fields. In such circumstances the scourges of violence mean that the give-and-receive rhythms of mutual power-with often need to become exercises in suffering-with our neighbor—and in that sense a priority of the other. Suffering-with (as distinct from suffering-from) is a voluntary, gratuitous act of standing alongside, empathic listening, affirming, speaking, and acting on behalf of.[62] It is what Levinas calls the "suffering for the useless suffering of the other person."[63]

In other words, the reality of rampant inequality, disadvantage, and outright oppression in our world means that the ethical symmetry of mutuality often calls for a priority in meeting the needs of others. Exercising mutuality means taking into account the position and circumstances of the other. When the other is "widow, orphan, stranger" (i.e., not able to be partner, whether through accident, need, impairment, lack of resources, etc.), there is what has been called in liberation theology the "preferential option for the poor." At the same time, when the other is engaged in acts of domination and injustice, an ethics of mutuality calls for acts of resistance and restraint. But this "asymmetry" is not an involuntary the-other-comes-first principle. Such "self-sacrifice" is not, I suggest, as with Niebuhr and Levinas, what it means to be quintessentially ethical. It finds its derivative place in an ethics of mutuality because of the brokenness and sinfulness of life. It is the compromise required by the breakdown of mutuality with the intention of making/restoring mutual partnerships. As Don Browning puts it, this makes "appropriate self-sacrifice as a transitional ethic on the way to restoring mutuality."[64] An ethics of being-with and suffering-with in this way also suggests that if maternity is to be the ethical metaphor *par excellence*, it would need to be recast not as the supreme emblem of self-sacrifice but (with paternity) as paradigm examples of mutuality in which life is created, given, and shared.

In the end my emphasis on "I-am-with" (power-with) instead of Levinas's "I-am-for" seems confluent with his (and my) intentions to envision a philosophy of non-violence. In his claim that the Face awakens me to responsibility, Levinas seems to assume that there is something in the ontological ego that urges or impels a journey into the exile of the "otherwise than being," giving rise to an awakening or birth of the moral self, not as "I am I," but as "I am for." Levinas stresses that this ethical "for" is not the social "with." However, "with" in my usage is not the social "being-with" of Heidegger. "With" carries the connotations of a humanity as a religious community-in-difference, gifted-with and called-to love, very similar to what Levinas calls "proximity" (OB, 81–99) as the religio-ethical place of responsibility, vulnerability, and non-violence (OB, 75–81).

Co-responsibility, care, and compassion are the key terms in a post-

modern ethic. Care goes back to the old Gothic word, *Kara,* meaning
"to lament, to weep with, to grieve." Compassion comes from the
Latin *com* and *pati,* meaning to suffer with. Suffering love as the voluntary willingness to suffer-with another person is required to restore
genuine relations of mutuality. We may even have to suffer at the
hands of the others for the cause of justice. In love we are moved from
the center to the margins where the lame and ill are gathered. But
such sacrifice of self is not done at whatever the cost to self, but is done
in tune with and at the behest of a self who, in wholeness and integrity,
wants to live out its convictions. In such circumstances, doing for the
other may be for the self, and doing for self may be for the other.
Thank God for such possibilities. I can come face to face with difference without effacement on my part or debasement on the part of the
other. Inspired and inspiring faces, shining, glowing, not fused, not
distant, but connected and connecting. In this broken world where
violence is so often overwhelming, disfiguring, and dismembering, we
are called to suffer-with, to sojourn together.

The poignancy and urgency of this call leads me to end this essay
with a spontaneous and forthright thank you[65] to Emmanuel Levinas
for raising again the vision of the widow, orphan, and stranger in a
world where compassion is too often in exile. May we all offer cups of
cold water to the other, gifts which we offer and say, "Drink" (Bois)![66]

NOTES

1. Jacques Derrida, *Specters of Marx,* trans. Peggy Kamuf (New York:
Routledge, 1994), p. 85.

2. Ibid., p. 83.

3. Tamara Wright, Peter Hughes, and Alison Ainsley, "The Paradox of
Morality: An Interview with Emmanuel Levinas," in *The Provocation of Levi-
nas: Rethinking the Other,* ed. R. Bernasconi and D. Wood (London:
Routledge, 1988), p. 176.

4. Derrida has an important discussion of justice in relation to law in
"Force of Law: The Mystical Foundation of Authority," trans. M. Quain-
tance, in *Deconstruction and the Possibility of Justice,* ed. Drucilla Cornell
et al. (New York: Routledge, 1992), pp. 3–67. For an earlier effort, on my
part, to give embryonic shape to a postmodern ethic in terms of a Gadamerian
narrative approach cross-pollinated by a deconstructionist ethics of dissemination, see "An Ethics of Compassion: Ethics in a Post-Modernist Age," in

What Right Does Ethics Have?, ed. Sander Griffioen (Amsterdam: VU Uitgeverij, 1990), pp. 125–46.

5. Emmanuel Levinas, "Morality Is Not a Branch of Philosophy, but First Philosophy," in *Totality and Infinity*, trans. A. Lingus (Pittsburgh: Duquesne University Press, 1969), p. 304, henceforth in text as TI. See also his "Ethics as First Philosophy" in *The Levinas Reader*, ed. Sean Hand (Oxford: Blackwell, 1989), pp. 75–87. See also *Ethics as First Philosophy*, ed. A. Peperzak (New York: Routledge, 1995).

6. As one of the first Levinas-inspired North American studies, Edith Wyschogrod's *Saints and Postmodernism* (Chicago: University of Chicago Press, 1990), appealing for a saintly ethics of self-sacrifice, also calls for attention. Today there is a growing spate of books taking up the issue of deconstruction and ethics. Three of special note are Simon Critchley, *The Ethics of Deconstruction* (Oxford: Blackwell, 1992); Zygmunt Bauman, *Postmodern Ethics* (Oxford: Blackwell, 1993); and John D. Caputo, *Against Ethics* (Bloomington: Indiana University Press, 1993).

7. Such an ethics, I submit, adds a fourth approach to Alasdair MacIntyre's three broad versions of ethical enquiry: the Enlightenment encyclopedic, the deconstructivist genealogical, and the Thomistic traditional. See his *Three Rival Versions of Moral Enquiry* (Notre Dame: University of Notre Dame Press, 1990).

8. Looked at from my perspective, Levinas could be said to have his own "compromise ethic" when, following recognition of the priority of the other, justice enters with the arrival of "the third"—another "other"—and I am permitted to see myself as the other of the other. Whereas for me, mutuality is the normative and self-sacrifice the compromise, for Levinas something like the opposite seems true. Normative is the priority of the other (with the sacrifice of the agentic self) and the political compromise is the reciprocity involving a third. On the other hand, the difference is somewhat muted when it is recognized that for Levinas equality is the goal of the priority of the other. That is, from his viewpoint, the priority of the other is not seen as a compromise, but the asymmetry of priority is considered the condition for the symmetry of equality.

9. Emmanuel Levinas, *Otherwise than Being or Beyond Essence*, trans. A. Lingus (Hague: Martinus Nijhoff, 1981). Henceforth in text as OB.

10. Stanley Hauerwas and David Burrell, "From System to Story," in S. Hauerwas and L. Jones, eds., *Why Narrative?* (Grand Rapids: Eerdmans, 1989), p. 163.

11. Perhaps the most influential contemporary effort to defend modern rationality (as it attempts to avoid modernity's pathologies) is Jürgen Habermas's "discourse ethics" with its goal of "communicative rationality." See his *Moral Consciousness and Communicative Action* (Cambridge: MIT Press, 1990).

12. See Lawrence Blum, *Friendship, Altruism, and Morality* (London: Routledge & Kegan Paul, 1980) for an incisive critique of the Kantian tradition.

13. MacIntyre, *Three Rival Versions*, p. 173.

14. Carol Gilligan, *In a Different Voice* (Cambridge: Harvard University Press, 1982).

15. Michel Foucault, *Power/Knowledge: Selected Interviews and Other Writings*, ed. C. Gordon, trans. C. Gordon et al. (New York: Pantheon, 1980).

16. " 'Religion' " is "the bond that is established between the same and the other without constituting a totality" (TI, 40).

17. Emmanuel Levinas and Richard Kearney, "Dialogue with Emmanuel Levinas," in *Face to Face with Levinas*, ed. Richard A. Cohen (Albany: State University of New York Press, 1986), p. 31.

18. In "A Medieval Lesson on Bodily Knowing: Women's Experience and Men's Thought," in *The Journal of the American Academy of Religion*, 57, No. 2 (1989), 341–72, J. Giles Milhaven has traced the impact of our limitation of knowledge to the rational.

19. Spinoza, *Ethics* in *The Chief Works of Benedict de Spinoza*, trans. R. Elwes (New York: Dover Publications, 1955), Part Three, Definition 3, p. 174.

20. See John D. Caputo, *Demythologizing Heidegger* (Bloomington: Indiana University Press, 1993), ch. 8, pp. 148–68.

21. Thus, Levinas worries that "Dasein in Heidegger is never hungry" (*Totality and Infinity*, p. 134.)

22. "The-one-for-the-other is the foundation of theory," *Otherwise*, p. 136.

23. Elsewhere I have called these fields of meeting the "wild spaces of love" to emphasize they are as free for love as they are for control and violence. See my "Crossing the Threshold: Sojourning Together in the Wild Spaces of Love," *Toronto Journal of Theology* 11/1 (1995), 39–57; chap. 9 below.

24. Despite the considerable debt owed to Merleau-Ponty for his recovery of the agent body, John Caputo points out that his analysis, by overlooking improper and unbecoming, vulnerable and suffering bodies, "is still a form of idealism against which he always fought" (*Against Ethics*, p. 202). Whereas for Merleau-Ponty it is the resemblance between self and other, for Levinas it is the asymmetrical, unsurpassable difference that opens up ethics and discourse.

25. Not to forget or minimize the restlessness or unrest awakened on contact.

26. Caputo, *Against Ethics*, p. 149.

27. Wyschogrod, *Saints*, p. xxiv.

28. Paul Ricoeur, *Oneself as Another*, p. 171. Chapters 7, 8, and 9 describe how for Ricoeur the ethical aim needs to pass through the sieve of the norm, even as, when the norm leads to situations of impasse, we go back to the aim.

29. In contrast to the "anonymous rustling" of Levinas (*Otherwise*, p. 3), the "incessant bustling" of the "there is [*il y a*], the horrible eternity at the bottom of essence" (*Otherwise*, p. 176).

30. Levinas does admit that "[t]here is a utopian moment in what I say: it is the recognition of something which cannot be realised but, which, ultimately, guides all moral action" ("The Paradox of Morality," 72).

31. In *Against Ethics*, by referring to a sentence of Derrida's in *Truth in Painting*, Caputo calls it "an impossible dream, even a dangerous dream, inasmuch as promises of what is absolutely unmediated are usually followed by the most massive mediations" (p. 82). When legitimate self-needs are denied, they have a way of coming back with a vengeance, often in disguised, underhanded, and dangerous ways.

32. In *Totality and Infinity* Levinas describes the importance of the "gentleness of the feminine face" (p. 150) in establishing the intimacy of home, making space for hospitality to strangers, and thus establishing a subjectivity capable of ethical relationships. The feminine other is also "the Beloved . . . an extreme fragility, a vulnerability" (p. 256). Since traditionally the woman too often has been considered the other who needs to be put down by the man as same, Levinas's acknowledgment of the significant place of women contributes to a new ethics of respect for women. However, at the same time, in *Totality and Infinity*, his ambiguity in regard to the feminine emerges when, in relating the erotic to the feminine, he sees the erotic with its "return to the self" (p. 266) as less than ethical, and when he talks of the "beloved," the feminine, as "without responsibility," fading into "ambiguity, into animality" (p. 263). Moreover, it is not clear whether, for Levinas, a woman can also be agent, the lover as well as the beloved. See Luce Irigaray's two essays on Levinas, "The Fecundity of the Caress," in Iragaray, *An Ethics of Sexual Difference*, trans. C. Burke and G. Gill (Ithaca: Cornell University Press, 1993), pp. 185–217, and "Questions to Emmanuel Levinas," in *Re-Reading Levinas*, ed. R. Bernasconi and S. Critchley (Bloomington: Indiana University Press, 1991), pp. 109–129. For a careful and nuanced discussion and critique of Levinas's portrayal of the feminine, see Atie Th. Brüggemann-Kruijff, *Bij de gratie van de transcendentie: En gesprek met Levinas over het vrouwelijke* (Amsterdam: VU Uitgeverij, 1993). Tina Chanter's recent *Ethics of Eros* (New York: Routledge, 1995) is also an excellent discussion of Levinas's views of the feminine and Irigaray's critique.

33. *Otherwise*, pp. 75–81. "Maternity, which is bearing par excellence, bears even responsibility for the persecuting by the persecutor" (p. 75). Although it is clear that the feminine, as the trope for subjectivity, is at the heart

of the ethical, I am deeply concerned about the felicity of employing feminine imagery for human subjectivity, which could, particularly by women, be heard not only as conflating being a woman with motherhood but also once more and once again glorifying their submission. Much better, it would seem, if one wants to emphasize the importance of committed caring for the other, the bearing of each other's burdens, to talk of paternity as well as maternity as ethical figures par excellence. See Morny Joy, "Levinas: Alterity, the Feminine and Women—A meditation," in *Studies in Religion*, 22, No. 4 (1993), 463–85.

34. "But egoism is neither first nor last," *Otherwise*, p. 128.

35. For Wyschogrod, "a saintly life is defined as one in which compassion for the other, irrespective of cost to the saint, is the primary trait," and "whatever the cost to the saint in pain and sorrow" (*Saints*, pp. xxiii, 34).

36. Levinas, *Ethics and Infinity: Conversations with Philippe Nemo*, trans. R. Cohen (Pittsburgh: Duquesne University Press, 1985), p. 98.

37. It is clear that in actual life, due to the third party, Levinas is able to justify pragmatically self-defense in the face of aggression. The point is that he seems on the highest ethical level to disallow any and all self-interest.

38. Vincent Brümmer, *The Model of Love* (Cambridge: Cambridge University Press, 1993), p. 210.

39. Jacques Derrida, "Violence and Metaphysics: An Essay on the Thought of Emmanuel Levinas," in *Writing and Difference*, trans. A. Bass (Chicago: University of Chicago Press, 1978), p. 126. "That I am also essentially the other's other, and that I know I am, is evidence of a strange symmetry whose trace appears nowhere in Levinas's descriptions" (p. 128).

40. In *Oneself as Another*, Paul Ricoeur also voices his concern that Levinas one-sidedly emphasizes the relation of the other to self (p. 335ff).

41. Levinas, *Ethics and Infinity*, p. 96.

42. In a context of narcissistic male domination, the hortatory use of such phrases would strikingly make the necessary point.

43. Cf. Joy, " Levinas . . . ," p. 484.

44. Levinas, *Ethics and Infinity*, p. 77.

45. Zygmunt Bauman reads this moral "before" as "better" (*Postmodern Ethics*, p. 72).

46. "*esse* is *interesse*; essence is interest," *Otherwise*, p. 4.

47. For Levinas, " 'I think' comes down to 'I can.' . . . Ontology as first philosophy is a philosophy of power" (*Totality and Infinity*, p. 46).

48. Paul Tillich, for example, defines power as "the possibility a being has to actualize itself against the resistance of other beings" (*The Courage to Be* [New Haven, Conn.: Yale University Press, 1952], p. 179). Paul Ricoeur claims that "[i]t is difficult to imagine situations of interaction in which one individual does not exert power over another *by the very fact of acting*" (*Oneself*, p. 220, italics added). Derrida concurs: "If it is true, as I in fact believe,

that writing cannot be thought outside of the horizon of intersubjective violence, is there anything, even science, that radically escapes it?" (*Of Grammatology*, trans. G. Spivak [Baltimore: John Hopkins University Press, 1976], p. 127). He considers "[s]uch violence may be considered the very condition of the gift. . . . *The violence appears irreducible, within the circle or outside it, whether it repeats the circle or interrupts it*" (*Given Time: 1. Counterfeit Money*, trans. P. Kamuf [Chicago: Chicago University Press, 1992], p. 147).

49. "But the moral priority of the other over myself could not come to be if it were not motivated by something beyond nature. The ethical situation is a human situation, *beyond human nature*, in which the idea of God comes to mind (Levinas and Kearney, "Dialogue," p. 25; italics added).

50. Anders Nygren, *Agape and Eros*, trans. P. Watson (Philadephia: The Westminster Press, 1953). "Eros is essentially and in principle self-love. . . . Agape, on the other hand, excludes all self-love"(pp. 216–17).

51. Reinhold Niebuhr, *The Nature and Destiny of Man* (London: Nisbet, 1943), p. 86.

52. Roger Burggraeve, *Emmanuel Levinas* (Leuven: Center for Metaphysics and Philosopy of God, n.d.), p. 56. This is an exceptionally clear and concise exposition of Levinas's thought.

53. In my view, the equality and reciprocity of justice with the emphasis on balanced exchange differs from the mutality of an ethical relationship (cf. below).

54. Levinas's recognition that there are always third parties and the necessary mediating structures again vividly raises the question of the practical viability of his ethics of priority.

55. Jessica Benjamin's *The Bonds of Love* (New York: Random House, 1988) is an articulate plea for "a new possibility of mutual recognition between men and women" in which both are empowered and mutually respectful.

56. Julia Kristeva, *Tales of Love*, trans. L. Roudiez (New York: Columbia University Press, 1987), p. 15.

57. See my "Crossing the Threshold: Sojourning Together in the Wild Spaces of Love," *Toronto Journal of Theology* 11/1 (1995), pp. 39–57; chap. 9 below.

58. See Introduction, pp. 3–4.

59. "Contact with the other . . . is neither to invest the other and annull his alterity, nor to suppress myself in the other" (*Otherwise*, p. 86).

60. For differences between manipulative, contractual (i.e., reciprocal), and fellowship kinds of relationships, see John Macmurray, *Persons in Relation* (Atlantic Highlands, N.J.: Humanities Press, 1991, chs. 5–7, and Vincent Brümmer, *The Model of Love* , pp. 156–73.

61. James H. Olthuis, "Being-with: Toward a Relational Psychotherapy," *Journal of Psychology and Christianity* 13/3 (1994), 217–31.

62. See ibid. for a discussion of what this means psychotherapeutically.

63. Levinas, "Useless Suffering," in *The Provocation of Levinas: Rethinking the Other*, ed. R. Bernasconi and D. Wood (New York: Routledge, 1988), p. 159.

64. Don Browning, *Religious Thought and the Modern Psychologies* (Philadelphia: Fortress Press, 1987), p. 153.

65. In the mutuality model I am developing, a free, unexpected, unsolicited, and uncoerced "thank you" escapes the economy of reciprocity and exchange. In contrast, since Derrida believes no gift can escape the economy of reciprocity and even the movement of gratitude returns to the Same, he ironically can thank Levinas only by being ungrateful and writing a faulty text. See Jacques Derrida, "At this very moment in this work here I am," trans. R. Berezdivin, in *Re-Reading Levinas*, ed. R. Bernasconi and S. Critchley (Bloomington: Indiana University Press, 1991), pp. 11–48. Simon Critchley incisively discusses Derrida's predicament in thanking Levinas in *The Ethics of Deconstruction*, pp. 108ff.

66. "Bois" is Derrida's final word in his text of homage to Emmanuel Levinas. "At this very moment in this work here I am."

6

Structures of Violence, Structures of Peace: Levinasian Reflections on Just War and Pacifism[1]

Jeffrey M. Dudiak

"THERE ARE no nonviolent structures." To acquiesce to this assertion is to find oneself within a milieu of thought that has come to be known as postmodernism.[2] This assertion is, I would argue, an assertion characteristic of postmodernist, as over against modernist, thought, among the indicators of a distinguishable intellectual *Zeitgeist*. While the modern, logocentric thinker may well recognize the (at least temporary, even if necessary) violence of whatever structures happen to govern life at any given moment, it is nevertheless an integral part of the modernist creed to believe that such structures are potentially (and, most often, inevitably) replaceable by ultimately true, ultimately just, and ultimately pacific ones. The postmodern thinker, on the other hand, has abandoned such faith, such faith having been deconstructed by the "recognition"[3] that violence constitutes a necessary element of the very structure of structure.

For the French, Jewish, postmodern philosopher and Talmudic scholar Emmanuel Levinas, this deconstruction, and its concomitant recognition of the essential violence of structure, derives from an encounter with the face of the Other, an event whose description cannot properly, for reasons that will become evident shortly, be designated as either an analysis or a phenomenology. I propose to trace this Levinasian discourse through a double movement, that is, through an initial movement that then doubles back upon itself in a second which constitutes a certain betrayal of the first, and then briefly reflect upon its possible implications for the just war/pacifism debate—a reflection not justified, surely, but perhaps given some credence, by the fact that it is a reflection upon the thought of a once interned Jew whose life and work have been, by his own account, perhaps first of all a protracted meditation upon the Holocaust.

STRUCTURES OF VIOLENCE

To reduce the other to the same, to make the other into a function of myself, is to do violence to the other. You are not the furniture of my world, to be arranged and manipulated according to my whims, to suit my pleasure. I cannot, ethically, murder you, rape you, enslave you, use you against your will to further my ends. I cannot, when my legs grow tired, insist that you kneel before me, to be used as a footstool. These are ethical banalities.

And yet, according to Levinas, "western philosophy has most often been an ontology: a reduction of the other to the same," a reduction effectuated "by interposition of a middle and neutral term that ensures the comprehension of being."[4] The middle or neutral term can appear to thought, variously, as sensation, as Being, as the *logos* itself; but in each case it places the other against a horizon in which I find myself, such that "the shock of the encounter of the same with the other is deadened."[5] Thus the theoretical relation, which "designates first a relation with being such that the knowing being lets the known being manifest itself while respecting its alterity and without marking it in any way whatever . . . also designates comprehension [intelligence]— the logos of being—that is, a way of approaching the known being such that its alterity with regard to the knowing being vanishes."[6] "To know ontologically is to surprise in the existent confronted that by which it is not this existent, this stranger, that by which it is somehow betrayed, surrenders, is given in the horizon in which it loses itself and appears, lays itself open to grasp, becomes a concept."[7]

"This primacy of the same," Levinas writes, in tracing its lineage to the onset of the classical period of our philosophical tradition, "was Socrates's teaching: to receive nothing of the Other but what is in me, as though from all eternity I was in possession of what comes to me from the outside—to receive nothing, or be free."[8] Yet this freedom is not the freedom of a "capricious spontaneity" but the freedom "that is the identification of the same, not allowing itself to be alienated by the other."[9] This doctrine, this "ontological imperialism," persists, according to Levinas, into our own century in the phenomenology of Husserl, for whom the idea of intentionality leaves the constituting subject the privilege of being the locus of meaning, the sense-giver, such that the other is constituted, after the fifth Cartesian Meditation, on an analogy of the body that begins with my experience of myself as corporeal. For Heidegger, too, for whom the existent is comprehended against the horizon of Being, "Being is inseparable from the comprehension of Being (which unfolds as time); Being is already an appeal to subjectivity,"[10] that is, Being is correlative with the freedom of the comprehending subject.

Of essential importance in all of this is, of course, the interposition of a third term that mediates between what might be perceived at first as a distance, as difference, as the otherness of the terms one to the other. This mediation, which according to Levinas is "characteristic of western philosophy,"[11] demands a surrender of the terms, cannot permit any genuine difference; for, Levinas asks, "how could intermediaries reduce the intervals between terms infinitely distant? Will not the intervals between the mid-points progressively staked out ad infinitum appear always equally untraversable? If an exterior and foreign being is to surrender itself to intermediaries there must be produced somewhere a great betrayal."[12] For the neutral third to do its job, for mediation to be effective, the other must surrender, must cease to be genuinely other.

What is more, the third term, allegedly middle and neutral, turns out, in the end, not to be neutral at all, but rather "a third term which I find in myself."[13] Whether the horizon against which the other is comprehended be Being, Truth, the *Logos*, or History, all totalities that reduce the other to a function of a greater whole, that lift from the other the power of dissent—in each case this horizon, this mediation—is mediated by *me*. Truth is always *my* Truth, or at least my conception of the truth, and to impose this conception upon the other is to make the other a function of myself, not of some neutral third. Levinas bases this assertion on the absolute impossibility of escaping one's own viewpoint, the impossibility of standing outside of the relation with the other and viewing it from above with a synoptic gaze, the impossibility of mediating a relation of which I am one of the terms as if I were at once inside and outside of the relation. My interposition of the third term is thus always the imposition of myself. "The ideal of Socratic truth thus rests on the essential self-sufficiency of the same, its identification in ipseity, its egoism. Philosophy is an egology."[14]

For Levinas, this identification of the same that is freedom, this essential self-sufficiency of the same that reduces all otherness, this

essential violence of the same, is called into question when it encounters an other, a genuine other, an other that it is incapable—at least
ethically incapable—of reducing to a function of itself, an other that
reveals the self to itself as murderous in its naïve spontaneity of living
the world as enjoyment and pleasure and subsuming the world to these
ends. This calling into question, this critique of the same, comes by
way of an encounter with the face of the other.

To encounter the face of the other is, after the description of Levinas, to encounter at once a supreme vulnerability to violence and a
supreme resistance to violence.

As vulnerability to violence, the face of the other is encountered as
exposure to the capricious whims of fate, of the faceless gods of pagan-
ism that Levinas describes with his notion of the *il y a* (there is), the
anonymous *il* of *il pleut*. What rains? *Il*. Mysterious, terrifying, because arbitrary, because beyond invocation, the face of the other is
encountered as exposure to the alien elements of a world that erodes
and corrodes the flesh. The face of the other is encountered as passive,
that is, incapable of asserting any final power with respect to the passing of time, vulnerable to its irremissible passing, to a senescence that
marks the face, with the marking of time, with lines that testify to its
impotence in warding off time, a time that marks, moreover, a passive
march toward a death that always comes too soon, that is always pre-
mature, that comes quietly in the night, a thief. It, *il*, steals from the
face what is to the face alone. But the face of the other is vulnerable,
too, to those who *fait face*, to those who face it, those who would
possess it, in tyranny, in oppression, those who, in doing it violence,
de-face, and those with a face who, in refusing to face, enmesh the
face in schemes not of its choosing, who make of the face a stake in a
game, or the hunted, or who implicate it in a crime it has not committed.

At the same time, the face is encountered as a resistance to this
violence, as an inviolable dignity, as a face that decries this violence
in its freedom, in its very humanity, and the violence that the face
resists first of all is *my* violence. Indeed, for Levinas, the commandment "Thou shalt not commit murder" does not require inscription in
any moral code, oriental or otherwise, to give it its ethical force; it
is, rather, inscribed in the face of the other *qua* face. Moreover, this
prohibition does not suggest only physical murder, though it certainly
does entail that, but also murder as the usurpation of the life of the
other by way of its reduction to the same, transgression with respect to

the dignity, freedom, and humanity of the other as other, as irreducible, such that physical murder is only one variant upon the prohibition. This first prohibitive ethical word, this call to "letting be," is yet accompanied by its positive companion in that it is at once a call to me to take responsibility for this face against all violence done to it. It demands of me an endless responsibility, a responsibility for the very responsibility of the other, a responsibility even for the evil the other does me, to the point of being servant to the other, being hostage to the other, to the point of substitution for the other. The face of the other informs me that I am indeed my brother's or sister's keeper.

While *what* the face signifies is important, what is most essential here is *that* the face signifies, that is, that it signifies not a *"what?"* but a *"who?,"* that the face first of all is giving sign of giving sign, or the very signification of signification. In signifying, the other does not give itself, as it is given over by way of the mediation that characterizes occidental thought, but gives sign, presents itself as immediate, and as the signification of signification the face is a donation of meaning *kat'-auto*, coming from itself, a donation of meaning that originates in a genuine transcendence, donates a meaning, a *sens*, a sign that could not have originated in me. As such, the face is a teaching, and first of all a teaching of that teaching itself. "Signification," where the other expresses herself or himself, is thus contrasted in Levinas with "manifestation," the latter signifying a showing, a disclosure, a presentation, a revelation where the other would be susceptible to my conceptual grasp, reduced, when fully known, to categories, to structures, to definitions that I already find in me. The encounter with the face of the other thus effectuates precisely a reversal of the vectors of meaning that emanate for philosophy from the same in recognizing a meaning that is outside of myself, a meaning that will, when Levinas has completed his argument for ethics as first philosophy, be posited as the very origin of all meaning.

The face thus deconstructs the self-same, self-identifying ego of sameness and its maieutic reduction by presenting the same with a transcendence, with difference, with an other, whose difference is not revealed to ontology but is produced as ethics. It presents itself in difference in that it demands of me non-in-difference, that is to say, absolute responsibility with respect to the other, to the other who as teacher, like the teacher contrasted with the Socratic maieutics in Kierkegaard's *Philosophical Fragments*, brings to me something absolutely new, absolutely different, and who, in the depths of his poverty and vulnerability, and because of them, approaches me from an ethical height as master, as the one who commands me and to whom I am servant.

To enter into relationship with the other without reducing the other to the same is called by Levinas "discourse," a "non-allergic relationship with alterity." In the ethical relationship of discourse, I do not speak *of* the other, but *to* him. "The invoked is not what I comprehend: *he is not under a category.* He is the one to whom I speak—he has only a reference to himself; he has no quiddity."[15] He is related to as independent of the relationship that I establish with him, as more than the relationship, as irreducible to the relationship. Language, as discourse, is "a relation in which the terms *absolve* themselves from the relation, remain absolute within relation."[16]

In the face, in the face that speaks, that expresses itself, therefore, is found the point of deconstruction of structure, the critique of structure, the ethical prohibition against any structure I might bring to bear to reduce the freedom and dignity and humanity of the other (terms that are the result of, and not the prerequisite for, the otherness of the other) to an ontological continuation of the same. In responding ethically to this other, in responsibility, is lived the pacific relationship of discourse. "Thematization and conceptualization, which moreover are inseparable, are not peace with the other but suppression or possession of the other. For possession affirms the other, but within a negation of his independence. 'I think' comes down to 'I can'—to an appropriation of what is, to an exploitation of reality."[17] The generalization that makes possible the sciences—sciences named for the *logos*, including the theo-*logos*—appropriates the otherness of the other for the same, denies the otherness that is expressed in the face. In the face of the other gleams the "thou shalt not commit murder," an absolute prohibition against the imposition of structures as fundamental as conception and thematization in her regard, an insistence, despite the everyday occurrence of the same, that violence with respect to the other is an ethical impossibility. The face of the other is an inviolable resistance to structure, to violence, to the necessary violence of *my* structures.

STRUCTURES OF PEACE

This absolute, unending responsibility, with its prohibition against structure, which the face of the other demands of me is yet troubled by the appearance on the scene of the third party (*le tiers*), the other of the other, for now I owe allegiance to two masters, and, as one wiser than I has said (and whom Levinas does not quote), no one can serve two masters.

It is interesting to note that in the whole of Levinas's philosophical corpus this question of the third party is given specific thematic attention only very rarely, remarkably rarely, and is almost completely overwhelmed by the extensive analyses of the self in its immediate face-to-face relation with the other, in its various aspects and articulations. This is particularly fascinating when we consider that, to believe Levinas, the third has always been present in the encounter of the face ("The third party looks at me in the eyes of the Other,"[18] he writes), although the latter has been exhaustively described *as if* the third were not yet present, and fascinating also in that, toward the end of his life, Levinas was particularly interested in discussing the implications of this question for his philosophy and its significance for social thought.

The following quotation raises the relevant issues:

> The third party introduces a contradiction in the saying whose signification before the other until then went in one direction. It is of itself the limit of responsibility and the birth of the question: What do I have to do with justice? A question of consciousness. Justice is necessary, that is, comparison, coexistence, contemporaneousness, assembling, order, thematization, the visibility of faces, and thus intentionality and the intellect, and in intentionality and the intellect, the intelligibility of a system, and thence also a co-presence on an equal footing as before a court of justice. Essence as synchrony is togetherness in a place. Proximity takes on a new meaning in the space of contiguity. But pure contiguity is not a "simple nature." It already presupposes both thematizing thought and a locus and the cutting up of the contiguity of space into discrete terms and the whole—out of justice.[19]

The appearance of the third, implicitly present at every encounter of the face, has two major consequences. First, it attenuates the service, if not that I owe, then at least that I am able to provide to any one other, in that I am as responsible to the other of the other, and to all others, as I am to the other, such that the introduction of the third party marks the "limit of responsibility." In this light, serving the other, even with all of the service that is his ethical due, to the exclusion of the third, turns into injustice. Language as discourse thus "refuses the clandestinity of love, where it loses its frankness and meaning and turns into laughter and cooing."[20] Rather, "Everything that takes place 'between us' [between the same and the other] concerns everyone, the face that looks at it places itself in the full light of the public order, even if I draw back from it to seek with the interlocutor the complicity of a private relation and a clandestinity."[21]

Second, in demanding a "comparison of incomparables,"[22] comes "the birth of the question: What do I have to do with justice?" "The relationship with the third party is an incessant correction of the assymetry of proximity[23] in which the face is looked at. There is weighing, thought, objectification, and thus a decree in which my anarchic relationship with illeity [the other] is betrayed, but in which it is conveyed before us. There is betrayal of my anarchic relationship with illeity, but also a new relationship with it."[24] That is to say that responsibility for the other in ethics becomes responsibility for the others in society—a responsibility that must be lived as justice, that is, that demands the very application of structure to the other that the encounter with the face, viewed as if in itself, forbids. Justice requires equality, control, law, the State, comparison and possession, thought and science, commerce and philosophy, and the search for principle(s). Further, it is through this societal equality that I am permitted to recognize and assert myself as an other of the other. Against the anarchical other as encountered in the face, the third demands synchronization, which is "the act of consciousness which, through representation and the said, institutes 'with the help of God,' the original locus of justice, a terrain common to me and the others where I am counted among them, that is, where subjectivity is a citizen with all the duties and rights measured and measurable which the equilibrated involves, or equilibrating itself by the concourse of duties and the concurrence of rights."[25] Thus, in society: "The poor one, the stranger, presents himself as an equal. His equality within his essential poverty consists in referring to the *third party*, thus present at the encounter, whom in the midst of his destitution the Other already serves. He comes to join me. But he joins me to himself for service; he commands me as a Master. This command can concern me only inasmuch as I am master myself; consequently this command commands me to command."[26] With the appearance of the third party, my servant self becomes itself a master.

I would, to end this section, like to suggest the possibility of a connection between the purportedly neutral and middle *third* term of ontology (*un troisième terme*) and the *third* party (*le tiers*) that gives rise to the justice of society. Levinas does not, to my knowledge, ever make this connection, and not surprisingly: the neutral third of ontology, a superstructural term emanating from the same, and the third party, an other, the other of the other, are not at all the same thing. And yet, in some respects, these two "thirds" play a parallel role: in each case the third, either the third term or the third party, plays a mediational role with respect to the face-to-face relation, and puts limits on my obligations to the other; and in each case the third gives me a point of reference outside of the face-to-face by which I am able to mediate my own relation with the other, transcending the absolute insistence of Levinas that no such point of view is possible for the face-to-face relation "in itself."

DISCUSSION

It is important to note that for Levinas the hierarchical relation of the face-to-face is in no way supplanted by the equality demanded by justice; rather, the former persists in the latter as its condition. Ethical inequality persists as the very foundation of social equality. Levinas writes: "In this welcoming of the face (which is already my responsibility in his regard, and where accordingly he approaches me from a dimension of height and dominates me), equality is founded. Equality is produced where the other commands the same and reveals himself to the same in responsibility; otherwise it is but an abstract idea and word."[27] And again, "Like a shunt every social relation leads back to the presentation of the other to the same without the intermediary of any image or sign, solely by the expression of the face."[28] Indeed, when the ethical relation is forgotten, when it no longer founds the social relation, the necessary and calculated "just violence" of society turns into blind tyranny. Levinas, in demonstrating the interconnections between ethics and justice, would seem to be encouraging us to live justly in society in the spirit of anarchical ethics. But does not a tension remain? For to respond to the other as face, a necessary condition of the social relation, is to respond, concretely, very differently from responding to the other as fellow citizen, which is demanded by the presence of the third.

Despite Levinas's formidable, even successful, attempt to demonstrate how the justice of society is founded upon a prior ethical relation, and how this pairing of ethics and justice remains simultaneously in operation, the tension between the two is nevertheless evidenced by the fact that Levinas himself uses such words as "contradiction," "betrayal," and "correction" to describe the "effect" of society upon ethical responsibility. I would argue that this fundamental tension in Levinas's analyses is irresoluble.

Perhaps, then, the question becomes: What should be made of this tension? Does its presence lead to a criticism, or even a refutation, of Levinas's work? Might it not rather reflect a philosophy that attempts to describe, first of all, a relationship with that which is transcendent to philosophy? Might we not rather expect to find, in such a situation, as a consistent inconsistency, a way of thinking that is, on its own terms, incapable of encompassing the unencompassable, and might this not be expected to issue in certain "systematic" tensions? Might it not also reflect a sensitivity of this thought to the profound reality of evil in our world, an evil that runs so deep that even the good itself is divided, such that one would have to choose, at least in certain concrete situations,[29] between what Levinas refers to as the ethical and the just? If Levinas's analyses indeed reflect our reality, and if structure, that is, one and the same structure, is at once necessarily violent and necessary to justice, then structure itself must be viewed as "pharmacological" (in the sense that Derrida gives to the term in indicating that *pharmakon* means both "poison" and "cure"), and the tension we discover with respect to embracing it should not surprise.

As a Quaker, I am particularly interested in the meaning of this tension for the just war/pacifism debate. Certainly Levinas's description of the face-to-face encounter gives a great deal of impetus to the argument for pacifism, and Levinas acknowledges this. Indeed, who could enter into war, perhaps the most extreme form of the imposition of violence (and a bizarre combination of the imposition and obliteration of structure), with a neighbor for whom I am responsible, responsible even for her responsibility, responsible even for the evil she does to me. And yet Levinas himself is not a pacifist. I asked him. And when I asked him why not, he answered: "*Il faut toujours lutter contre le mal*" ("It is always necessary to fight against evil"), where *lutter* clearly implied military struggle, and his response was contextualized in terms of an appeal to the third. Our highest calling, he informed me, is not to a "wild philanthropy," but to be about building just institutions. I, on the other hand, despite the analyses with respect to the third party, and no doubt influenced by my own prejudices, believe that the weight of Levinas's work suggests precisely the opposite stance as the most appropriate one. Which way to turn?

The tension remains, and results for me in this crudely put question: Do we allow, in the last resort, in the name of nonviolence, in principled courage that refuses to repay violence for violence, the slaughter of the innocents, or, in the last resort, in the name of justice, in principled courage that refuses to permit the slaughter of innocents, do we impose an order that will necessarily oppress even in its very lifting of oppression? Both irresistible choices, both painful choices, both impossible choices, both glorious choices, and, in either case, a beautiful and treacherous risk.

It occurs to me that historically, within the domain of Christian traditions, our various denominational communities have made more or less consistent decisions along such lines, with the reformed traditions, for instance, finding themselves more at home with the ability of structure to effectuate justice, and the anabaptist traditions finding themselves far more suspicious of structure because more sensitive to its oppressive aspect. Historically, of course, one of these views had to be right and the other wrong. But in the more nuanced theoretics of postmodernism (at least when it comes to issues of truth), perhaps it can credibly be argued that both—and neither—are "right." Given the nature of structure as posited in postmodern theory, perhaps the tension must remain. Perhaps, given the course of events in our century, we should all be suspicious of anything purporting to be, or going by the name of, "The Final Solution."

In a world where the painful and persistent reality of evil plagues us to the point that even our responses to it seem to implicate us in it or leave us helpless before it, in a world where redemption seems to be fleeting and rare, we cannot, perhaps, expect to find a response to evil that is simple, univocal, straightforward, and free of the suffering it hopes to redeem. What I am suggesting is that perhaps we need one another, those of us who insist upon pacifism and those of us who opt for just war. We need those who are willing to be active in our world in "fighting against evil," those willing to make the cut that cures, those seeking to institutionalize justice. And, at the same time, we need the uncompromising ones, those who refuse to be implicated in a violence that, as violence, can never ultimately heal, those who remind us of the structural violence that always forms a part of even our most cherished institutions. Perhaps in the interplay of these nonintegratable callings a community committed to a non-articulable good is engendered, a community founded not upon creedal acquiescence but upon the responsibility for the other that gives sense to fraternity and sorority. As Levinas has said, only the genuinely other can teach me.

NOTES

1. This chapter is based on a paper presented at the annual meeting of the Canadian Theological Society on June 8, 1993, Carleton University, Ottawa. (Emmanuel Levinas was still living at the time; editorial changes have been made in light of his death in 1995.)

2. This is, of course, just one of my possible ways to characterize post-modernism, which, far from being a unified movement, is a term used to designate a wide variety of discourses which are collectible under this term perhaps only because of their shared reactionary relationship to "modernism" and its faith in the efficacy of universal Reason.

3. This, too, entails a faith, even be it a loss of (a certain other) faith, for even if every version of modernist, self-grounding Reason were to be "decon-structed"—internally disturbed by the pointing out of uncontrollable ele-ments necessary to its self-control (or internal stability)—this would not prove a priori that any such project would necessarily fail, even if we could not presently conceive of the success of such a project. It is not a matter of "dis-proving" modernist paradigms (which would be, paradoxically, to reinforce a logic that is being called into question) as much as it is a matter of these paradigms, as Lyotard says, having "lost credulity."

4. Emmanuel Levinas, *Totality and Infinity: An Essay on Exteriority*, trans. A. Lingis (The Hague: Martinus Nijhoff, 1979), p. 43.

5. Ibid., p. 42.

6. Ibid., p. 42.

7. Ibid., pp. 43–44.

8. Ibid., p. 43.

9. Ibid., p. 42.

10. Ibid., p. 45.

11. Ibid., p. 44.

12. Ibid., p. 44.

13. Ibid., p. 44.

14. Ibid., p. 44.

15. Ibid., p. 69.

16. Ibid., p. 64.

17. Ibid., p. 46.

18. Ibid., p. 213.

19. Emmanuel Levinas, *Otherwise than Being or Beyond Essence*, trans. A. Lingis (The Hague: Martinus Nijhoff, 1981), p. 157.

20. Ibid., p. 213.

21. Ibid., p. 212.

22. Ibid., p. 158.

23. "Proximity" is a locution adopted in *Otherwise than Being* that, for our present purposes, can be taken to indicate the face-to-face relationship.

24. Levinas, *Otherwise than Being*, p. 158.

25. Ibid., p. 160.

26. Levinas, *Totality and Infinity*, p. 213.

27. Ibid., p. 214.

28. Ibid., p. 213.

29. For instance, do I devote myself to the construction of a more just social order, or do I spend myself attempting to attend to those crushed by whatever order is currently in place? Few of us, it seems to me, are superhumanly capable of doing both, let alone one or the other, well.

7

Again Ethics:
A Levinasian Reading of Caputo
Reading Levinas[1]

Jeffrey M. Dudiak

CAPUTO AGAINST ETHICS

IN HIS RECENT BOOK *Against Ethics* (along with its companion piece, *Demythologizing Heidegger*[2]) Professor John Caputo argues, with wit, grace, and a clarity of style rare among postmodern thinkers, that we would do well to give up on "ethics" and limit ourselves to the far more humble task of responding to "obligation."

Ethics, he claims, is too Greek, which is to say that it is the effect of a dream, a Greek-philosophical dream of perfect clarity, of unambiguous principles that would provide answers to all of life's questions regarding responsibility, such that one need not think (or at least not think much, and certainly not much about individual cases), need not struggle, but simply apply rules for behavior that would guarantee satisfactory results. On Caputo's reckoning, this Greek dream has become a nightmare for all those who are not "Greek," who do not share in the dreaming (who are not selected to play on the metaphysical "dream team"), who do not participate in the drawing up of the principles, who do not become privy to the power exerted in the name of the dream. To recognize the worth of these "others," these non-Greeks that Caputo, after Lyotard, likes to refer to as *les juifs*, is to recognize that things are not quite so simple as the Greek dream would have us believe, that a responsible life does not consist in the straightforward application of true ethical principles, but is a much more confusing, miscegenated mix of odds and ends, not of individuals participating in universals, but of singularities that call for a singular, rather than a "principled," response and that obligate us in their singularity. *Against*

Ethics is an attempt to stir us from our Greco-ethical dream and to awaken us to the suffering that occurs both out of the sight of ethics (which is too focused upon rules and getting them right to see the lame lying nearby) and as a result of ethics (which, in reciting to itself the law, drowns out the voices of those who protest that they are being crushed underfoot). I read *Against Ethics*, then, as a continuation of the project set forth by Caputo in his *Radical Hermeneutics*: the project—explicitly borrowed from one Johannes de Silentio and applied in *Against Ethics* to the area of ethics and obligation—of "making life difficult."[3] A little bit, or perhaps a lot, of humility, it seems, will hold us in good stead when it comes to our responsibilities to our neighbors. Agreed.

In place of a new philosophy, in place of another set of philosophical principles (which would be too Greek, which would implicate him in that which needs to be, as much as possible, avoided), Caputo offers up instead a "poem on obligation," a poem whose purpose it is "to make [obligation] look as strong as possible," which, he says, under the circumstances, is "the best anyone can do."[4] Caputo's poem, a great, lyric poem of "Paradise well lost"[5] and unable to be regained, of the deconstruction of metaphysics in favor of a hermeneutics of facticity, is indeed beautiful. In the course of this poem, parts are written for a number of characters whose philosophical personae we recognize: Kierkegaard, Nietzsche, Heidegger, Derrida, Lyotard, Deleuze, to name only a few of the principals. My contention in this response to Professor Caputo is that one of the parts in his poem, the part written for Emmanuel Levinas, a character who figures prominently in the work, has been poorly written, and that this (on my view) mis-writing, the result of a (on my view) mis-reading, has important implications for the effectiveness of the poem as a whole. I offer to Professor Caputo, then, these public comments, from one reader of Levinas to another, in the interest of *les juifs* of all creeds and races.

APPROACH /AVOIDANCE: CAPUTO READS LEVINAS

Caputo follows Levinas (or follows Derrida and Lyotard, who, in this, follow Levinas) in asserting that it is the call (face/flesh) of the other that elicits my response and that is the (non)site of obligation; he follows Levinas in asserting that our responsibility is not to some abstract philosophical formula, not to "ethics," but precisely to this other. It is this idea that pervades his text. In fact, if the sections of *Against Ethics* that not only refer explicitly to the work of Levinas but that depend upon this work (including by way of Derrida and Lyotard) were to be extirpated, the book would, I maintain (and perhaps Caputo would concur), be a mere heartless shell of what it is, a still-clever hymn to polymorphism, but without (much) *caritas*. Despite this dependence, however, Caputo remains uncomfortable with the work of Levinas, or at least with this work on the terms in which Levinas (at least on Caputo's reading) presents it. Caputo gratefully acknowledges his debt to Levinas, but wishes to recontextualize this work (that is, to demonstrate that "the other" is the result of a textual operation, namely, is the effect of *différance*), to strip it of its pretention to have "located" infinity, to deconstruct it, and to make life more difficult for Levinas — whom Caputo nevertheless loves. Caputo claims that we cannot take Levinas straight, that we cannot quite believe Levinas, and suggests instead that Levinas's ethics must be taken not on its own terms but as a hyperbolic myth — albeit a myth that Caputo also loves.

Caputo's sundry disagreements with Levinas (almost[6]) all, it seems to me, stem from the single contention that, in the end, according to Caputo, Levinas's formulation of the relationship with the other, despite its great contribution to contemporary thought, nevertheless remains "ethics," that it fails to escape, or reverts back into, metaphysics — a charge perhaps suggested, and facilitated, by the fact that Levinas uses the terms "ethics" and "metaphysics" to describe this relationship. Caputo maintains that Levinas's "other," as infinite, as commanding me unambiguously, participates in the dream of Being without difference, without *différance*. This single charge assumes a number of formulations, or manifestations, in Caputo's texts, and it is, I think, worth enumerating briefly the most persistent among them and demonstrating their relation to this single criticism.

Levinas Is Too Pious

The first hint in *Against Ethics* that something in Levinas's work might be problematic for Caputo arises in the context of Caputo's laudatory comments regarding Levinas's having performed "the greatest deconstruction of ethics since Johannes de Silentio." We are told that Levinas has performed this great gesture:

> Even though Levinas thinks that everything is or turns on ethics and that ethics is first philosophy, even though he is very "pious" and loves

ethics like a rabbi, and even though, despite his admiration for Derrida's "formidable questioning," he would defend the priority of "ethics before Being," not the "deconstruction" of ethics. . . .[7]

In the footnote that follows upon the word "pious," we are told:

> By "piety" I mean not only a discursive style but a discourse which is centered and homological, which makes everything turn on something central, unique, and one, like the Other (Levinas) or the *Ereignis* (Heidegger). Eccentricity is no less a form of centering than concentricity. Levinas's piety is centered not on the True but on the Good and can be seen in the monopoly of ethical discourse, its hegemony over other discourses.[8]

The charge of piety[9] thus stems from Caputo's insistence that there is nothing that can be successfully stabilized as central to a discourse, nothing that can avoid being subject to the de-centering (quasi)law of *différance*: neither the True nor the Good nor the Other. *Différance*, as the condition of the im/possibility of everything, in demonstrating that every term, in being posited in a discourse, implies and therefore relies upon its excluded opposite, which can therefore no longer be effectively excluded but must also be made "central" to the discourse (thereby creating a second "center," which deconstructs the very notion of center), is essentially (if it has an essence) de-centering, deconstructive of all presumed centers.[10]

The Other Cannot Be "Absolutely" Other: Otherwise-Than-Being Cannot Avoid Being-Otherwise

The argument, *pace* Levinas, that there can be no "absolutely" other, and therefore that Levinas's "otherwise-than-being" cannot avoid "being-otherwise," is Caputo's most frequent, and perhaps central, complaint against Levinas, or at least against Levinas "taken straight."[11] Against Levinas's claim that it is only "the other as absolutely other" that would be capable of breaking up the egology of the Same and its constituted world by calling it into a relationship of responsibility, Caputo insists that this relationship between the same and the other must be a "correlation," since these terms are related—not dialectically, mind you, but related nevertheless—ethically, absolutely. Caputo then asks:

> But how can you have an absolute relation to an absolute? Would not the very relation and correlation dissolve the absoluteness? How could

anything be cor-related to what is ab-solutely Other, since the absolute absolves itself of all relation and correlation? If something were, properly speaking, absolutely Other, then it would not be a matter of concern for us and we would simply ignore it, being quite oblivious to it.[12]

Caputo correctly recognizes that ignoring the other is not quite what Levinas has in mind, so he concludes that in laying its unconditional claim on us "the Other is related to us after all," such that "in fact the absolutely Other is only relatively absolute, almost absolute, not quite absolute."[13]

Along the same lines, Caputo deconstructs Levinas's otherwise-than-being down to being-otherwise, correlating the Levinasian gesture of claiming the status of otherwise-than-being for the other to Eckhart's claim that God is not a Being. Caputo finds the confession he is searching for in Eckhart: " 'When I said that God was not a Being and was above Being,' Meister Eckhart said, 'I did not thereby contest his Being, but on the contrary attributed to him a *more elevated Being*.' "[14]

So, for Caputo, who does not believe it is possible to twist free of Being:

> the commanding claim of the Other . . . is not beyond Being because it is less than Being but rather because it is *more* than Being, because it exceeds Being. It is beyond Being because it is so radically, so absolutely, so fully, that it cannot be contained by Being (so long as Being means *physis*). That is why it is preeminently and paradigmatically metaphysical. . . . Against Levinas, . . . I would say it is impossible for what is otherwise-than-Being to avoid being-otherwise. To say that the other comes to us from on high, in a way that is higher and more eminent than Being (*physis*), is to attribute to the Other a higher being, a being higher.[15]

Caputo insists, therefore, that the face of the other is not totally other, not otherwise-than-being, but comes to us across "quasi-hermeneutic forestructures," and that Levinas is not to be believed—at least, not quite.

> For this absolutely Other, this infinite alterity, is, as it stands in Levinas, the dream of virgin lands and arctic snows, of absolute nonviolence, of full presence utterly unmarked, unmediated, unmodified. It is the dream of absolute presence in the mode of absolute absence, the dream of a world without *différance*, without textuality, without phrases, without horizons, contexts, settings, frameworks, or any form of media-

tion—all this delivered up in *le dire*, not in *le dit*, that is, in phrasing. So it is an impossible dream, even a dangerous dream, inasmuch as promises of what is absolutely unmediated are usually followed by the most massive mediations.[16]

Levinas Is Actually a Kind of Neoplatonic, and Not Really a Postmodern

The previous point makes it easy to see why Caputo can say: "I do not think that Levinas intended a breach of metaphysics in a 'postmeta-physical' style, as in Derrida. I think he intended a more Neoplatonic or 'hypermetaphysical' radicalizing of metaphysics, in the style of Plotinus or Meister Eckhart."[17] Caputo's claim would, moreover, seem to be corroborated by Levinas himself, who, after defending *Totalité et Infini* as a dissertation for his *doctorat d'Etat*, published a summary in the *Annales de l'Université de Paris* in which he claims that we must "recover Platonism" and calls for a new Platonism as antidote against a world disoriented and "dis-occidentalized."[18]

Now, if we are to grant that simply not "being postmodern," if indeed Levinas is not, is nothing to get into a worry about (and why should it be, unless "postmodernism" is some kind of salvific orthodoxy?), then Caputo's concern along these lines can be seen to revert to the same, persistent problematic. According to Caputo, Levinas gives us a "metaphysics of the Good,"[19] rather than a deconstruction of metaphysics, and this because he conceives, on Caputo's view, of "the absolutely Other in terms of Neoplatonic infinity."[20] Caputo (following Wyschogrod) also sees Deleuze as a kind of Neoplatonic, and thus, regarding these two philosophers of excess, he claims:

> Both of these views proceed for me from the dream of being without *différance*, from a kind of neo-Neoplatonism of being-to-excess which lacks the restraint of *différance*. I find myself, factically speaking, moving in the limited space between these two infinities. That space of finitude is the field in which my odd 'Heterologist' roams about.[21]

Levinas Backs Up the Claim of the Other, Guarantees It, with Recourse to God

For Caputo, as we shall see, obligation simply "happens," without any backup, metaphysical, divine, or what have you. *Es gibt* obligation. That is all. Caputo is therefore naturally suspicious of Levinas's claim that the other is capable of stilling the *es gibt* (of which, for Caputo, the other is a part), of breaking up the anonymity of the *es gibt*, or, on Levinas's terms, the *il y a*.

> I do not think that anything can "deaden the heartrending bustling of the *il y a*." I am more inclined to believe Levinas when he says that obligation comes "from I know not where" (*je ne sais d'où*). I am more inclined to believe that we cannot separate the *il* which is Him, God, which is God's own utter illeity, from the *il* of *il y a*, from the rumble of the *il y a*. "God" is not the "apex of my vocabulary," something which would organize and stabilize my vocabulary, but another word that puzzles and disturbs my sleep.[22]

So, when Caputo claims that Levinas sees in the infinity of the other "a categorical command cutting through the film of appearances and putting us in contact with the noumenal world,"[23] or "a trace of a still more absolute and more infinite infinity,"[24] he sees an attempt at discovering a "divine backup" for obligation, at discovering a depth structure—going from the trace of the other to the trace of God—that would circumvent undecidability, that would put us, "thanks to God," in touch with Being without *différance*.

Caputo sees infinity in Levinas, therefore, as "expressly something metaphysical and even theological, something ethico-theo-logical."[25] "Indeed," Caputo comments, "I think that what Levinas provides is above all a metaphysics of the religious, of faith, which organizes faith around the trace of the Infinite Other." Caputo is not opposed to faith, but makes it clear that there can be no (theory of) faith without *différance*. "I take the notion of *différance* as a propaedeutic to a theory of faith."[26]

Levinas Rejects Politics as War

Caputo's criticism of Levinas's politics follows from the same basic objection in that Caputo sees Levinas trying to keep ethics pure with respect to politics, sees Levinas desiring an ethics with clean hands, uncontaminated by the impurity that results from an (on Caputo's view, unavoidable) exposure to *différance*.

> For Levinas, it is not politics that is first philosophy [as it is for the Platonic philosopher-architect] but ethics; politics, on the other hand, is war. That is not a deconstruction of politics, I think, but a riding roughshod over it that will not do because it does not take into account the fact that we are always inside/outside political totalities.[27]

Caputo proceeds with a rather *ad hominem* attack on Levinas's personal political views in order to sustain his "philosophical" point, to show that Levinas's ethics are, when push comes to shove, indeed contaminated by politics, to show that Levinas, too, would have to admit, if he were honest, that it is necessary to deconstruct ethics.

> That he sometimes does, like it or not. If you can get him to talk about politics, about jewgreek ethics and Israeli politics. About the Palestinians. If you ask him about infinite responsibility to the Other, about being held hostage to the Other, about the infinite *me voici* which opens itself to the unconditional command of the Other, and in particular about whether there are any Others other than the Others defined by antisemitism. Then he talks freely of the desirability of "a political unity with a Jewish majority . . . a State in the fullest sense of the term, a State with an army and arms, an army which can have a deterrent and if necessary a defensive significance." Then the Other to whom you are responsible turns out to be "[m]y people and my kin," my own. That is, the Other ends up being the same. As to the Other who is not the same, who is the enemy, then it is better to keep an army.[28]

Caputo assures us that he is not trying to make Levinas (whom he loves after all) look bad, but that he is "trying to situate his discourse, to mark off its limits, to delimit the discourse on ethics and infinity,"[29] in short, to deconstruct Levinas's ethics of infinity.

Over against this Levinas taken straight, Caputo prefers a certain impiety with respect to "the other" (after Lyotard), prefers an other that is not "purely" other, that is, a deconstructed other, an other whose manifestation is always already a function of the play of *différance*, always already presented across the trials of undecidability, always already inside/outside of politics (after Derrida), and who has no metaphysical backup—not in God, not in Truth, not in Reason. In other words, Caputo wants to (has to, I would maintain, in order to sustain his argument) retain the discourse on alterity that emerges as the fulcrum of the Levinasian corpus, wants to (has to) maintain what he refers to as the heteronomic—the law of the other that gives rise to obligation—but he wants to disturb the purity of this law by exposing it to what he refers to as the heteromorphic—the pure play of difference in the plenum of Being, without the absolute hierarchy established (albeit in favor of the other) in Levinas's curved space of obligation. Caputo wants to admit that the face of the other does indeed command me (though not quite so unambiguously as Levinas suggests), does indeed obligate me, but that this command always comes to me across a miscegenated blur of signifiers. Yes, Caputo confesses, obligation happens, but so do a lot of other things. "It (obligation) happens." "Shit happens," too, as some of our less delicate friends sometimes remind us. (Sh)it happens. With all of this happening "happening," it is never easy, or even ever really possible, to tell what exactly is happening. In the face of all of this perturbation, in the face of all this difficulty, all of this interpretation, and interpretation of interpretation, with all of this radical hermeneutics happening, Levinas's version of the face as piercing the confusion, as cutting through the anonymous (sh)it, as commanding me unambiguously—to the point of making me a hostage to it in my obligation, to an obligation that cannot be avoided—strikes Caputo as too "pure," as not sufficiently immersed in the play of *différance*, as trying to cut free from the depths of undecidability—in short, as too metaphysical, not sufficiently "postmodern."

To an undeconstructed Levinas, Caputo attributes a transcendental move, a maximizing of the phenomenal face and the finitude of obligation, pushing them to a transcendental completion, beyond any limits, and thus a kind of totalizing, a totalizing of otherness.[30] Such a discourse, Caputo insists, clearly cannot be taken straight, and needs to be deconstructed. And yet Caputo loves (and needs) this discourse, so he retains it, but not on its own terms. Caputo therefore deconstructs Levinas's philosophical discourse down into a prophetic one, calling Levinas's infinity a piece of prophetic hyperbole, a myth, stripping Levinas of his philosopher's garb and replacing it with that of a prophet (which, while not necessarily insulting, is nevertheless done without Levinas's consent!).

> I would say that what we find in Levinas is prophetic hyperbole. If it is taken seriously, held to the canons of philosophical discursivity, it cannot be believed or defended and it lapses at strategic points into the most classical Neoplatonic metaphysics and negative theology. So it is a mistake to take Levinas on his own terms, in the way that Levinas himself demands—metaphysically—for then Levinas is vulnerable to all of the criticisms that beset metaphysics, for this is a metaphysics indeed, a metaphysics of the Good not the true, a metaphysical ethics, not a deontology, but a metaphysics still.[31]

Moreover, Levinas *as prophet* is not supposed to be believed. "[I]t is not necessary to believe the stories that prophets tell, not literally," because "cognitive phrases and poetic phrases belong to different regimes."[32] Levinas tells beautiful stories, stories that need to be told. He is a great poet of obligation, *the* great prophet of obligation to the postmoderns, but it would be "a degradation and a distortion of mytho-prophetic discourse" to take it straight, for we are rather to be instructed otherwise by such impossible, unbelievable stories. These stories belong, Caputo claims, not to the realm of the true but to the myth of justice.[33]

So Levinas's discourse is, for Caputo, "an excess, an excessive statement, a bit of hyperbole, which is an operation of *différance*."[34] In the end, for Caputo, Levinas's discourse on infinity and the totally other are simply (although this is still quite a lot) a poetic, prophetic, hyperbolic myth, a way of saying that obligation happens.

> The absolutely other is a poetic and hyperbolic name for the fact, as it were, of obligation, of heteronomy, that we do not belong to ourselves, that we are always already held fast in the grips of something I know not what, *je ne sais quoi*, something *heteros*, something absolutely *heteros*— almost. It is a way of saying: obligation happens, *emphatice!*[35]

Challenging the Hegemony of *Différance*

Before proceeding with what I imagine might be Levinas's response to these criticisms, or rather to this multifaceted, single criticism, let me first attempt to raise a few questions regarding Professor Caputo's position in order to create a framework from out of which Levinas's thought might better be able to be evaluated.

As I have just indicated, Professor Caputo's major point of contention with Levinas is that Levinas, in making my responsibility to the other "absolute," in arguing that "ethics" is outside of the auspices of Being, transgresses the "law of *différance*," that is, that Levinas permits the other to stand outside of the economy of *différance*, which for Caputo is impossible because, on his reckoning, *différance* is the condition of the impossibility of "everything."[36] Now, Caputo is correct, I think, in believing that "the other" of Levinas's discourse transgresses this law. The question that interests me at this point is whether this law is legitimately hegemonic with respect to "ethics" as Levinas uses the term.

For Caputo, following Derrida, *différance* is the condition of im/possibility for everything, in that all discourse, in signifying, in engaging a signifier, enters into a field of signifiers that is predicated upon the possibility of distinguishing one signifier from another. Engaging any particular signifier, therefore, necessarily implies (negatively) engaging the signifiers that are not explicitly employed, and this because the meaning of any particular signifier is determined by its relation to all of those from which it is distinguished, which are, as such, drawn into the discourse even as they are (seemingly) excluded. Deconstructive reading is, therefore, and perhaps among other things, a demonstration of the manner in which the "excluded" from any particular discourse is necessarily implicated in this discourse, and in which a discourse in fact feeds off of that which it attempts to exclude, and thus disrupts or "deconstructs" the claim of "presence" asserted in the discourse, since that which is "present" (the included sign) implies that which is "absent" (the excluded sign). As such, anything that enters into discourse, anything that can be said, therefore, is the "effect" of *différance*, made possible by the "spacing" of signifiers that *différance* names, even as that "effect" is made impossible as a pure presence in that it is eroded, or deconstructed, by that which it (necessarily) attempts to exclude.

Différance is thus, according to Caputo, a "kind" of transcendental, a "kind" of principle, but as it makes any kind of unity simultaneously possible and impossible (or im/possible, as Caputo prefers to say), it is neither a transcendental nor a principle in any strong sense, and Caputo, again following Derrida, prefers to call it a (quasi)transcendental, or a (quasi)principle. The use of "quasi" here is also meant to signal a certain caution in thinking of *différance* as a transcendental or a principle or a law, for it is, according to Caputo, to whatever extent it functions transcendentally, a strange sort of transcendental. It is, he claims, a "transcendental without a subject," an anonymous, impersonal field, that "is neither a name nor concept and possesses no nominal unity."[37] That is to say, according to Caputo, that *différance* is a transcendental — almost.

The (quasi)law of *différance* is, as such, correlative with, or determinative of, another (quasi)law, that of "undecidability." For if entering into the play of signifiers at any given point implicates one in all of the excluded signifiers, implicates one in the play of signifiers, then we can see that there can be no privileged place in this differential field, no place where one could stand as if at the center around which the field might be organized, and no place outside of this field that would provide, as a "transcendental signified," a privileged point of entry — for we are always already within language. As each of the signifiers involves all of the others, there is no priority of one over another, and any choice of one and exclusion of another is therefore without criteria. The possibility of choosing a place within this field is, therefore, made possible by the differential (quasi)structure of the field, while, at the same time, as any given choice also implies the non-chosen, to choose (to make present without invoking the implied absence) is also made impossible. The (quasi)law of undecidability therefore, paradoxically, makes choice both possible and impossible, which does not, Caputo emphasizes, make choice any less pressing or necessary; it "simply" makes choice more difficult, without (philosophical) criteria—which makes choice a genuine choice—and, precisely, im/possible.

As the condition of im/possibility for everything, as that upon which "everything" becomes im/possible, *différance* functions, I would argue, as Caputo's "principle of all principles," or since it is not really a principle,[38] as his "(quasi)principle of all (quasi)principles." As that which opens up the field of undecidability, as that in terms of which everything becomes im/possible, I am not sure how else to refer to this (quasi)law/principle/transcendental. In response to those who might argue that faith, or obligation, or ethics, or justice, or what have you, might challenge the all-pervasive reach of this (quasi)principle/law, Caputo assures us that nothing can escape exposure to *différance*, that we cannot get beneath undecidability and find something more primordial because "undecidability goes *all* the way down,"[39] or all the way up, or out, or all the way in whatever direction or into whatever modality one might seek in order to get outside of it.

But does undecidability really go all the way down? If it does, as Caputo assures us, then must we not be consistent and insist that, as going all the way down, there must therefore be a certain undecidability at the heart of undecidability itself (if it has an "itself"), a certain undecidability with respect to undecidability? Must there not be a difference at the heart[40] of *différance*?[41] And if this were the case, would one not have to "decide" for undecidability, at least insofar as one wanted to take "undecidability" as the (quasi-)transcendental condition for "everything"? Would the "choice" for undecidability as a (quasi)-principle of all (quasi)principles not also be im/possible? Would such a choice not also imply *its* other—namely, *not* choosing for undecidability, that is, choosing for "decidability?" And if one were to "decide" for undecidability in the throws of this deeper undecidability (an ever deepening, ever receding undecidability, as at each level of "undecid-

ability with respect to any decision for, and resting in, undecidability"
a "deeper" undecidability would, *ad infinitum*, be required), what
would be the criterion by which such a decision would be made?
Would not a "decision" for undecidability, at any of these "levels" (as
that which will function as the condition for everything else) be as
"undecidable" as any other decision? Would it not be equally arbitrary,
equally im/possible?

Now, it is of course a foolish mistake that I am making at this point
(I admit it!), a category mistake. For how could one even conceivably
ask whether *différance* could be the condition of *différance*? Is it not
necessarily the case that a condition is a condition for the conditioned,
and never for the condition itself? How can something be its own
condition, short of being God?[42] Still, I intentionally commit this error
in order to dig a little more deeply into what might be going on here.
For what sort of power play, what sort of appeal to truth, or even
Truth, must be taking place if the enforcement of this categorical law
is insisted upon? (Have we at long last landed upon a postmodern
unconditional?) For if undecidability, in fact, goes all the way down,
then must it not, as I have already suggested, in revealing a certain
undecidability at the heart of undecidability itself, create the possibility
(im/possibility) of deciding against undecidability, or perhaps of deciding for something "other" than undecidability? And if undecidability
does not, in fact, go all the way down, that is, all the way down into
undecidability itself, does not *différance* itself escape the play of *différance*, and thus—irony to end all ironies—fulfill the dreaded dream of
perfect presence (albeit in the form of presence/absence)? In order to
avoid the charge that *différance* is its own condition, which would
make it "unconditional" and most metaphysical, must not Caputo
maintain that *différance* is the condition of im/possibility for everything
except différance itself? But is not the appearance of such an "exception" precisely the site at which Caputo locates the metaphysical? Is
not this "except" always followed by a designation of that which would
claim to be Being without difference, without *différance*, and—Caputo
will hate this—is this not the old metaphysical dream that Caputo
hopes to disturb?[43] Caputo will, of course, insist that *différance* "is
neither a name nor concept and possesses no nominal unity,"[44] that
it is not really a transcendental, but merely a (quasi)transcendental.
But does the thin protection of the prefix "quasi-" really help here?
"Quasi-" or not, the law of *différance* remains the condition of, and
thus *governs*, however purportedly neutrally (anonymously) or be-

nignly, the im/possibility for everything.[45] The hegemony of the law of *différance* is enforced, whether it is prefixed with "quasi-" or not. Must one not wonder how much metaphysics is being transacted underneath the veil of this little prefix?[46]

Of course, I am not really chiding Caputo for this "philosophizing," for he himself confesses that it is not a matter of not doing metaphysics, but of doing so only minimally. "If one has to philosophize, one has to philosophize; if one does not have to philosophize, one still has to philosophize (to say it and think it). One always has to philosophize." Monsieur Derrida, Caputo's mentor, said that.[47] What I am curious about is whether Caputo's philosophizing, his insistent recourse to a discourse on *différance*, is really as metaphysically minimal as he would have it,[48] especially given its "priority" (and this does not seem to be too strong a word) with respect to all other discourses, as the (quasi)transcendental condition for their very im/possibility. Is it not strange that the discourse of *différance*—a discourse that claims to be the advocate of a plurality of discourses—can refuse to accept another discourse "on its own terms" (as Caputo refuses the discourse of Levinas on its own terms), but can accept it only as mediated (made im/possible) by the discourse of *différance*? That seems to me to be a promotion of a rather limited diversity, a rather attenuated polymorphism, a diversity within rather strict confines, and gives me to wonder whether that can be called a promotion of plurality in any meaningful sense at all.

Indeed, does not Caputo find himself, in this respect (as a post-liberal?), in the same sort of awkward position that liberalism is vulnerable to, that is, as having to discipline, by means of censure or reinterpretation according to its own tenets, certain positions in order to make space for all positions (some of which will, of course, no longer be able to recognize themselves), and carrying out this operation from an ostensibly neutral meta-position (or in the case of Caputo, an ostensibly neutral meta[quasi]position)? Caputo is explicitly for the proliferation of discourses: "Let them be!" But, mind you, do not necessarily let them be themselves. "Oh my fellow democrats, there are no democrats."[49]

A LITTLE LEVINASIAN APOLOGIA

Coming off the offensive, this troubling of the troubling (quasi)law of *différance*, it is now possible to offer a brief *apologia* for Levinas, as I would like to argue that *différance* is not necessarily *the* (quasi)transcendental, that is, that *différance* is not the only (language) game in town. On the contrary, it is my contention that Levinas is more sensitive to the problematics of postmodernism than Caputo gives him credit for being, and that, upon re-reading, Levinas's view is, therefore, closer to the view that Caputo himself proposes (despite its problems—problems that apply equally to Levinas, or Derrida, or, I think, to views *tout court*) than Caputo expects (but which is not surprising, given Caputo's [cautious] dependence upon Levinas).

On Not Circumventing Levinas's (Quasi)Transcendental

On my reading, it would be erroneous to interpret Levinas as meaning by "ethics" what Caputo means by ethics,[50] and I believe that Caputo's criticism(s) of Levinas depend(s), at least in part, upon such a reading. Levinas's discourse on ethics, the discourse that dominates his philosophical writings, I maintain, is in no way an attempt at fashioning a metaphysics of morals or at delineating an ethical principle. It is, rather, an extended investigation into the transcendental condition *for* "ethics" as Caputo wishes to employ the term, a description of the conditions of possibility for such an ethics (as well as for friendship, for politics, for truth—indeed, for anything "intersubjective"), and not a description of any particular ethics, or of the principles governing any one of them. To read Levinas as proposing an "ethics" in Caputo's sense would be to read Levinas either along empiricist lines or as committing the same move that Caputo accuses Heidegger of when the latter finds an historical instantiation (or a dual historical instantiation: Greece and Germany) for the "meaning of Being," whereas it cannot, on its own terms (which Caputo maintains, against the later Heidegger, were argued correctly in *Being and Time*), have such an instantiation, because the "meaning of Being" is "a transcendental theory *about* the history of metaphysics, not a theory which assumes a place *within* that history."[51] It is such a transcendental status, which Caputo also attributes to Derrida's *différance*, that I would attribute to Levinas's "ethics."

When Levinas does begin to write about what Caputo refers to as ethics (and he only ever just begins, as this is never his focus), he calls it "justice," and consistently shows how such becomes possible only by way of its relation to its transcendental condition, which is "ethics" in his own sense. But in Levinas, too, justice is not quite possible, but, like Caputo's ethics, im/possible. This is because, as Caputo perceptively notes, justice in Levinas (as is the case for Derrida's "law") is put in place not in order to restrict injustice, but to restrict ethics (in Levinas's sense, or what Derrida refers to as justice). Justice demands that I turn my attention to all of the others, and not just to *le premier venu*, although it is my responsibility to "the first comer," and to all subsequent comers, that is the *condition* for justice, and that responsibility can never be forgotten if there is to be justice. Still, perfect justice would mean absolute responsibility to the other, which, as forgetful of the other others, would be patently unjust. Perfect justice (a justice that would equal "ethics," a justice that would be the instantiation of ethics) would, strangely enough, be unjust. Therefore, ethics is not able to be instantiated, but remains, nevertheless, the condition of possibility of justice, and, indeed, since perfect justice would be unjust, remains the condition of im/possibility of justice. I maintain, therefore, that as a condition of im/possibility, Levinas's ethics should be seen not only as transcendental, but precisely as a (quasi)transcendental.

Levinas does not, then, *pace* Caputo's reading, reify ethics. Ethics never *is*, but as a (quasi)transcendental condition, like *différance*, creates the conditions of im/possibility for being. It, like Derrida's "justice,"[52] is an "ideal," not in the sense of conforming to an Idea, but in the sense of responding ethically to the singular other, to all singular others, and as such is perhaps "a dream of virgin lands and arctic snows, of absolute nonviolence, of full presence utterly unmarked, unmediated, unmodified"; but it harbors no illusions about treading upon this sacred and infinitely distant tundra, even as it attempts, always and again, in eschatological hope for a future always future, to complete the journey. For Levinas, the third person already gleams in the eyes of the other, calling ethics to justice, though still by way of ethics, that is, in responsibility to the third as to yet another other. For Levinas, ethics never *is*.

Now, the importance of getting Levinas straight on this score shows itself most clearly, I think, in respect to the criticisms that Caputo makes of Levinas's politics. For when Levinas opposes ethics to politics, and refers to politics as war, he is in no sense, as Caputo suggests, opposing politics as a "factical life world" activity that might somehow be circumvented by recourse to some "pure" ethics, nor is he denying that we are always inside/outside political totalities, nor is he is denying the necessity of both constructing and deconstructing political institutions. He is, rather, or so I am suggesting, engaged in a description of the conditions of possibility for such things as politics.

For Levinas, the politics that is war goes back to a description of the tendencies of the Same to totalize, the tendencies of the ego, as a function of its centered-in-self *jouissance,* to assimilate its "world" in a manner commensurate with its needs, to make of all alterity an extension of itself. Now, the description of the Same, like that of ethics, is, in Levinas, a transcendental description. There is no ego living in pure *jouissance* whose "world" is not already disturbed by the other, but, like ethics, this transcendental is, according to Levinas, an ideal, namely, the ideal of Western philosophy—an ideal that finds its essence in an aspiration to autonomy that Caputo, following Nietzsche, nicely sums up in what can be taken as "philosophy's opening and characteristic gesture": "I, Plato, am the truth."[53] It is in attempting to "meet" this impossible ideal that politics is war, war in Levinas being the forcing of a singularity to play a role in which she no longer recognizes herself.[54] Politics as war is thus a strange mix of recognizing the otherness of the other, and yet trying to suppress this otherness by nevertheless remaining the Same, by bringing the other into this sameness, by ruse, by rhetoric—as the other attempts to reduce the singularity of the same to her sameness. To the extent that politics is a function of this ideal, a function of war, is politics as war, Levinas opposes it, and contrasts it to ethics as the recognition of the other as other. But Levinas is in no sense opposed to politics as the "getting one's hands dirty" work of trying to effectuate justice—institutional, "political" justice.[55] Levinas does not try to transcend this latter kind of politics by fleeing to some sort of pure ether of ethical height. On the contrary, ethics (as the condition of justice) demands such politics.[56]

So for Levinas (and this, I think, goes against Caputo's reading) there is no recourse to a "pure" ethics that would put him in a position to "ride roughshod" over politics, no "ethics" (in Caputo's sense) that would not already be political. Such an ethics, such a politics, would be, rather, like deconstruction, "between" the universalizing, totalizing, systematizing Same and the singular, heteronomic, system-refusing Other, always already both at once. It is in this space that Levinas advocates "justice," the perpetual but non-dialectical play (although for Levinas such "play" is, in the face of suffering, always [and I think appropriately] serious, a *jeu* that involves an *enjeu*) that seeks to respond to the singular, but, as necessarily responsible to all singularities, does so by way of universal law, from which the singular *qua* singular recedes again and again—and it is this movement, I would maintain, that makes deconstruction possible, or that is deconstruction, if such a thing exists. As we shall see shortly—and, according to Caputo, we have it on good authority—"Deconstruction is justice."

A recognition of the (quasi)transcendental character of Levinas's ethics answers too, I think, Caputo's concerns regarding Levinas's "practical" politics, for there could then no longer be any question of a "pure" ethics being corrupted (deconstructed) by exposure to "practice." There simply *is* no such purity to be corrupted. For in the "factical/existential life world" where I am always already presented with the other of the other, justice and equality are demanded (albeit as conditioned by the asymmetrical ethical relationship), such that not only is the other of the other the equal of the other, but I too come to be the other of the other, and an equal. Here law and its enforcement are required, necessitating the presence of the police (despite Caputo's reluctance to call them), and also international law (if politics means, in our time, that we have nations) and its enforcement, necessitating the presence of an army.[57] Justice also, as Caputo confesses, demands judgment, and while I with Caputo (in goyish solidarity) might well disagree with Levinas's judgment regarding the Palestinians, I would maintain that Levinas's statements on this score contain no "in principle" hypocrisy with respect to his philosophy. One needs to talk justice and politics and make judgments, even if one is careful to remain vigilant to the ethical transcendental that conditions their im/possibility.

On Not Circumventing the Totally Other

It is in the context of the aforementioned interplay between "the same" and "the other," languaged by Levinas in the later writings as "being" and "otherwise-than-being," that Caputo's objection that there can *be* no "totally" other, no otherwise-than-being, but only a partially (though still quite a lot) other, or a being-otherwise, needs to be addressed.

On Levinas's description, the same is marked by an egoism which is, if left to itself, without the checks of the other, essentially and naïvely assimilative. This egoism, which lives as *jouissance*, "consumes" all that is around it in accordance with its needs, that is, "worlds" its world as an extension of itself, setting itself up in a "home" that centers space such that all space, as surrounding this center, is a unified space, a single space, so that the "there" differs from the "here" only superficially, in that every "there" is in effect only an extension of the "here." Time is likewise collected into a "now" that mediates the "then" of past and future, time's extases gathered into, in being related to, a central "present." All difference, in this scheme, is thus only superficially different, is a difference that either is, or is potentially, assimilable to the same. So long as the other, even the human other, enters into this space and is consumed by the same, assimilated into the world of the same, it cannot be said to be other, to be different, in any meaningful sense, in any sense that would challenge the naïve domination of the *conatus essendi*.

For Levinas, therefore, no partially other, no superficially other, would suffice to pose a challenge to, to inaugurate critique in, the monopolistic, totalizing same. So we cannot, on Levinas's view, have (quasi)transcendental forestructures sufficient for the Other (*l'autrui*, the human other)—for then the human other would be reduced to an intentional object, drawn into the domain and dominion of the same. Even if the Other were to be constituted as an alter ego—that is, not reduced to an intentional "object" but recognized as a co-intentional "subject," albeit arrived at by way of an analogy to the same (as in Husserl's famous fifth Cartesian Meditation)—Levinas claims that he is still reduced to the same, for what could be more "the same" than another "me"?

Now, in pointing out that other human beings enter into our (quasi) hermeneutic forestructures, Caputo is clearly correct. Other human beings *are* a lot like me, and this very recognition permits me to identify them as other human beings, to identify with them as fellow human beings. It would seem that such forestructures must indeed be in place for such an identification to be made. But Levinas does not claim that the other is totally other in her nature, or in her attributes, or in her being. The notion of totally other can be correctly read, it seems to me, only in relation to the notion of the same as Levinas employs the term. The other is totally other not with respect to her being, but in that she presents herself as refusing the domination of the same, as refusing (ethically) to be nothing more than an extension of my (quasi)hermeneutical, transcendental forestructures. The other is thus encountered (not "experienced," which for Levinas is still too phenomenological) precisely as a resistance to the same, as incapable (ethically) of being fitted into the forestructures that constitute my centered-in-self world, as resistant to the center that is the same and that would center the other in itself. To demand that this relation be mediated by forestructures, to ask how such a relation might "make sense" or "be possible" from the side of the same, is already to miss Levinas's point, already to miss the relation.

The other *qua* totally other is absolutely so, despite all anthropological similarity, as an ethical prohibition (that is at once a positive ethical command). The question of the totally other cannot, therefore, be approached, as Caputo approaches it, by asking how one could possibly enter into a relation with an absolutely other (who would by definition absolve itself of all relation), but by seeing that absolute otherness is "produced" in the ethical relation, by terms already in relation, and this as the ethical resistance of the other with respect to the consumptive egology that characterizes the same.

So, in response to Caputo's claim that the other cannot present itself to me as otherwise-than-being but only as being-otherwise, that there can be no totally other but only a partially other, a Levinasian response might be to insist yet again that otherwise-than-being cannot be merely a "more than Being, because it exceeds Being . . . beyond Being because it is so radically, so absolutely, so fully that it cannot be contained by Being," as Caputo claims, bolstered by his proof-text from Meister Eckhart. The other in the ethical relation is quite precisely otherwise-than-being (and not a more than or exalted being), and this because Being itself is, on Levinas's reading, a category of the same.

Caputo's incredulity kicks in at this point, for, as he tells us, he does not believe that it is possible to twist free of Being. But what is Being? Caputo suggests (at least in the passages relevant to his discussion of these issues) that it is perhaps *physis*. But if it is *physis*, then is not any thought of Being, including the thought of a being from which it is impossible to twist free, not already *meta-physis*? And how would we know what Being is, whether as *physis* or as something else, to know that we could not twist free of it, if Being were not manifested to a knowing ego?[58] Is not "Being," then, be it *physis* or something else, be it noun or verb, always already someone or other's "conception" of Being? And is such "conception" not precisely the activity that characterizes "the same" in Levinas? (Has Being really got a hold on us, as Caputo claims, or is this claim just another way of keeping a hold on Being, of regulating what Being is permitted to signify, and of subjecting all beings to this notion?) To claim that we cannot twist free of Being, to claim that the other cannot *se presente* as otherwise-than-being but only as being-otherwise, is, from Levinas's perspective, to continue to reduce the other to the thought of the same, to bring the other within the "thought of Being" (which need not be reduced here to the specifically Heideggerian meaning), which is always my (or somebody's) thought of Being. To be unable to twist free of Being is to be unable to twist free of the same.

So when Caputo tells us that if he were asked to rewrite Levinas's *Totality and Infinity* he would rename it *Totality and Partiality*,[59] Levinas might well question whether the "part" of Being which Caputo relies upon to be the site of obligation is really up to the task. For is not a "part," by definition, a part of a "whole," and if so, then just exactly whose "whole" (or whose conception of the whole) are we talking about when we refer to its part? Must not the fact, as it were, of obligation (even as Caputo formulates it) presuppose an other who can refuse "my whole," my tendencies as ego to totalize, and to reduce the other to a part of my totality—the other who is, *ethically* speaking, totally other, that is, capable of declining my kind offer to make him merely an extension of what is mine (including making him a function of my ideas of Being [or whatever] formulated by me)? I am inquiring, in short, as to whether Caputo's poem on obligation does not, after all, require the totally other he is so determined to refuse (a refusal that is the result, I am arguing, of a commitment to *différance* that precedes and governs any commitment to the other), even as his discourse makes repeated appeals to it.

It seems to me that Caputo consistently wants to have it both ways: he needs an other, but he does not want this other to be genuinely other.[60] For instance, in *Against Ethics*, we read, first of all: "*We are always on the receiving end* of such obligations; we cannot trade places with the sender and put ourselves in a position to know the source of the message being sent. Otherwise we would be in a position of autonomy, which is a cognitive model, and we would be back in the position of the solitary soldier on the drill field congratulating himself on his ability to take orders."[61] While *on the facing page* we read: "The Other is not an absolute, not a transcendental fact, not a pure reason, but *a factical fact that I have construed* in a hermeneutics of facticity that includes a section on the poetics of obligation and that has made its mind up to have a heart."[62] Obligation requires passivity, but this passivity turns out to be my activity. Can we really have it both ways? Perhaps the site of the total otherness of the other is not exhausted by the options offered by Caputo: either as transcendental fact or as pure reason.

On Not Circumventing the Priority of the Other

It is, finally, in the context of this coming of the other which disturbs the *conatus essendi* of the same that Levinas's comments regarding the Good beyond being, and God, need to be understood, for I would argue that the Platonic or Neoplatonic and theological language that Levinas employs is always (at least in the philosophical writings) a way of speaking, within philosophy and, of course, in an always inadequate way, about the singular other to whom I am responsible, and never an attempt to make the other a subset of some divine Other, or some grand Good, or some overarching Infinity. To take the singular other in this way, as a "part" or "participant" in the Good beyond being, or as the trace of *the* Trace which is God (and this appears to be Caputo's reading[63]), Levinas would have to have forgotten almost the whole of the rest of his discourse where the other's resistance to any such totalities is precisely and consistently at issue.

On my reading, the language of the Good beyond being, the language of Infinity, and the language of God, and the correlation between this language and the other, is not to be taken to mean that the other is or partakes of these as if they were totalities that governed some realm that ran parallel to the realm of Being—Levinas is, on the contrary, expressly opposed to any such *arrières mondes*. This language serves, rather, to indicate from within philosophy—within which the singular other is incapable of showing itself (philosophical discourse being, like all language, predicated upon universalization)—that philosophy is not all, that it has failed in its attempts to complete the System, to indicate that *Cronos* (the all-embracing time of philosophy, of the same), "thinking he swallows a god, swallows but a stone."[64] This philosophical language indicates, from within philsophy, that the other of philosophy leaves its trace even within philosophy, and that at certain moments this recognition has, perhaps even inadvertently, been made (Plato's Good beyond Being and Descartes' infinity as a thought that thinks more than it can think being among Levinas's favorite examples), even if the mainstream of the tradition, including the thinkers who gave us these indications, has ignored them. But these indications are only negative ones (as the other signifies positively only ethically), are a trace of an other in the System, and cannot be taken as "descriptions" of that other, or as descriptions of some totality in which the other participates.

Caputo does not want to take Levinas straight, but here he takes

Levinas too straight, missing, I think, the function of this kind of language in a thought that wishes to keep itself open always to the singularity of the other, not to reassign the other for duty in yet another totality, be it the kingdom of the Good or the kingdom of God.[65] Such a language is a function of the singular other; the other is not a function of the terms of this language reified into *arrières mondes*.

AN IMPOSSIBLE RAPPROCHEMENT

Could it be that Levinas and Derrida are not really so far apart as Caputo seems intent upon insisting, that their respective projects might be conceived of as being more complimentary, that is, less antagonistic, than Caupto's readings demand? I should like to make just such a suggestion, and this by way of a reading of a Derridian pericope that Caputo deals with at some length.[66] This seemingly scandalous "hard saying," taken from Derrida's "Force of Law," reads as follows:

> Justice in itself, if such a thing exists, outside or beyond law, is not deconstructible. No more than deconstruction, if such a thing exists. Deconstruction is justice.[67]

Several pages later, Derrida writes:

> If I were to say that I know nothing more just than what I today call deconstruction (nothing more just, I'm not saying nothing more legal or more legitimate), I know that I wouldn't fail to surprise or shock not only the determined adversaries of said deconstruction or what they imagine under this name but also the very people who pass for or take themselves to be its partisans or practitioners.[68]

After recalling the first of these quotations, Caputo asks, with rhetorical incredulity: "Undeconstructible justice? What can that be if not an ageless truth, an unshakable foundation, a *fundamentum inconcussum* lying beneath the surface of deconstruction?"[69] As is already evident from the objections Caputo raises against Levinas, undeconstructible justice could not, for Caputo, be any such thing. So Caputo undertakes to interpret this "hard" saying, indeed, both of these hard sayings, by arguing what, on his reading, "given the presuppositions of deconstruction,"[70] Derrida *must* mean by them. Caputo reads them, I am arguing, in such a way that the "surprise or shock" Derrida was aware that such statements would effect is largely reduced; he reads them in the context of Derrida as the "unflagging adversary of the dream of perfect presence"[71] against the Derrida who, in this statement, appears to desire to "surprise and shock" even deconstruction's partisans (including Caputo himself?). Against his own rubric, "Derrida's Scandal: The Undeconstrutibility of Justice,"[72] Caputo proceeds, it seems to me, to attempt to eliminate the scandal Derrida anticipates and perhaps even seeks to effect.[73]

Caputo takes up his discussion of these statements in the context of the article from which they are taken, Derrida's "Force of Law," wherein Derrida distinguishes between law (*droit*) and justice. Law, Derrida tells us, and Caputo recounts, concerns itself with universality, with the drawing up of regulations and structures (a political *techne*) that are properly blind to the particularities of the singular individual to whom they are "applied," and indeed must do so in order to be just (in the sense of unprejudicial). Justice, on the other hand, concerns itself precisely with the "frailty of action" (is a *praxis* rather than a *techne*), with the singular individual, with the one who calls to me out of her singularity, with that which I owe to the other in her singularity. These terms, however, despite the fact that they would appear to work at cross purposes—the one aiming at a universality that necessarily excludes singularity and the other at a singularity that eludes universality—are nevertheless implicated with and in each other. To see this we must remember that for Derrida, as for Levinas, the law is not fundamentally a constraint against injustice, but a constraint against justice, against spending all of my justice on one particular "other," to the exclusion of "the third," the other other, and all other others, which would, of course, be unjust. The law is properly conceived of, then, as aiming at justice, as an attempt to respond responsibly to the need, not only of the singular other, but of all of the singular others. The law, therefore, requires justice, lives "on credit"[74] from the responsibility for the other that justice demands, and justice, if it is to be just, requires the law, requires what Levinas refers to as the "comparison of incomparables," lest it, in Levinas's terms, degenerate into a "community of two," into the cooing of love forgetful of the universe, that is, forgetful of the other others.[75]

That is why, for Derrida, the law, which is necessary, is not to be destroyed, but deconstructed, that is, recognized as having been constructed, and constructed as a response to the call of justice issuing from the other, and "the third." It is because laws have been constructed—because they have been " 'drawn up,' 'made,' 'written': [because] they do not fall from the sky but are woven from the fabric of *écriture*"[76]—that they can be deconstructed, that they call for deconstruction, that is, can be called upon to account for their fidelity, or lack of such, to justice. This "deconstructibility of law" is, thus, one of the conditions of possibility for deconstruction. The other condition of deconstruction's possibility, Derrida tells us, is the "undeconstructibility of justice." "The result: deconstruction takes place in the interval that separates the undeconstructibility of justice from the deconstructibility of law (authority, legitimacy, and so on)."[77] Deconstruction, therefore, according to Derrida, takes up a position "between" law and justice, traversing the terrain that separates deconstructible law and undeconstructible justice, deconstructing rather than destroying the law, keeping the law supple for the sake of the fragile singularities for which the law has, in fact, been constructed but which, in its striving after universality, it nevertheless continually threatens to crush.

"Deconstruction," Caputo recounts, "is possible only insofar as justice is undeconstructible, for justice is what deconstruction aims at, what it is about, what it *is*."[78] We are left with the question, however, of "what undeconstructible justice can possibly *be* or *not be* or *be otherwise than*."[79] Rejecting the possibility that by undeconstructible justice Derrida ("unless he has simply lost his senses"[80]) could mean either a Platonic *agathon* or an Idea in the Kantian sense or some "categorical imperative"—all of which would implicate Derrida in asserting the idea of perfect presence and engaging in the metaphysics against which he has always fought—Caputo makes the following assertion, one that will interest me further shortly:

> Nor can he mean that "justice," the sign that includes both the signifier and the signified, unlike every other signifier, stands outside the economy of *différance*, and so is not implicated in its opposite, injustice and inequality. He cannot mean that "justice" always produces justice, that there is a justice that is never unjust, that innocent blood has never been spilled in the name of justice. Surely the name of justice is no more or less venerable than that of God or truth or peace or freedom, in whose name the most unspeakable atrocities are committed with unfailing regularity.[81]

These possibilities rejected, Caputo proceeds to review the "one comparison that Derrida allows (aside from Kierkegaard)," namely, the comparison to Levinas, although "even this is to be held at a distance."[82] Caputo's reasons for insisting on this "distance" (which have already been reviewed at some length in sections II.2 and II.3 above), despite Derrida's extensive taking over of Levinas's language of infinity, come down, we will recall, to the fact that, for Caputo (who, remember, does not think it is possible to slip free of being), Levinas's otherwise-than-being cannot be but a being-otherwise, a more elevated Being, which, as we have seen, Caputo believes needs be interpreted as a Neoplatonic gesture, which, he claims, is "completely classical."

> That is why undeconstructible justice in Derrida cannot be assimilated to Levinas's infinity, which, if it is neither Platonic, Cartesian, or Kantian, is rather more Neoplatonic, like the One Beyond the *nous*, like an inexhaustible Neoplatonic infinity. . . . For if it is neither a Platonic Good nor a Neoplatonic One, neither a Cartesian infinity nor a Kantian noumenon, *there is just no accounting for Levinas's infinity.*[83]

"There is no accounting," Caputo tells us, "—unless one were willing to say that it is hyperbole. . . ."[84] Hyperbole: this will be Caputo's explanation of both Levinas's infinity and of Derrida's undeconstructible justice. Caputo writes:

> I propose to locate what Derrida does not hesitate to call deconstruction's "infinite demand for justice" in a grammatical operation, a rhetorical trope, a work of grammar and linguistic invention, which arise by way of a response to the demands that are placed upon us by the singularity of the Other.[85]

Unlike Levinas's infinity, which Caputo interprets as a reification, an attributing of actuality or reality to that which he valorizes, Caputo reads Derrida's "quasi infinity of undeconstructible justice" as "neither Being nor otherwise than Being; the excess is not the excess of being but the excess of a linguistic performance, an excess within the operations made possible and impossible by *différance*, in response to the singularity lying on the edge of *différance*," such that, "[i]n Derrida, infinity means a hyperbolic responsiveness and responsibility, a hyperbolic sensitivity."[86] On this reading, Derrida's "scandal" has been removed (at least for those who are not scandalized by deconstruction), justice has been shown its place (as an "effect" of *différance*, like everything else) and deconstructive "orthodoxy" is restored.

It is, as I have indicated, just this concern with orthodoxy (although perhaps Caputo would insist upon its being called a quasi-orthodoxy), just this concern to stay devotedly within the "presuppositions of deconstruction," just this lack of scandal, that makes me nervous. In this context, let me briefly revisit the challenge posed earlier to the hegem-

ony of *différance* on the way toward suggesting a different reading of
Derrida's "hard saying," and a possible *rapprochement* between Levinas and Derrida.

If one were, by means of an experiment, to take the quotation cited
earlier—"Nor can he mean that 'justice' . . ."—and substitute deconstructive terms for justice, would one not find *différance* itself susceptible to all of the same difficulties that Caputo raises with respect to
"justice?"

> Nor can he mean that *"différance,"* the sign that includes both the signi-
> fier and the signified, unlike every other signifier, stands outside the
> economy of *différance*, and so is not implicated in its opposite, an econ-
> omy of the Same. He cannot mean that deconstruction always produces
> deconstruction, that there is a deconstruction that is never deconstruct-
> ible, that other systems of thought will never be suppressed in the name
> of deconstruction. Surely the name of deconstruction is no more or less
> venerable than that of God or truth or peace or freedom, in whose name
> unspeakable atrocities are committed with unfailing regularity.

It seems to me pointless, and perhaps even a little naïve, to try to
suggest—as Caputo, it seems, must—that *différance* is not such a sign,
a sign among signs, and that rather it *alone*, unique in this respect
among signs, it seems, is "neither a name nor a concept and possesses
no nominal unity."[87] Along these lines, Rorty comments that this term
"was, indeed, not a word, but only a misspelling" the first time Derrida
employed it, but that "around the third or fourth time he used it, it
had 'become' a word," that is, it would have been integrated into a
matrix of differentiated signs along with all other signs.[88] However
clever the introduction of this Franco-Latinate (and thus very much
derived) neologism might be, it would not, of course, have lasted as a
non-word even for the first few gratuitous usages that Rorty graciously
allots it; it would not, in fact, have survived even its first usage, which,
I take it, is what Rorty is humorously pointing out.[89] Now, I fully
suspect that Caputo would be perfectly content to confess that the sign
"différance" is indeed an effect of *différance*, but in order for this theory
(and it is a theory—although Caputo will confess only to Derrida's
having a "kind of theory") to have any explanatory efficacy, it is necessary that the sign designate a field of differences, a differential play,
that is not the equivalent of the sign itself, lest the sign be its own
effect, which is somewhat more foundationalist than Caputo would
appear to want to be. Of course, the field of differences that *différance*

names is not a "thing," but rather a condition of the possibility of things—in short, a quasi-transcendental. But if the sign that is *différance* is capable of designating such a quasi-transcendental, is capable of designating that which stands outside of the economy of *différance* (for the economy of *différance* can hardly be an effect of the economy of *différance*, can hardly cause itself—which would be even more metaphysical than an Unmoved Mover, rather more like the God of a process theology), if *différance* is "neither a name nor concept," if *différance* is "neither Being nor otherwise than Being" (despite the fact that Caputo does not think it possible to slip free of being!), then might it not be possible that other signs, too, might designate quasi-transcendentals (even while maintaining their status as signs), that, for instance, justice might have a designation that is not reducible to the *sign* "justice" (which in turn takes it meaning from its place in a field of differentiated signifiers), just as the differential field designated by the *sign* "*différance*" (if deconstructive theory is to have any sense) cannot be reduced to its sign. Why should the economy of *différance*, designated by, but not equatable with, the sign "*différance*," be granted hegemonic priority over any other "contender" for quasi-transcendentality? Why is the field of *différance* alone allowed to stand outside of the economy of *différance*?

It is as such quasi-transcendentals that I propose we read both "the other" (and the responsibility that such an other demands) in Levinas, and "justice" in Derrida, that is, like *différance* itself, other than as a *mere* effect of *différance*, even if it is also always the case that the *signs* "justice" and "the other" are such effects. This, it seems to me, is the claim that Levinas is making: that the other, and its call to responsibility, produces a meaning *kath'auto* that is not dependent upon being placed in any prior context of meanings; indeed, it makes such contexts possible. So while it remains always possible to read such meaning as coming out of, and finding its place within, a web of linguistic signifiers, it is not necessary that the meaning of such a term be reduced[90] to the meaning it accrues by being so located.

Indeed, I think Levinas might ask whether the field of *différance* is really prior to justice (as Caputo, after Derrida, uses the term), producing justice as an effect, or whether, on the contrary, it is the encounter with the other that opens up the field of *différance*. For Levinas, whose discourse is hinged between the Same and the Other, the encounter of the other, of a non-integrative alterity, is the introduction of difference, the introduction of an authentic difference that would not be

immediately reintegrated into the system of the Same.[91] The encounter of the other thus introduces into thought a "difference that makes
a difference,"[92] introduces the notion of height, of "non-indifference"
(this is one of Levinas's favorite words) into a horizontal field of "indifferent" differences—indifferent because equally effects of the same
(non)system. And is not such a difference necessary to the very opening
up of a field of genuine differences, differences that are not, in the
end, reducible to the Same (system), and necessary to the introduction
of the notions of responsibility and justice owed to an "other?"

Caputo, in speaking of deconstruction as being between law and
justice, and arguing that the two columns of Derrida's text *Glas* reflect
these terms and deconstruction's (non)place between them, demonstrates very well, I think, just how the priority of *différance* over that of
alterity (in that alterity is its effect) produces such a reduction of alterity
to the same.

> So then we are tossed back and forth between two impossibilities: the
> failed universal and the impossible singular, *which both belong to the*
> *same system.* For it is only in virtue of having language at all, a set of
> coded repeatable traces, a network of universals, that it is possible to
> pick out the singular, to sound their names, to summon them up, to
> call upon them, to call their *glas*. *Language is nothing but a system of*
> *universals,* of iterable signifiers, even as a truly concrete universal is an
> impossible dream. The singular always steals away even as the concrete
> universal always leaves something singular out. Pure singularity and a
> perfectly concrete universality: two impossibilities, two unerectable col-
> umns, *belonging to the same (non)system.* That is the argument of
> *Glas.*[93]

In rejecting as im/possible the universalizing and Systematizing pretensions of the Hegel column in *Glas* with its "philosophical" aspirations to *Sa* (*savoir absolu*), does Caputo (after Derrida) not introduce a
new System, be it a non-system, whose claims to totality are just as
pretentious, that appeals instead, but correlatively, to *Da* (*différance*
absolue)? Does Derrida, under Caputo's reading, become DerriDa?
Différance is described as a field of differences, but what kind of difference is really possible among differences that "belong to the same system," or "same non-system?" If *différance* is to describe a field of
differences that represent genuine differences, differences that make a
difference, and that are not simply (of) the same (system), where might
such differences come from?

I would like to suggest—and in this I believe I am following Levinas—that a case could be made for "the other" (and not just the sign "other") and her call to justice as being a condition of possibility for genuine difference and thus of the differences productive of meaning that the term *différance* seeks to describe. If such were the case, then *différance* would not be the condition of possibility of justice and everything else, which it would produce as its effects, but justice would be the condition of possibility of *différance*. And language would not be "nothing but a system of universals," as it is for Caputo; although it is a system of universals, it would also be "expression," interpellation (and this for Levinas is the "essential" of language),[94] an address, a response, a responsibility, to an other who is not himself an effect of the language with which one addresses him, but whose alterity makes the notion of language (as communication) meaningful in the first place. (Or else we end by claiming that language is really language speaking to language, which finishes in perfect [because complete] silence, which is not only the fruition of philosophy's dream of perfect unity and self-presence, but, as Caputo himself recognizes, a strange sort of thing for a theory of language to aim at.)

But my purpose here is not to take up the very phallo-centric project of suggesting that we pull down our philosophical pants and argue about whose quasi-transcendental is bigger than whose, of seeing whose (non)system—on "philosophical" grounds, which may not, I am arguing, provide the most pertinent criteria[95]—can be erected more impressively than whose. Could it be, instead, that Levinas and Derrida have both caught a glimpse of the problematic nature of "ethics" (in the derogatory sense that Caputo gives to the term) in the discourse of Western thought, and that each seeks, from differing adumbrational perspectives, in mutually critical rigor that nevertheless places them at times "in the heart of the *chiasmus*,"[96] to open up that discourse to its "other," even while recognizing the impossibility of the "closure" of this discourse and the correlative impossibility of any *pure* "opening" toward a new, non-Greek (as opposed to jewgreek) discourse. Derrida, the dean of deconstruction, who, vigilant to the ever-present danger of being subtly implicated in the Tradition in attempting to escape it, attempts to create an opening for the other from within, setting the Tradition to work against itself in his readings, but never naming its other in realizing that singularities, like Genet's transvestites, are dead as singularities in being drawn into the universality that naming entails.[97] Levinas, no less aware of the dangers, nevertheless takes *un beau risque* and "names the beyond essence" despite the steepness of the access, its "failures and renewed attempts," and his admitted "breathlessness."[98]

I would like to suggest, moreover, that such an opening toward the other cannot but aim at an "otherwise than being," because the discourse of Western philosophy is the discourse of Being, is ontology, and to point toward or to create a space for an "other" of that discourse, even from within that discourse itself, to an other who is not immediately reintegrative back into the system of that discourse, is to point toward an "otherwise-than-being"—not beyond being where being is *physis*, as Caputo seems to insist (and which assumes there is a *"physis an sich"* that is not already an interpretation), but where being is the totality of what "is" (or the process of its "being") according to the philosophical discourse that aims at an integrated totality.

And it is along these lines that I read Derrida's "scandalous" comments about justice. For Caputo, the qualifying phrase "if such a thing exists" that modifies "Justice in itself . . . outside or beyond law" is taken to call into question the reality of such a thing as "Justice in itself," such a thing as *pure* justice, a justice uncontaminated by injustice. On my reading, the qualifying phrase does not call "justice in itself" into question so much as it questions the status of "justice in itself" as something that could be said to "exist," calls into question its having the status of an existent, its participation in "Being." The same would then hold for deconstruction ("No more than deconstruction, if such a thing exists"), whose status as an existent is also called into question in that, as a discourse that strives to open itself to singularity, it is a discourse that attempts to situate itself outside of (or beyond) the philosophical/ontological discourse of the occident (*différance* being "neither a name nor concept"), even as it is necessarily implicated in this discourse. And while the employment of the copula in correlating justice and deconstruction is enigmatic in this respect ("Deconstruction is justice"), that is, if the "being" of both terms is in question, it nevertheless appears clear that the "is" so employed cannot be taken in any straightforward sense, for the simple reason that if deconstruction traverses the space "between" law and justice, it clearly cannot be "equated" with one of the terms it is placed between. I suggest instead that this statement be taken to mean that "deconstruction is *just*," just in that it aims at justice, is sensitive to the singular other to which it responds, and not that it "effects."

It is my contention, then, that Levinas, like Derrida, attempts to situate his discourse between that which Derrida calls law and justice, or what Levinas calls totality and infinity. Both are aware of the difficulties, the im/possibility, perhaps the very impossibility, of transcending philosophical language, of not speaking Greek; but each, in his own way, attempts, in philosophical discourse, to make audible the voice of philosophy's other. Neither is "against" the universalizing tendencies of law/politics/ethics (even if they are both against the founding of such in some or other transcendental signified), which are always necessary (if justice is to be just), even as they must be perpetually deconstructed in the face of the call of justice, of the singular, of the other.

A FINAL PENSÉE: A VIEW FROM PORT ROYALE

In the end, I must confess that I am somewhat troubled by the prospect of giving the discourse of *différance* the last word, or the first word, however deferred and differentiated and disseminated this word as a word would be. As much as it is the case that justice is always troubled by its inevitable miscegenation with "ethics," I must nevertheless confess that I sense in Caputo's "decision" for undecidability, in his devotion to the (quasi)law of *différance*, a strong possibility for a sort of postmodern *divertissement*—an anesthesia for the pointed pain of obligation in a deflection effected by the ambiguity concurrent with a (quasi)ultimate *différance*.[99] Derrida himself refers to the dangers of the "illusion of illusion," wherein the "facticity" of pain is deflected by a too critical analysis, a too skeptical, or unflagging, deconstruction.[100] For while Caputo's impressive efforts to continue to make life difficult for those who seek overly easy answers to the problems of obligation (who seek their *divertissement* in metaphysical security) are unquestionably necessary and much appreciated (not to mention very beautiful), does the poem of obligation not risk—in its contextualization of obligation—another kind of *divertissement*? It seems to me that Caputo is trying to put justice in its place, whereas the whole "experience" of justice, even according to Caputo himself, is precisely that it puts us in our place.

That is to say that I, at least, am more existentially (factically) impressed with the face of the suffering child than I am with any theory about the inversion of textual effects into (quasi)transcendental conditions, however rigorously pursued, especially if the latter, even supported by the best of intentions, serve to blur the force of the former.

That is my hermeneutics of facticity, or the facticity that inaugurates my hermeneutics. If this is the debate, I must respectfully decline Caputo's kind invitation (to be against ethics) and side with Levinas (for ethics, ethics again, and again, ethics always deconstructed, always "on the way," but ethics, nevertheless).

For me, the true difficulty of life is in neither the construction nor the deconstruction of metaphysical frameworks regarding obligation, but in trying to respond to, and dealing with my failure to respond appropriately to, the face of the other. It is this responsibility, and my hypocrisy with respect to it, that disturbs my sleep, and not, as with Caputo, the specter of a cold Nietzschean universe. Does a deconstructed face, a call to justice in the throes of undecidability, not, and perhaps even unwittingly, risk taking the edge off obligation and making life just a little easier, and therefore just a little too easy?

NOTES

1. This article first appeared in *Joyful Wisdom: A Journal for Postmodern Ethics*, 3/2 (1997), and is reprinted here by permission.

2. John D. Caputo, *Against Ethics: Contributions to a Poetics of Obligation with Constant Reference to Deconstruction* (Bloomington and Indianapolis: Indiana University Press, 1993). John D. Caputo, *Demythologizing Heidegger* (Bloomington and Indianapolis: Indiana University Press, 1993). In *Demythologizing Heidegger*, see in particular the chapter entitled "Hyperbolic Justice," which can, I think, be fairly taken as a précis of, or primer for, *Against Ethics*.

3. Or is this love of difficulty (also) the result of Caputo's long exposure to the Heideggerian texts valorizing *Kampf*?

4. Caputo, *Against Ethics*, p. 38.

5. My apologies to both Milton and Rorty.

6. Other charges are made, but not emphasized, and I have not attempted to trace these relatively minor points back to Caputo's central charge against Levinas, although this might be able to be done. For Caputo's claims that Levinas demands the (impossible) negation of the "I," see *Against Ethics*, pp. 124, 125, 219; that Levinas is too patriarchal, see pp. 145, 259n68, and that Levinas excludes animals from being "others," see pp. 145, 198.

7. Ibid., p. 14.

8. Ibid., p. 252n50. References or allusions to "Levinas's piety" can be found on pp. 14, 32, 61, 65, 83, 84, 125, 223, 236, and 252n50. I will ask momentarily whether Caputo's discourse, centered as it is on the notion of *différance*, as the condition of im/possibility for everything, is any less hege-

monic, which raises the question as to whether there can in fact be any "discourse" that is not centered on something or other, and whether the question then becomes one of what one prefers in terms of a center, be it a (quasi)-center.

9. This charge also has the advantage of at least implicitly associating Levinas's discourse with something that most contemporary people are highly suspicious of and not inclined to want to be associated with, as piety has come to be associated with something that is old-fashioned, boring (or at least not much fun), and perhaps even a bit hypocritical. It is associated with being religious in a rather dull and unsophisticated way. Even given the precision that Caputo gives the term in his footnote, he cannot be entirely unaware of the emotional impact that the label, at least potentially, also produces. Does he mean this, too?

10. I will discuss the use that Caputo makes of Derrida's notion of *différance* in greater length presently. I will try here to limit my discussion of *différance* to the way in which it is received and put to work by Caputo without concerning myself with the faithfulness, or lack thereof, to Derrida in this reception.

11. This disagreement is taken up, in one form or another, in *Against Ethics*, pp. 18, 19, 64, 74–75, 80–82, 145, 179, 191, 221–22, 236, 237, 264n73, and in *Demythologizing Heidegger*, pp. 198–99.

12. Caputo, *Against Ethics*, p. 80.

13. Ibid., pp. 80–81.

14. Caputo, *Demythologizing Heidegger*, p. 199.

15. Ibid., pp. 198–99.

16. Caputo, *Against Ethics*, p. 82. The last sentence of this quotation is taken from Derrida's *Truth in Painting*.

17. Caputo, *Against Ethics*, p. 257n52.

18. See *Annales* 31 (1961), 385–86; and Adriaan Peperzak, *To the Other: An Introduction to the Philosophy of Levinas* (West Lafayette, Ind.: Purdue University Press, 1993), pp. 38–39. For references to Levinas's "Neoplatonism" see Caputo, *Against Ethics*, pp. 63, 81, 252n51, 257n67, 263n67, and 267n26.

19. Ibid., p. 257n52.

20. Ibid., p. 263n63.

21. Ibid., p. 63.

22. Ibid., p. 226.

23. Caputo, *Demythologizing Heidegger*, p. 206.

24. Caputo, *Against Ethics*, p. 75.

25. Caputo, *Demythologizing Heidegger*, p. 200.

26. Caputo, *Against Ethics*, p. 287n29. For texts relating to this point see ibid., pp. 75, 226, 274n2, 278n29, and *Demythologizing Heidegger*, pp. 200, 205–206.

27. Caputo, *Demythologizing Heidegger*, pp. 197–98.

28. Caputo, *Against Ethics*, p. 123. Caputo quotes from: Emmanuel Levinas, "Ethics and Politics," in *The Levinas Reader*, ed. Sean Hand (Cambridge, Mass.: Basil Blackwell, 1989), p. 292. For other references to Levinas's politics see *Against Ethics*, pp. 123–26, 273n47, 274n2, and *Demythologizing Heidegger*, pp. 197–98.

29. Caputo, *Against Ethics*, p. 123.

30. Ibid., p. 84.

31. Caputo, *Demythologizing Heidegger*, p. 201.

32. Caputo, *Against Ethics*, p. 80.

33. Caputo, *Demythologizing Heidegger*, p. 201.

34. Caputo, *Against Ethics*, p. 82.

35. Ibid., p. 83.

36. This is made clear, for instance, when Caputo claims: "As with everything else, *différance* is the condition of the im/possibility of faith" (ibid., p. 286n6). I am less interested at this point in what the object of the condition is than in the assertion that *différance* functions as a (quasi)transcendental condition for faith, justice, and "everything else," providing any other discourse with its "uncircumventable limits."

37. Caputo, *Demythologizing Heidegger*, p. 25.

38. As will become increasingly clear as this section proceeds, I am not sure that I quite believe this assertion about *différance*, at least not in terms of how it functions (quasi-)transcendentally. My persistent (and perhaps annoying) "bracketing" of the "quasi-" with which Caputo prefixes such terms as "transcendental," "principle," and so on, is intended to (half-playfully) express my (relative) incredulity about the possibility for *différance*, or any term, to function non-metaphysically.

39. This phrase is taken from a personal letter sent by Prof. Caputo to Prof. James Olthuis, but the belief it expresses is found throughout Caputo's recent works.

40. And Caputo assures us that deconstruction does, at least, have a heart, a *caritas*.

41. Up to a certain point, Caputo, after Derrida, recognizes this. Referring to *Of Grammatology* (pp. 57–63), Caputo writes: "For it belongs to the very idea of differential play that the play is of itself self-differentiating, disseminating, and that any such formal rules as one could devise would be themselves 'effects' of the play not the 'basis' of it, subsets of the play of signifiers, not rules which govern it." John D. Caputo, "On Not Circumventing the Quasi-Transcendental: The Case of Rorty and Derrida," in *Working Through Derrida*, ed. Gary Madison (Evanston: Northwestern University Press, 1992), p. 158. We would seem to have here, therefore, something of a deconstruction of deconstruction—almost. But since this deconstruction of deconstruction is carried out in terms of deconstruction itself, it does not seem to mean much,

for the postulates of deconstruction always return intact, at a deeper level, even after they have been deconstructed. So deconstruction is, at least on these terms, never really deconstructed, even if its own tenets insist that it can/must be, and it never can be deconstructed so long as it is "deconstructed" only on its own terms, so long as it continues to play the same language game, so long as it remains, even if self-differentiating, "the same." Might the im/possibility of deconstructing deconstruction not "signify otherwise" than as the eternal return of the same (deconstruction)?

42. Depending, of course, on one's conception of God. At the time of the writing of this paper, God him/herself was not available for comment.

43. Here we see, I think, the danger of making the shift from deconstruction as a textual operation, as a protocol for reading, to deconstruction as providing a principle (be it a [quasi]principle: *différance*) that conditions things or events, which implicates it necessarily, it seems to me, despite all possible precautions, in metaphysics.

44. Caputo, *Demythologizing Heidegger*, p. 25.

45. Despite claims to the contrary, I am arguing that Caputo's employment of *différance* at least *functions* as if it were some sort of neutral "factical fact" (or names such)—moreover, as *the* factical fact, as if, in being proffered as the field in which difference and interpretation become possible, it were not itself already an interpretation. If Caputo's discourse teaches us anything, it teaches us to be vigilant in our incredulity with respect to any such claim, even if it be made implicitly.

46. It is my (perhaps naïve) belief that Derrida himself is more sensitive to these conundrums than Caputo appears to be, and this at least in part explains, perhaps, why Derrida's own criticisms (and are they criticisms?) of Levinas appear to be more humble than those of Caputo.

47. Jacques Derrida, "Violence and Metaphysics: An Essay on the Thought of Emmanuel Levinas," *Writing and Difference*, trans. Alan Bass (Chicago: University of Chicago Press, 1978), p. 152. The "voice" is that of a Greek, and Derrida immediately adds: "Levinas knows this better than others." Levinas responds to this quotation in: Emmanuel Levinas, "God and Philosophy," in *The Levinas Reader*, pp. 166–89.

48. And, consequently, whether there is, in fact, the possibility of a "minimalist metaphysics." Perhaps it is a matter not of not doing metaphysics, or of doing metaphysics minimally, but of confessing that we are doing, and must do, metaphysics (if we are to think in the occident), that we cannot have a hermeneutic, however radical, however purportedly attuned to "facticity," that is not metaphysical—and then retaining the hope that we can do metaphysics in a manner that produces, or reveals, an excess, a supplement, that might signify other than metaphysically, an other than metaphysics, a "signification" that would trigger a deconstruction of metaphysics even if always already from within metaphysics.

49. Caputo, *Against Ethics*, p. 121. This section is in part my attempt to respond to the charge that Levinas's philosophy is too "pious," too "homological," resulting in "the monopoly of ethical discourse." My contention is that Caputo's discourse, as claiming to describe the conditions of im/possibility of any other discourse, is equally pious, homological, and monopolistic. Certainly, Caputo wants his discourse to open up space for a plurality of discourses, but this is also the goal of Levinas, evidenced, I think, by his (very humble) criticism of Buber in claiming that the latter's thought "does not enable us to account for (except as an aberration, a fall, or a sickness) a life other than friendship: economy, the search for happiness, the representational relation with things," in short, does not open us up to a plurality of discourses, including the non-specifically ethical ones. (Emmanuel Levinas, *Totality and Infinity: An Essay on Exteriority*, trans. A. Lingis (The Hague: Martinus Nijhoff, 1979), pp. 68–69. My suspicion is that any "discourse" needs be homological. The question is what "facticity" one is going to privilege as determinative of it.

50. Roughly speaking, I think that when Levinas uses the term "ethics" he is referring, *mutatis mutandis*, to that which Caputo means by "obligation" and Derrida means by "justice." When Levinas uses the term "justice" he is referring to that which Caputo means by "ethics" and Derrida means by "law." The parallels are, of course, not perfect, and I therefore do not think that it is possible to standardize this vocabulary, even for the purposes of this essay, which would have been a very useful thing to do as I sense that Caputo's (on my view) misunderstanding of Levinas stems in part from some small confusion along these lines. I shall do the best I can to keep things straight.

51. Caputo, *Demythologizing Heidegger*, p. 10.

52. Levinas's ethics cannot be aligned perfectly with either Derrida's *différance* or Derrida's justice, because, for Derrida (at least on Caputo's reading), justice is an im/possible "ideal" that is the effect of *différance*, whereas for Levinas the condition and the "ideal" are of a piece.

53. Caputo, *Against Ethics*, p. 12.

54. Levinas, *Totality and Infinity*, p. 21.

55. When I personally asked Levinas (in the spring of 1992) the question, "What, according to your philosophy, at the end of the day, are we to be about in this world?" his response was: "Building just institutions." The academic impropriety of quoting a private interview aside, this did not sound to me like a philosopher eschewing politics.

56. As it demands its deconstruction, because the "comparison of incomparables" that justice demands, that politics administers, is haunted always by the ethical responsibility to the singularity that inspired it, but to which it cannot be adequate.

57. Levinas is not a pacifist. I asked him, getting the answer I expected but not necessarily the one that I wanted. Caputo's reading of his philosophy suggests, I think, that he should be.

58. *"Being and Time* has argued perhaps one sole thesis: Being is inseparable from the comprehension of Being (which unfolds as time); Being is already an appeal to subjectivity." Levinas, *Totality and Infinity*, p. 45.

59. Caputo, *Against Ethics*, p. 19. Caputo does confess that, at least so far, no one has asked him to do so. If I were asked to rewrite *Against Ethics*, I would rename it *Again Ethics* (for reasons I will raise later), but, at least so far, and strangely enough, no one has asked me to do so, either. In terms of a discussion of this title, my point in the previous section was to argue that Caputo reads Levinas as if his book were called *Not Totality But Infinity*. It is not. I checked the translation myself.

60. Caputo would object that a partially other can be genuinely other, and that is what I am disputing here. I might even want to argue, in this regard, that, in the end, the phrase "partially other" is an oxymoron, while "totally other" is a pleonasm. Shared characteristics do not suffice for identity.

61. Caputo, *Against Ethics*, p. 84 (emphasis added).

62. Ibid., p. 85 (emphasis added).

63. Caputo might well be right in saying that Levinas is not a "postmodern," if by postmodern one means someone who is about deconstructing metaphysics, although there is certainly a strongly deconstructive side to his work with respect to the metaphysical tradition. Levinas would not (and I confess that I am speculating here) believe that the closure of metaphysics is "possible." He believes that "Greek philosophy cannot be eliminated," as "the Greeks have taught us how to speak. Not to speak, not the saying [*le dire*] but to rediscover ourselves in the said." "The Paradox of Morality," *The Provocation of Levinas: Rethinking the Other*, ed. Robert Bernasconi and David Wood (London: Routledge, 1988), p. 178. He does seem to believe that it is, however, possible to open metaphysics up to its other, and that this can/must be done from within metaphysics itself. (But is this really so different from the deconstruction of metaphysics that attempts to think the closure of metaphysics from within metaphysics by thinking its closure? Is that, too, not a form of opening metaphysics up to its other?)

64. Levinas, *Totality and Infinity*, p. 58.

65. Such talk, of the Good or of God or of Infinity, is for Levinas, I would argue, a way of giving the singular other—who cannot make an appearance in the universalizing language of philosophy—something of an idiom within philosophy. The Good is only ever a way of saying "responsibility to the other," and there is never any content to the Good outside of such service; the Good is not something that pre-exists the other and my obligations to him in which my particular goodness (or lack thereof) might participate (or fail to participate). Likewise, God is not the justification or backup for my responsibility for the other; rather, the word takes on meaning only in my responsibility to the other. "The existence of God, the *Sein Gottes*, is sacred history itself, the sacredness of man's relation to man through which God may pass."

"Dialogue with Emmanuel Levinas," *Face to Face with Levinas,* ed. Richard A. Cohen (Albany: State University of New York Press, 1986), p. 18.

66. Caputo deals with this in both *Against Ethics,* pp. 85–92, and in *Demythologizing Heidegger,* pp. 192–206. It is the latter of these discussions upon which I will focus. While Caputo's references to "Force of Law" are to its publication in the *Cardozo Law Review* 11 (1990), 919–1078, mine shall be to: Jacques Derrida, "Force of Law: The Mystical Foundation of Authority," in *Deconstruction and the Possibility of Justice,* ed. D. Cornell, M. Rosenfeld, D.G. Carleson (New York and London: Routledge, 1992), pp. 3–67.

67. Ibid., pp. 14–15.

68. Ibid., p. 21.

69. Caputo, *Demythologizing Heidegger,* p. 193.

70. Ibid., pp. 196–97.

71. Ibid., p. 192.

72. Ibid.

73. Caputo could, of course, maintain that it is the other "partisans" of deconstruction—specifically, those who fail to take account of Derrida's concern for justice—that Derrida anticipates "shocking" with these sayings, and not readers such as himself. One of the things that I am attempting to (perhaps presumptuously) propose in this essay is, however, that a deconstruction that is too bound by deconstructive "orthodoxy," too concerned with promulgating deconstruction's "presuppositions," is perhaps too little deconstructive, not to mention too little just.

74. Caputo, *Demythologizing Heidegger,* p. 195.

75. Levinas, *Totality and Infinity,* p. 213.

76. Caputo, *Demythologizing Heidegger,* p. 193.

77. Derrida, "Force of Law," p. 15.

78. Caputo, *Demythologizing Heidegger,* p. 193.

79. Ibid., p. 197.

80. Ibid.

81. Ibid.

82. Caputo, *Demythologizing Heidegger,* p. 197.

83. Ibid., p. 199 (emphasis added).

84. Ibid., p. 199.

85. Ibid., p. 200.

86. Ibid.

87. Ibid., p. 25.

88. Richard Rorty, "Deconstruction and Circumvention," in *Essays on Heidegger and Others: Philosophical Papers* II (Cambridge: Cambridge University Press, 1991), pp. 102–103.

89. Caputo recognizes the problem, and comments: "But of course it is also true that anything Derrida himself would say about the differential play would be in the same predicament, an effect of the play, not the play itself.

. . . It is always already too late for Derrida too. That is why he devised the strategy of inventing words like '*différance*,' with the purely graphic alteration, which is not a word or a concept—at least not for the first three or four times he used it, as Rorty rightly points out—after which it is too late again. But at least for the first couple of times he uses . . . you see what he is up to, what he is pointing to. Once it sediments and becomes part of the established vocabulary of 'deconstruction,' he has to move on and try it another way. In his earlier works Derrida tended to spell this out; in his later works he takes it for granted. In '*Glas*,' which is his major work, he is just putting it to work" (John D. Caputo, "On Not Circumventing the Quasi-Transcendental: The Case of Rorty and Derrida," in *Working Through Derrida*, ed. Gary Madison [Evanston: Northwestern University Press, 1992], pp. 158–59). I wonder, with respect to this quotation, (1) whether Caputo thinks Rorty is serious about actually having the first couple of usages free, that is, whether Caputo fails to get the joke, and (2) more importantly, whether this "having to move on and try it another way" does not presuppose that there is "something" (a "play," an "economy," a "field") that *différance* (as a sign inadequately) names that just simply is "the way things are," or "the way language works." For just as "there is just no accounting for Levinas's infinity" if this idea is held to the canons of philosophical discursivity, and I agree there is not (but disagree that there should be), on the same criteria there is also "just no accounting" for Derrida's *différance*, simply because the presuppositions of a philosophical discourse are incapable of justifying themselves. Unless Derrida has been (miraculously) capable of simply "reading off the way things are" on the basis of certain textual effects, whereas presumably everyone else has had to "interpret" the data, then Derrida, too, must make some sort of philosophically non-justifiable "cut" in order to begin philosophizing at all, and this cut is always already an interpretation, always already a decision (or incision) about "the way things are." (Such an appeal would seem to have to at least implicitly accompany the deconstructionist's claim that deconstructive reading [at least to the extent it is extended into assertions regulating the limits of other discourses] is not an active interpretation but rather a more or less "passive" witnessing of the text's autodeconstruction. But is deconstruction really so far above [or below] the fray, and moreover, is it not a most metaphysical move to claim to be so attuned to some or other "facticity" that everyone else is left to [mis]interpret?) Freed from any illusion of reaching theoretical ground-zero, might not such a decision be called religious, and might not this be the point at which religion infiltrates philosophy, disrupting its reasoned rigor and its claim to being even its own final court of appeal?

90. I would argue that the charges of "reification" (like that which Caputo levels against Levinas's "infinity") and that of "reduction" (like that which is being brought here against Caputo) are equal and opposite criticisms, and, moreover, that there are no philosophical criteria for deciding the truth of

either, since each charge arises out of a discourse whose presuppositions are incommensurable with the discourse the respective charge is brought against. Thus, for Nietzsche, pity is the "effect" of a (frustrated) will to power, and the altruist could be said to "reify" pity, whereas the altruist could accuse Nietzsche of "reducing" pity to his particular form of vitalism. Since there is no neutral, objective discourse that might mediate between these claims, since each discourse determines what is to be granted "status" (as "being," as "real," or what have you) according to its own presuppositions, charges such as these have little persuasive power. I make this charge, therefore, (1) to counter Caputo's charge against Levinas (which is no less parochial than my charge of reductionism against Caputo—for deconstruction is a discourse, with presuppositions), and, more importantly, (2) to indicate that if Caputo wishes to apply his charge of "reification" convincingly, he should not do so equally across the board and should not exempt that which for him is ultimate, in the sense of being a propaedeutic for any other discourse: *différance*.

91. Caputo would claim, of course, that these terms, the Same and the Other, are already an effect of *différance*, and therefore could not be a condition of *différance*. I am arguing that alterity (difference) is presupposed by the notion of *différance*, that a play of differences presupposes differences, that a relation productive of sense requires *relata*. Of course, the Same and the Other are not identifiable as "the Same" and "the Other" until they are caught up in the play of signifiers that gives them a linguistic sense, but this does not mean that they are a creation (effect) of the play—unless the play is ultimate, unless the play is the Play, unless "the Play's the thing."

92. I borrow this felicitous phrase from James Olthuis.

93. Caputo, *Against Ethics*, p. 204 (emphasis added).

94. Levinas, *Totality and Infinity*, p. 67.

95. See note 89.

96. This phrase comes at the end of one of Levinas's articles regarding Derrida: Emmanuel Levinas, "Wholly Otherwise," trans. S. Critchley, in *Re-Reading Levinas*, ed. R. Bernasconi and S. Critchley (Bloomington and Indianapolis: Indiana University Press, 1991).

97. Caputo, *Demythologizing Heidegger*, p. 205.

98. Emmanuel Levinas, *Otherwise than Being or Beyond Essence*, trans. A. Lingis (The Hague: Martinus Nijhoff, 1981), p. xlii.

99. Caputo could no doubt object that it is ridiculous to assert that the (quasi)law of *différance* might keep us from "experiencing" the full weight of obligation when it is this law that is the condition for the im/possibility of obligation in the first place. But, for reasons I have attempted to articulate in this essay, I do not quite believe him.

100. In speaking of the "constructed" information transmitted by way of the media, Derrida warns: ". . . il ne faut pas que la déconstruction nécessaire de cette artefactualité serve d'alibi. Elle ne devrait pas céder à une surenchère

dans le simulacre et neutraliser toute menace dans ce qu'on pourrait appeler le leurre du leurre, la dénégation de l'événement: 'Tout, dirait-on alors, et même la violence, la souffrance, et la guerre et la mort, tout est construit, fictionné, constitué par et en vue des dispositifs médiatiques, rien ne se passe, il n'y a que simulacre et leurre.' " "Derrida: La déconstruction de l'actualite," interview conducted by Brigitte Sohm, Cristina de Peretti, Stéphane Douailler, Patrice Vermeren, and Emile Malet, *Passages* (Septembre 1993), 62. It seems that perhaps for Derrida, too, the "reality" of pain somehow trumps the realization that our "reception" of pain (either in suffering [passion] or in suffering with/for an other [compassion]) is always already a "construction," the "effect" of a discourse.

A GOD WITH/FOR THE OTHER

8

How to Avoid Not Speaking: Attestations

James K. A. Smith

HOW SHALL WE SPEAK of God? *Shall* we speak of God? How shall we tell others about God? Or shall we? If we speak of God, do we not claim to speak *from* God? But who knows God? Who could speak for God?

Can God speak? Would God speak?

What is speaking? Is speaking not tied up with language; and does not language attempt to encompass and enframe, thereby leaving an excess, requiring a supplement? Would not speaking of God, then, limit the Absolute, de-fine the infinite? Should we not then remain silent about God, in order to avoid doing violence to God? Perhaps it would be best if we were to avoid speaking of God.

But is it not already too late?[1] In recommending silence, have I not spoken of God? Can we help speaking of God? Can we avoid speaking?[2] So we find ourselves in a double bind: not wanting to do violence to God by reduction to language, yet unable to escape speaking, language, textuality. Silence is impossible, but it functions as a "regulative ideal."[3]

Such is the case as sketched by Jacques Derrida, and, following in his footsteps, by John Caputo. Both emphasize the "violence" of language, inasmuch as language "cuts," excludes, leaves an excess and a supplement in its attempts to conceptualize. "God-language" is guilty of this same reduction. Nevertheless, we cannot help speaking, we cannot get outside of language, we cannot escape textuality. Caputo would like to be silent, but he knows that it is impossible.

I do not want to give silence the exalted status of a "regulative ideal." With Caputo and Derrida, I, too, want to emphasize the violence of conceptual language[4] and the textuality and mediacy of our knowledge. As such, I want to avoid speaking in a certain manner: I want to avoid speaking violently.[5] But I do not want to avoid speaking altogether.

I want to avoid not speaking: I want to tell a story, announce some good news (*eu-angelion*). I want to evangelize (*eu-angelizō*)—not because I have *the* good news, or because my story is *the* story, or God's story (I do not claim to speak for God). I want to tell a story—which is avoiding not speaking—because it is a good story, a healing story, a helping story. And so in my ev-angelism I simply *attest* (Ricoeur) to how the story has helped me. I bear witness, testify (*martyreo*) to the healing power of the story.

In this essay, I will trace what deconstruction has pointed out to theology regarding language, and god-language as a result, viz., the violence of conceptual language and our inability to attain to immediate knowledge. I will then sketch two possible responses to this dilemma: the first is silence about God (which is impossible); the second is a vigilance in speaking about God, attempting to avoid not speaking, but also to avoid speaking violently. Such an approach will mean telling stories, announcing some good news, or, as I have called it, "ev-angelism," meaning, good-story-telling.

I

One would not expect to find a critique of theology in a collection of love letters, but such an unlikely correspondence is one location of Jacques Derrida's delimitation of theo-logical discourse. In *The Post Card*, a collection of love notes is preserved in a section titled "Envois." But contained in these letters—letters from one lover longing to see another face to face—is a sustained critique of what we might call the "postal system" as a metaphysical superhighway of information, a communications network where the communication always arrives.

The author would like to address himself (herself?) directly, "without *courrier* . . . but I do not arrive, and that is the worst of it."[6] In expressing his love, he must communicate through this postal system. But he does not trust it. He is even terrified of it: he is scared he may have the wrong address, or the letters in the wrong envelope, or that the letter will go astray. Because of this fear he sometimes finds himself chasing the postman, trying to get the letters back. His suspicion of the postal system is a suspicion (fear) of the Heideggerian *Seinsgeschick*, the sending of Being, the destiny of Being, the destination of Being.

Being's letters always arrive, at the proper destination (as destiny would have it).

But for Derrida this is a myth, a postal story of the sort that Cliff Claven would tell: a tall tale about Being's love notes that never get lost in the mail. Derrida's love notes and postcards point out the mythology in Being's epistles:

> If the post (technology, position, "metaphysics") is announced at the "first" envoi, then there is no longer A metaphysics, etc. . . . , nor even AN envoi, but envois without destination. For to coordinate the different epochs, halts, determinations, in a word the entire history of Being with a destination of Being is perhaps the most outlandish postal lure. There is not even the post or the envoi, there are posts and envois. . . . In a word, . . . as soon as there is, there is differance . . . and there is postal maneuvering, relays, delay, anticipation, destination, telecommunicating network, the possibility, and therefore the fatal necessity of going astray, etc.[7]

Communication between lovers is left in the hands of an unreliable postal system. As soon as I drop the letter in the mailbox (as soon as I seal the envelope!), my expression of love is subject to the whim of the postal gods, of whom Hermes is in charge.

But this is true for more than love letters, or postcards, or even junk mail. It is the case of language and communication itself. Derrida's point is that "within every sign already, every mark or every trait, there is distancing, the post, what there has to be so that it is legible for another, another than you or me, everything is messed up in advance."[8] The post "has to be": we cannot escape the postal system. This distancing, creating a space of dif-ference and de-ferral, is necessary for enabling others to read the envelope and direct the correspondence to the proper destination. Signs must be "repeatable" or "reiterable," which forces every discourse into the universalizing world of language. Language can never speak the absolutely singular, for "as soon as language has arrived on the scene the singular has already fled, already slipped out the back door."[9] This necessary space of repeatability constitutes the postal system. We are always already posted and postal: we can never destroy or "overcome" the postal system. But the inescapable interpolation of the postal system means that there is a possibility that letters can be lost. And the "possibility" of going astray becomes a "fatal necessity."

But where did *that* come from? When did a possibility become a "fatal necessity"? Why, because it is possible that a letter will not arrive, is it necessary that it not arrive?

Derrida admits that he cannot demonstrate that something never arrives at its destination; rather, he will always say, "a letter *can* always *not* arrive at its destination."[10] That is certainly a weaker reading, but Derrida doesn't really mean it. He betrays such in a postscript (to a postscript), noting that "in order *to be able* not to arrive, it must bear within itself a force and a structure, a straying of the destination, such that it *must* also not arrive in any way."[11] The problem, for Derrida, is built into the very structure of the postal system; which is also to say that it is an inherent element of the structure of the sign and system of signifiers. The "possibility" of going astray is a *structural* matter, which means that it must (necessarily) be the case. (This is Derrida's logic, not mine.) So once again, we are back to the "fatal necessity" of going astray. But isn't this a lot of talk about structure for a poststructuralist?

John Caputo's reading of Derrida on this point is very interesting. According to Caputo, the "(a)thesis" of *The Post Card* is that "a letter is always *able not* to arrive at its destination," that "the letter may always not reach its destination."[12] Now, Caputo is an excellent commentator (and I am not being facetious), but I think here he offers us a watered-down Derrida, one who is not really Derrida but rather another Derrida. It is a Derrida that I like but must confess that I know is an imposter. Caputo's Derrida does not convert possibility into fatal necessity. But the Derrida of *The Post Card* makes the conversion, transforming "may" to "must."

I think we may be able to get a handle on what is going on here by going back to an old theological debate, a medieval conundrum. In Augustine's discussion of sin, his sinful discussion, the Western theological tradition inherited three categories which would figure into the conversation for centuries to follow, and would also be introduced into Christological discourse. Augustine, outlining Adam's capacity to sin, described him in his original state as *posse non peccare et mori* (able not to sin and die). Had he obeyed, he would have passed to the condition of being *non posse peccare et mori* (not able to sin and die). But having disobeyed, he entered into the state of being *non posse non peccare et mori* (not able not to sin and die). These categories were then applied to Christological discourse concerning the impeccability of Christ, instigating considerable debate.

I think we can helpfully apply these categories to our present discussion. Is the letter *non posse advenire* (not able to arrive)? Is it, rather, *posse non advenire* (able not to arrive)? Or is the letter *non posse non advenire* (not able not to arrive)?

For Western metaphysics, and for fundamentalist theology (which is very modern), the letter is not able not to arrive; that is, the letter *always* arrives. Metaphysics and fundamentalism have an extremely reliable—I should say "infallible"—postal system. It is a telecommunications network equipped with unbreakable lines, virus-proof computers, and the latest in technological advances. The receiver of the communication experiences more than virtual reality: she experiences reality itself, without distortion, interruptions, or static on the line. Theology in the West was very fortunate in being able to acquire this technology for its task. This meant always receiving God's word unmediated, undistorted, in no way affected by the postal/telecommunications system. God's word received a privileged place outside of the tangled chain of signifiers, and theology itself (which spoke/speaks for God) communicated this God to us, itself immune to linguistic or historical conditioning.[13] The letter always arrives, "without *courrier*": right on time, perfectly intact. The letter is never torn, or lost, or delayed by postal strikes.

It is this impeccable postal service that frightens Derrida. Such a (theological) system, built on a flawless telecommunications network, knows God and speaks for God *without mediation*. But for Derrida and Caputo this is impossible, because there is nothing outside of the text. This is not to say that texts lack reference, but rather that "there is no reference that can escape the influence of texts, textuality, language."[14] As Derrida wrote to his lover, "as soon as there is, there is *différance*." All discourse is historically and linguistically conditioned, including theological discourse.

This is the point (and it is awfully sharp at times) of Caputo's sustained attack on Jean-Luc Marion's *God Without Being*. Marion wants to liberate God from the condition of "being," to situate our discourse *sans l'être*: with-out Being, outside of Being.[15] He wants to deliver God from the conceptual idol of Being and to conceive of God via the icon of love.[16] In this icon, God is released from conditions, particularly the condition of Being and metaphysics. The idol of Being, according to Marion, submits God to an anteriority, but in the icon of love, God is allowed to be God.

But, Caputo asks, "Is that not to reproduce the gesture that submits God to an anteriority, but this time to a more adequate anteriority?"[17] In releasing God from the condition of Being, Marion sought to release God from conditions altogether, because love is unconditional.[18] But is that not merely switching to another, different condition rather than escaping conditions and arriving at unconditioned discourse? Marion appeals to revelation, where God speaks to us on/in his [*sic*] own terms. But are not the Scriptures conditioned and mediated? The New Testament was written by people who lived in a particular world, at a particular time, speaking a particular language. Is *koine* Greek the language of heaven? And are those Greek stories not already a translation of events that happened in a Hebrew culture and of words spoken in Aramaic? Even "good Catholics" (and Marion certainly wants to be a good Catholic) recognize the historical and linguistic conditionedness of Scripture.[19]

We cannot speak of God outside the text, which is to say that our discourse about God is also subject to textuality. We cannot escape that. Our discourse, if it is to be intelligible, is confined to a system of repeatable signifiers, which is simply to say that we cannot collapse the space necessitated by language itself. As soon as we speak we make a universalizing gesture which necessarily excludes and cuts, leaving a supplement and an excess. "The universal never quite fits."[20] In speaking, we inevitably exclude something, for we can never say everything, particularly when we are speaking of God. As Heidegger noted, as soon as philosophizing is committed to words, it exposes itself to an "essential *misinterpretation of its content*."[21] Therefore, it is impossible for the letter to *always* arrive, to be not able not to arrive, because the perfect postal system—a system of immediacy—is a dream: a dream of no postal system at all.

But such a desire for immediacy is not only impossible, it is dangerous, because those who have such privileged access speak *for* God and consider themselves God's private police force. The rest of us should cringe in terror whenever someone claims to have an unconditioned revelation, Caputo warns,

> [f]or what we always get—it never fails—in the name of the Unmediated
> is someone's highly mediated Absolute: their Jealous Jahweh, their
> righteous Allah, their infallible church, their absolute Geist that inevitably speaks German. In the name of the Unmediated we are buried in
> an avalanche of mediations, and sometimes just buried, period. Somehow this absolutely absolute always ends up with a particular attachment
> to some historical, natural language, a particular nation, a particular
> religion. To disagree with someone who speaks in the name of God
> always means disagreeing with God. Be prepared to beat a hasty retreat.
> The unmediated is never delivered without massive mediation.[22]

Marion, for instance, claims that he is writing *theology*,[23] that his logos is God's logos. His *theology* informs us (and we should thank him for this) that God sides with Neoplatonism over Thomism: this is God's point of view, written in inspired French; and any who disagree are disagreeing with God—and the bishop.[24]

The position of metaphysics, and of fundamentalist theology (whether Protestant, Catholic, Islamic, etc.), that the letter is *non posse non advenire* (not able not to arrive) is an impossible dream and a dangerous delusion: impossible because of the reality of textuality and the tangled chain of signifiers which no discourse can escape; and dangerous because of the oppressive nature of an "unmediated" oration. Against this, Derrida's position is that the letter is *non posse advenire* (not able to arrive): built into the structure of the postal system is the possibility and "therefore fatal necessity" of going astray.[25]

This is Derrida's point of contention with Hans-Georg Gadamer. Derrida thinks Gadamer is too optimistic; he hears Gadamer saying that the letter is not able not to arrive, that it always arrives, so long as we have the good will to understand. (The postal system must be very efficient in Germany.) But, according to Derrida, this is just more metaphysics; the good will is always already the good will *to power*, subsuming the otherness of the other in a fusion of horizons. "[O]ne needs to ask," Derrida comments, "whether the precondition for *Verstehen*, far from being continuity of *rapport* . . . , is not rather the interruption of *rapport*, a certain *rapport* of interruption, the suspending of all mediation?"[26] Gadamer seems ultimately unable to account for or appreciate the ruptures and interruptions in discourse, the differences and misunderstandings that occur in the midst of speaking.[27] Gadamer has a crew of exceptional engineers constructing the magnificent bridge of language, which will provide a superhighway of communication and understanding. Or perhaps more accurately, discourse is an engineering feat constructed with the exceptional raw materials of "natural language." But, Derrida would remind him, language is sometimes a barrier, or rather, *always* a barrier. The letter (returning to the postal metaphor) is not able to arrive because it "necessarily" goes astray.

But is that the case? Does the letter necessarily go astray simply because there is a postal system? Now, I think Derrida is right about Gadamer (almost). On Gadamer's hermeneutical superhighway, there are (in the end) no interruptions, delays, barriers, or bridges out. That is just more German optimism and oblivion to otherness and difference of the sort we see in Hegel's *Aufhebung* and Heidegger's pure *Judenrein* myth of great Greek (i.e., pre-Socratic) beginnings. The letter does not always arrive; we do not always understand. And the metaphysical postal system, especially the German model, has delivered some terrifying letters.[28] But must we say that the letter never arrives? Is that not to miss something as well, to miss the reality of communication and the miracle of understanding? Is Derrida oblivious to the moments of connection amidst the interruptions? If Gadamer sees language as an indestructible bridge, does Derrida not erroneously concede language to be an insurmountable barrier? Did he not send his love letters, containing the critique of the postal principle, *via* the postal system? In disagreeing with Gadamer about "understanding," did he not direct three questions to him which were intended to be understood?[29]

This is where Caputo's reading of Derrida becomes interesting. I have tried to point out that, in (his) texts, Derrida is saying that the letter *"must . . .* not arrive in any way." The letter is not able to arrive, not ever, never. But Caputo reads Derrida differently: he hears Derrida saying that the letter is *"able not* to arrive." That is certainly a "weaker" reading, offering to us a more optimistic Derrida, a Derrida that I like very much, although I do not think it is the Derrida of the text. Nevertheless, I think it is a faithful reading of Derrida; that is, in his texts he claims that the letter never arrives, that there are always interruptions, that language is a barrier. But he also writes letters and sends them in the mail, he writes texts and receives the royalties from them, and he poses questions which are intended to be understood.

In the end, those who posit that the letter is *non posse advenire* (not able to arrive) send us a letter (or text or journal article) which tells us this. But then the gig is up. It's too late: a letter has arrived. Just as the metaphysical postal theory is a dream, so too is the deconstructionist a/postal hypothesis. Caputo's reading strikes a helpful balance. The letter is *posse non advenire* (able not to arrive). Sometimes letters do arrive—it is possible; but sometimes they do not. There are moments when we experience connection and understanding, but interruptions are also a reality. It is not that letters always arrive, or that they never arrive: sometimes they do, sometimes they do not. There are times when the bridge is out, but there are also times when we can make it across the abyss, though carefully, on a bridge made of rope and logs— one certainly not engineered by German scientists.

And yet a young German philosopher has a great deal to contribute to the discussion. Heidegger, in his early Freiburg years and into his tenure in Marburg, wrestled with these same questions regarding language. Heidegger's sweeping critique of the Western metaphysical tradition chastises philosophy for treating the "world" (which it has in fact forgotten) as a collection of present objects, available and accessible to the knowing subject who stands over against the world. In this framework, truth is narrowed to assertions that claim to point out (*Aufzeigen*) the "entity itself." The assertion is a "predication" whereby "the 'subject' is *given a definite character* [*bestimmt*] by the 'predicate.' " This "logical prejudice" is based on an understanding of being as sheer presence, and treats the world as "present-at-hand," which is immediately accessed. [30]

But, Heidegger challenges, we never have such pure access; we always encounter other selves, other things, and other texts in the context of a totality of involvements. All of these others come to us through the mediation of a "postal" system. As Heidegger formulates it, we always "see" objects "as" something:

> In dealing with what is environmentally ready-to-hand by interpreting it circumspectively, we 'see' it *as* a table, a door, a carriage, or a bridge; but what we have thus interpreted need not necessarily be taken apart by making an assertion which definitely characterizes it. Any mere prepredicative seeing of the ready-to-hand is, in itself, something which already understands and interprets. . . . Whenever we see with this kind of sight, we already do so understandingly and interpretively. [31]

In contrast to a predicative discourse rooted in a metaphysics of presence, Heidegger understands philosophical concepts to be *formally indicating* (*formal anzeigend*), as a revisable way of pointing to some phenomenon. [32] In this sense, concepts are seen not as predications but rather as indications which signal that which is referred to in a *revisable* manner, as opposed to the *definitive* character of the predicating assertion. As Daniel Dahlstrom observes,

> A philosophical concept is accordingly "empty" in a certain sense and hence purely "formal"—"formal" because it points in the direction of something that must be performed or gone through and even fulfilled or perfected by the philosopher, a direction, moreover, that springs from the philosophical "object" or "theme" itself. [33]

But one must not conclude that, as a result, philosophical concepts are completely devoid of content and therefore unable to preclude errant interpretations. On the contrary, philosophical concepts refer (point) in a manner that is "binding" and "principled."[34]

In this early period, Heidegger was attempting to avoid an objectifying philosophical discourse by which concepts are understood as predicating that which is true about the world. But at the same time, Heidegger was himself engaged in a philosophical discourse. Is not Heidegger's own philosophy then open to the criticisms that he levelled against the Western tradition? Is not the analysis of Dasein an objectifying discourse inasmuch as it employs theoretical concepts?

In response, Heidegger contends that not all concepts (or use of concepts) are objectifying: there is a distinction between theoretical assertions that objectify nature as present (Western metaphysics) and theoretical assertions that point or signal (formally indicate). Just because something is theoretically articulated does not mean that everything is taken to be present-at-hand. Understanding concepts as "formal indicators" would seem to allow one to avoid not speaking, and at the same time to avoid speaking violently. Heidegger's emphasis on the "pointing-function" of concepts points us to the limitations of theoretical discourse while at the same time affirming the access provided by such a discourse. Concepts understood as *Anzeigen* signal a framework which honors the mediation of the postal system and yet avoids contending that letters never arrive.

It is possible for the letter to arrive. In being able not to arrive (*posse non advenire*), it is also able *to* arrive. Such a reading does not commute on German *Autobahns*, but neither does it get swallowed up in a Parisian pothole. I would offer that this position can be found in Gadamer, in another side of Gadamer: a demythologized Gadamer. In trying to communicate, Gadamer admonishes, "One must look for the word that can reach the other person. And it is possible for one to find it."[35] He does not say that one *always* finds it (though such a metaphysical Gadamer could certainly be found in his texts), but, rather, that it is *possible*. That is a Gadamer that I like very much, a Gadamer that is not very far from Derrida (or at least Caputo's reading of Derrida).

Western theology has consorted with metaphysical post*men* [sic] for a long time. And if this is true of classical and medieval theology, it is also true of modern theology. Schleiermacher is not only the father of modern theology but also the father of hermeneutics.[36] It was he who started the German postal optimism of hermeneutics which infected Dilthey, Heidegger, and (metaphysical) Gadamer. As such, Derrida's

deconstruction of the postal principle wreaks havoc not only on fundamentalist theology (whether Catholic or Protestant), but on "liberal"
theology as well.

The deconstruction of this system which was thought to be so reliable would seem to culminate in the radical a/theology of someone
like Mark Taylor: a theology which Caputo calls "a more ruthlessly
atheistic theology, an atheism with a Saussurean twist."[37] But I think
Taylor takes Derrida too seriously, reading him *ad litteram* and missing
the hyperbolic nature of his texts. When Derrida claims that the letter
necessarily goes astray, that it must not arrive, he is exaggerating: he is
speaking in hyperbole, almost like a prophet.[38] Such a discourse if
taken literally can never hold together, for inevitably these discourses
proposing that the letter never arrives do arrive in the form of a text or
journal article. Taylor's reading misses this (almost) prophetic element
of exaggeration and, as such, goes "beyond" Derrida. "Deconstruction," Caputo comments, "is *not* the latest version of death of God
theology." He goes on to propose what this deconstruction of the metaphysical postal system means for theology:

> I do not think that Derrida undoes the very idea of religious revelation
> but that he undoes a lot of the ideas of revelation that religious writers
> have proffered for some time now. He thinks that all immaculate con-
> ceptions are always already contaminated with writing. He would in-
> sist—patiently, ruthlessly, indefatigably—that textuality sticks like glue
> to what religious traditions hold dear, that textuality insinuates itself into
> religious "positions." . . . Deconstruction wants to cut off the illusion
> of immediacy—of immediate experience, immediate revelation.[39]

We do not have the Tradition or the Word of God in pure form,
fallen from the sky, unmediated; and the desire for such a deposit only
results in violence—to God, and too often to other human beings. But
this mediation—the interpolation of a postal system (i.e., the space of
dif-ference and de-ferral)—opens up the possibility for misunderstanding and lack of connection. The letter may get lost, or effaced in tran-
sit, or delivered to the wrong address. Such possibilities ought to keep
us from dogmatically announcing the "meaning" of a letter. Sometimes we do not know where it came from (*Je ne sais d'ou*): perhaps
the letter is a forgery. The fact of mediation keeps us from immediately
enforcing our meditation.

But the conditions of textuality and mediation, though limiting, are
also *enabling*. Caputo, in a moment of surprising affirmation, asserts

that we "gain access" to the things themselves via the text. Language enables us to "put things in a meaningful perspective."[40] Such is not a pure perspective, or the "true" perspective, or God's perspective, but a meaningful perspective, which, if nothing else, is a helpful perspective. In our god-language, in our talking of God, we cannot employ a syllogistic vocabulary which is identical with God's. God does not have a vocabulary, a language; God is not tangled in a chain of signifiers. That is why Caputo cringes when Marion claims to let God speak *à partir de lui*, in God's own terms. God has no terms, and those who offer God to us "in his own terms" are proffering a highly mediated God. (It is interesting that, at the beginning of his book, Marion sends us an "envoi," a letter, which is *the* letter. I would prefer, with Derrida, to have *envois* (in the plural): a multitude of letters, the more letters the better. Let many letters come! *Viens!*)

II

Seeing the violence which postal theology wreaks on God, and on God's children who are not privileged enough to receive these German epistles, we are faced with two avenues. One possibility would be to be silent, to not speak about God. But silence itself "speaks," "sometimes joy, sometimes contempt, sometimes pleasure, sometimes fear, sometimes consent, sometimes renunciation, sometimes impotence, sometimes honor."[41] And, "in fact, with regard to God, overwhelmingly, we speak."[42] We say too much, too often, too soon, making promises that we cannot keep. Silence, for Derrida, is impossible; but despite (or perhaps, because of) its impossibility, Caputo wants to keep silence around as a "regulative ideal." But is silence somehow non-violent? Is it not possible that silence may do more violence than speaking? Aren't many silenced in the name of Silence, sometimes in a very violent way? Are not those who are silent, silent because they have a *secret*, and do they not often set up their secret societies in a very hierarchical (and often patriarchal) manner?[43] Is silence, then, the best (i.e., least violent) way to respond to the violence of speaking?

Even Heidegger, despite the "mystical element" in his thought and his affinity with Eckhardt, concedes that silence does not escape the harm of metaphysical discourse. Recounting a conversation from the early 1970s, German theologian Eberhard Jungel discloses Heidegger's thoughts on silence and speaking:

"And God," I asked, "should we not also *think* God?"

Heidegger answered: "God is what is most worthy of thought, but here language fails."

I contradicted him. He accepted my contradiction, knowing that theology cannot honor the mystery entrusted to it by remaining silent.[44]

Christian mysticism, which attempts to escape the conditions of metaphysics via negative theology, seeks the One beyond Being and seeks to honor the One by silence. But, Derrida contends, "this movement toward hyperessentiality" must move within Being, presuppose Being; as such, apophantic theology remains defined by metaphysics, and therefore plagued by the violence of metaphysics.[45]

In the final portion of this paper, I want to offer another option which attempts to avoid the violence of both metaphysical theology and negative theology. Having (well) lost the immediate access of metaphysics, we cannot speak *for* God, using God's own terms, as it were. But a negative theology, a silent theology, also falls into a violent trap. I will propose instead a vigilant theology which seeks to avoid violence, or at least keep violence to a minimum. But how can we do that? How can we avoid speaking violently? If we want to avoid violence, how can we avoid *not* speaking? If we speak *of* God, do we claim to speak *for* God?

Perhaps we could tell a story. I want to tell a story, announce some good news (*eu-angelion*)—not because it is *the* story, or *God's* story (I do not claim to speak for God). I want to tell a story—or better, many stories—because they are good stories (*eu-angelia*), healing stories, helping stories. Recognizing that "certainty" is (and always was) an illusion, and having lost any postal/metaphysical backup, we tell our stories, but not without hesitation. These are, after all, only our stories, not tall tales that have fallen from the sky or been recorded from the mind of God. We do not demonstrate, but rather testify or bear witness (*martyreo*) to that which we have seen and experienced for ourselves. In Paul Ricoeur's very biblical word (though he would not want to admit it philosophically[46]), we *attest* to the truth,[47] point to it (*anzeigen*). The truth is in (the) pointing.

Such a theology would be very ev-angelical (*eu-angelikos*), proclaiming good stories of healing and helping, told to people in the tears and tears of life. It would be hard to distinguish such theology from ev-angelism (*eu-angelismos*). Not traditional evangelism, of course, which tends to be very violent, but rather an ev-angelism which is simply good story-telling: in the sense of telling good stories, and also in the sense of telling them well.

I may even be so pious as to propose that this is very old theology, even—dare I say it?—apostolic, albeit an "early apostolic," when the apostles were still on the shores of Galilee rather than ruling the empire. The disciples were committed to a theology (and a Christology) from below: they attested to that which they had seen, telling their stories to any who would listen. In the ev-angelistic theology that I am proposing, we too simply point others to the One whom we have embraced. We take them to see him, show them who he is. We do not come with postal/metaphysical backups, nor are we silent in the face of their trials and burdens; rather, we simply say, "Come and see" (John 1:46). Come and see the One who has healed us and helped us and fed us. We can point to the Lamb (John 1:29) and lead others to him (John 1:42). As such, we are only imitating the early Christian community, who were sent as witnesses—attestors—to testify concerning that which they had seen and heard and experienced (Matthew 28:19–20; Acts 1:8).

But we must be vigilant in guarding against the shift from ev-angel-ism as good-story-telling to evangelism as telling-*the*-story. We must constantly remember that our story (*angel*) is *ours*, in our own terms, not God's in God's own terms. We must avoid making our good news *the* good news, lest it become bad news for many others.[48] If our stories are not healing stories, then they are not good (*eu*-) stories.

In telling stories we can avoid speaking violently and also avoid not speaking. Story-telling as a discourse avoids violence because it is a discourse of praise rather than predication, a "praise that feeds on the impossibility or, better, the impropriety of the category."[49] The aim of good-story-telling is to point (*indicare*), not to comprehend (*comprehendere*); as such, our stories point to or signal (*anzeigen*) that about which we speak. In this ev-angelical theology we attempt to navigate between metaphysical (non)postal systems and a complete lack of communication; between *non posse non* and *non posse*. The way to avoid not speaking is by attesting to what we experience as truth, by telling those stories which have meant good news for us. Such stories offer the hope of healing to others in the brokenness of life. In rethinking theology in this framework, perhaps we could conclude that the world needs a few more ev-angelists, a few more good-story-tellers.

NOTES

1. Throughout this essay I am playing with the discourse of Jacques Derrida, "How to Avoid Speaking: Denials," trans. Ken Frieden, in *Derrida and Negative Theology*, ed. Harold Coward and Toby Foshay (Albany: SUNY Press, 1992), pp. 73–142, henceforth abbreviated as HAS; and John D. Caputo, "How to Avoid Speaking of God: The Violence of Natural Theology" in *Prospects for Natural Theology*, ed. Eugene Thomas Long (Washington, D.C.: The Catholic University of America Press, 1992), pp. 128–50, henceforth abbreviated as HASG. On this point, see Caputo, HASG, p. 128.

2. On this question in general, see Jacques Derrida, *Of Spirit: Heidegger and the Question*, trans. Geoffrey Bennington and Rachel Bowlby (Chicago: University of Chicago Press, 1989), pp. 1–3 and passim.

3. Caputo, HASG, pp. 128–29, 148–49.

4. This violence occurs when language attempts to definitively grasp something (the world? the self? God?), attempts to comprehend (*comprehendere*), thereby enframing, which necessarily means excluding, leaving something outside of the frame. See Derrida's discussion of these themes in *The Truth in Painting*, trans. Geoffrey Bennington and Ian MacLeod (Chicago: University of Chicago Press, 1987). I would not, however, say that this violence is inherent to language, as Derrida asserts. Instead, my proposal outlines a way of speaking which is not violent but also recognizes the violence of certain modes of speaking, particularly conceptual language construed as immediate grasping.

5. I would emphasize, with Derrida, that it is a question not of *what* to say, but of *how* to speak. It is a question of speaking *well*. See HAS, p. 85.

6. Jacques Derrida, *The Post Card: From Socrates to Freud and Beyond*, trans. Alan Bass (Chicago: University of Chicago Press, 1987), p. 23, henceforth abbreviated as PC.

7. Ibid., p. 66.

8. Ibid., p. 29.

9. John D. Caputo, *Demythologizing Heidegger* (Bloomington: Indiana University Press, 1993), p. 202.

10. PC, p. 123.

11. Ibid.

12. John D. Caputo, "Derrida and the Study of Religion 2," *Religious Studies Review* 16 (1990), 22.

13. Of course, theology's immune system is intact in this modern/fundamentalist paradigm, which will have nothing to do with those who have Acquired Immune Deficiency Syndrome.

14. HASG, p. 143. Caputo has also done a wonderful job of clearing up

this pervasive misunderstanding in his "The Good News About Alterity: Derrida and Theology," *Faith and Philosophy* 10 (1993), 454–57.

15. Jean-Luc Marion, *God Without Being*, trans. Thomas A. Carlson (Chicago: University of Chicago Press, 1991), pp. xxii, 44–45.

16. Ibid., pp. 47–48.

17. HASG, p. 136.

18. Marion, *God Without Being*, p. 47.

19. I am thinking of *Dei Verbum* (secs. 12–13), Vatican II's Dogmatic Constitution on Divine Revelation.

20. Caputo, *Demythologizing Heidegger*, p. 203.

21. Martin Heidegger, *Die Grundbegriffe der Metaphysik*, GA 29/30, ed. Friedrich Wilhelm von Herrmann (Frankfurt am Main: Klostermann, 1983), p. 422.

22. HASG, pp. 129–30.

23. Marion, p. 139.

24. Ibid., p. 153; HASG, p. 138.

25. This is against Caputo's watered-down reading discussed above, which I will consider once again below.

26. Jacques Derrida, "Three Questions to Hans-Georg Gadamer," in *Dialogue and Deconstruction: The Gadamer–Derrida Encounter*, ed. Diane Michelfelder and Richard Palmer (Albany: State University of New York Press, 1989), pp. 52–53. Interestingly, the French title of Derrida's response was *"Bonnes Volontés de Puissance"* (The Good Will to Power).

27. A word of qualification: Many would find it an odd (or rather, erroneous) move to associate Gadamer with fundamentalism and metaphysics. After all, is it not Gadamer who has pointed out to us the conditionedness (and traditionedness) of our understanding? Hasn't Gadamer, if anyone, sought to honor the reality of mediations and textuality? Is it not Gadamer who has opened our eyes to the fact that our understanding is always already an interpretation? Yes and no. Gadamer certainly honors the historicity of knowing, and I am greatly indebted to him in many ways. But in this essay I am pointing to some hesitations I have concerning how seriously he takes misunderstanding and disconnection. Though we never have perfect understanding, Gadamer would say, there is an (almost eschatological) appeal to a future "fusion" of horizons, which seems to function in a manner similar to Habermas's "ideal community," which is the archetype for the "real community." Caputo (following Joseph Margolis) refers to this as Gadamer's "closet essentialism": " 'Closet'—because up front there is a lot of brave talk about history and change, time and becoming—but still 'essentialist'—because when the truth is told, that is all just a front for a theology of lasting essences" ("Gadamer's Closet Essentialism: A Derridean Critique," in *Dialogue and Deconstruction*, p. 259).

28. Heidegger's rectoral address in 1933 at the University of Freiburg had

a lot to say about the destiny (*Geschick*) of the German people, a destiny sent their way by Being (and the pre-Socratics). See Martin Heidegger, "The Self-Assertion of the German University," trans. Lisa Harries, in *Martin Heidegger and National Socialism*, ed. Gunther Neske and Emil Kettering (New York: Paragon House, 1990), pp. 5–13. For Heidegger's discussion of *Geschick*, see *Being and Time*, trans. John Macquarrie and Edward Robinson (New York: Harper & Row, 1962), pp. 434–39.

29. Gadamer, "Reply to Jacques Derrida," in *Dialogue and Deconstruction*, p. 55.

30. Heidegger, *Being and Time*, p. 196.

31. Ibid., p. 189.

32. Ibid., pp. 108, 152. See, more importantly, Heidegger, *Phänomenologische Interpretation zu Aristoteles: Einführung in die Phänomenologische Forschung*, GA 61, ed. Walter Brocker and Kate Brocker-Oltmanns (Frankfurt am Main: Klostermann, 1985), pp. 19, 32, 56–60, 140–41; and *Ontologie (Hermeneutik der Faktizität)*, GA 63, ed. Kate Brocker-Oltmanns (Frankfurt am Main: Klostermann, 1988), pp. 79–80. For two helpful essays on this notion, see Daniel Dahlstrom, "Heidegger's Method: Philosophical Concepts as Formal Indications," *Review of Metaphysics* 47 (1994), 775–95; and Theodore Kisiel, "Heidegger (1920–21) on Becoming a Christian: A Conceptual Picture Show," in *Reading Heidegger From the Start: Essays in His Earliest Thought*, ed. Theodore Kisiel and John van Buren (Albany: SUNY Press, 1994), pp. 175–92.

33. Dahlstrom, 782.

34. See Th. C. W. Oudemans, "Heidegger: Reading Against the Grain," in *Reading Heidegger From the Start*, p. 41.

35. Gadamer, "*Destruktion* and Deconstruction," in *Dialogue and Deconstruction*, p. 106.

36. Paul Ricoeur, "The Task of Hermeneutics," in *Heidegger and Modern Philosophy*, ed. Michael Murray (New Haven: Yale University Press, 1978), p. 145. It must be noted, though, that one may point to a "demythologized" Schleiermacher as well: a Schleiermacher who posits that words are "infinitely analyzable," open to a multiplicity of meanings, and lacking precise determination. See F. D. E. Schleiermacher, *Hermeneutics: The Handwritten Manuscripts*, ed. Heinz Kimmerle, trans. James Duke and Jack Forstman (Missoula, Mont.: Scholars Press, 1977), pp. 70–76. My thanks to Doug Hallman for showing me the other side of Schleiermacher.

37. Caputo, "Derrida and the Study of Religion 2," 25.

38. Caputo warns against taking someone like Levinas too seriously. You must remember: he is a prophet, and prophets were never intended to be interpreted *ad litteram*. Prophets tell fabulous stories and powerful poems to make a point. They are storytellers, not reporters. Caputo sees a similar device in Derrida (*Demythologizing Heidegger*, pp. 186–208).

39. Caputo, "Derrida and the Study of Religion 2," 25.

40. HASG, p. 148.

41. James H. Olthuis, "Crossing the Threshold: Sojourning Together in the Wild Spaces of Love," *Toronto Journal of Theology* 11 (1995), 43; Chap. 9 below.

42. Marion, p. 55.

43. Note Pseudo-Dionysius' *Ecclesiastical Hierarchy*. The inter-relatedness of secrecy and hierarchy is explored by Derrida, HAS, pp. 88–92.

44. Jungel, "Letter to Gunther Neske, 18 August 1988," trans. Lisa Harries, in *Martin Heidegger and National Socialism*, p. 249.

45. Derrida, HAS, pp. 77–79.

46. This is because Ricoeur is still clinging to the hope that his philosophy is autonomous, free from faith and theology. See Ricoeur, *Oneself as Another*, trans. Kathleen Blamey (Chicago: University of Chicago Press, 1992), p. 23. For a discussion of his methodological agnosticism, see Pamela Sue Anderson, "Agnosticism and Attestation: An Aporia Concerning the Other in Ricoeur's *Oneself as Another*," *Journal of Religion* 74 (1994), 65–76.

47. Ricoeur, *Oneself as Another*, pp. 21–23.

48. This is not to say that good news will never mean bad news for some, or excluding some. I don't think Derrida or Caputo would deny that sometimes we need to exclude others (e.g., homicidal rapists or Adolf Hitler). As Caputo comments, "The mistake is to think that deconstruction cannot oppose cruelty or oppression because then it would be 'excluding' or 'marginalizing' someone, viz. the oppressors." The Other, rather, is always a victim: "Exclusion and marginalization . . . are never merely formal ideas; they always have to do with damaged lives and disasters." (*Against Ethics* [Bloomington: Indiana University Press, 1993], p. 119.)

49. Marion, *God Without Being*, p. 76.

9

Crossing the Threshold: Sojourning Together in the Wild Spaces of Love

James H. Olthuis

In the wake of the eclipse of the divine, darkness . . .
  sacred darkness lingers . . .
lingers endlessly.
Night
Sacred night
Night that is not day
Night beyond
Night
Night
From which we never
Awake[1]

WE LIVE in a "time between times," a "place which is no place,"[2] where, as Mark C. Taylor describes it, "sacred darkness lingers . . . endlessly." Like it or not, the Enlightenment dream of a world increasingly controlled by the light of pure rationality is fading fast over the horizon. Control through reason and science has left wide swaths of destruction in its wake: systematic violence, marginalization, oppression, suffering, domination of the "other." It is that sorry history that both lies at the root of the postmodern attack on the totalizing power of reason and gives shape to the postmodern ethical imperative to include the "other" and to make room for the "different." But what now—at the end of reason, after virtue, after philosophy, after God? What if there is neither a religion nor a morality within the bounds of reason alone? Was Taylor right when he recently exclaimed: "Though it continues, theology is as dead as the God for which theologians search"?[3] If the "sacred escapes the strictures of ontotheology,"[4] unattainable by either the *via positiva* or the *via negativa*, is the sacred beyond reach?

The questions are formidable. But they are also exciting, especially for those of us involved in the theological enterprise. The kinds of questions and queries about claims to certainty and warrants to power which postmodernism is raising are precisely the kinds of limit questions[5] that lie at the heart of the theological endeavor. In the modern era the declaration of human autonomy was also the announcement of God's death. But now, paradoxically, since postmodern voices are declaring that the death of God finds its completion only in the death of the self,[6] questions of how to talk of self and God are once more taking center stage. As I see it, new spaces are opening up for theologians to be once again relevant players and significant voices in the public realm.

I suggest that Jacques Derrida's emphasis on undecidability, the secret, and the *khôra* open the way to a new post-secular discourse about faith and God. However, Mark C. Taylor's figure of the erring, serpentine wanderer as a liberated being in carnivalesque release abandons us only to isolation, wounds, and tears, and asks that we give up on any possibility of meeting, healing, and mending. I therefore propose that we replace an ontology of being—with its question, "To be or not to be?"—with a vision of love—with its basic question, "To love or not to love?"[7] In the priority of love, agency returns, not as a self-construction but as a gift to be received and a call to be heeded. I conclude by intimating that sojourning (rather than settling or wandering) in the wild spaces of love is an apt metaphor for a genuine postmodern theology.

THE HOUSE OF BEING: POWER

In philosophical theology the concept of being has traditionally played a central role, and God has been considered the highest Being and the ground of every being. Since metaphysics needed a centerpiece, a keystone, in its house of being, it may be credibly said that the advent of "God" in philosophy arose less from God than from metaphysics. As Heidegger has described, this concept of God finds its full formulation in the modernity of Descartes, Spinoza, Leibniz, and Hegel with the *causa sui*: "The Being of beings is represented fundamentally, in the sense of the ground, only as *causa sui*. This is the metaphysical concept of God. . . . This is the right name for the god of philosophy."[8]

Heidegger concludes: "Man can neither pray nor sacrifice to this god. Before the *causa sui*, man can neither fall to his knees in awe nor can he play music and dance before this god."[9] In other words, the *causa sui* is only an "idol" of God, and so-called "god-less thinking is more open to him than ontotheologic would like to admit."[10] In another place Heidegger makes the same point. "[A] god who must permit his existence to be proved in the first place is ultimately a very ungodly god. The best such proofs of existence can yield is blasphemy."[11] In a 1951 seminar at the University of Zurich, Heidegger summarized: "If I were yet to write a theology—to which I sometimes feel inclined—then the word *Being* would not occur in it. Faith does not need the thought of Being. When faith has recourse to this thought, it is no longer faith."[12]

But the problem is not simply that as *causa sui* God becomes a prisoner of our concepts, metaphysically chained in the ontotheological abode of being.[13] The category of being itself as the institutionalization of reason, with its claims to full presence, is fraught with difficulty. For at least since Descartes set out to establish the ego as point of absolute certainty, being has been characterized with what Spinoza termed the *conatus essendi*: "Everything, in so far as it is in itself, endeavours to persist in its own being."[14] Since for him all things are modes of God, this *conatus essendi* emerges by necessity out of the eternal and infinite essence of God. Since "God's power is identical with his essence,"[15] power becomes the central concept of modern ontologies.[16] Here theology is the keystone in a theory of absolute power.

Even when the human ego replaces God as the apex of the system, the self-maintaining ontology of power takes center stage, whether as Leibniz's monads of power, Nietzsche's will to power, Freud's libido, Dasein's care (in Heidegger), or the striving for being (in Sartre). In other words, as Derrida and Levinas have argued, what has developed is a process of totalizing with reason as the instrument by which an ego or society of egos overpowers and totalizes, appropriates and disempowers anything that is "other" or different.[17] Whatever the details and variety, being is a system of maintenance, control, domination: power-over.[18] One either dominates or is dominated—as Freud, Hegel, and Sartre in particular emphasize.[19] Thus, Paul Tillich defines power as "the possibility a being has to actualize itself against the resistance of other beings."[20] To be a self is to have enemies. Implicitly, if not explicitly, one is always at war. This apotheosis of the self is seen to crest in the idealism of Hegel in which everything becomes itself in and through its own other. In the end, since the "other" has a utilitarian function in relation to the self, relationship to the other is, finally, self-relationship. When an "other" resists this role, failing to mirror the self, when it resists being used and consumed, it must be invaded and dominated.

There is one more telling aspect of this picture that needs to be noted before we continue with the deconstructionist critique. In the world of being-as-power, suffering has no legitimate place.[21] Spinoza again voices the dominant tradition: "Pain is the transition of a man from a greater to a lesser perfection."[22] Pain and suffering are diminutions of being. Pain weakens the power of activity and suffering is powerlessness. Even Heidegger, an archcritic of the ontotheologic tradition, by considering that the essence of pain cannot be painful in a feeling sense, takes the suffering out of pain.[23] Strikingly, some postmodernists do the same. Deleuze and Guattari, for example, champion "the schizophrenic process" in its "potential for revolution"[24] without any attention to the actual psychological pain and suffering of schizophrenics.

ERRING

In our day, prefigured by the masters of suspicion, Marx, Freud, and Nietzsche, the imperial self has also been declared dead. More precisely, the self as the child of enlightment, fully present to itself, self-conscious, sovereign, absolute agent, given power over the world as object, is revealed to be itself a production of this very world and the processes it was said to master. All we have left is a decentered, deconstructed "self," the self as a product and effect of the crossings and interfacings of impersonal cosmic forces.

Mark C. Taylor has given in *Erring*[25] perhaps the fullest description of such a non-self self: postmodern persons are "transitory 'points' of intersection," " 'sites' of passage," "erratic markings" (137). A human subject is a "wanderer" (150), an "errant trace" (144), a "drifter" (157), "attached to no home and always separated from father and mother" (156), "deindividualized" (135), "anonymous" (143). "Everyone becomes no one" (142), "always suspicious of stopping, staying, and dwelling" (156). "Rootless and homeless" (156), deprived of "origin, center, and conclusion" (156), "the subject is *always* both 'stained' and 'wounded,'" and the marks are "incurable" (139). The "life of erring is . . . nomadic" (156) and the "serpentine wandering" (150) is "purposeless and aimless (endless)" (157). This "careless wanderer" yearns neither for "completion" nor for "fulfillment" (147), and therefore is not unhappy but free from "anxious searching" (157) and no longer preoccupied with past and future. Indeed, for Taylor, although such liberation means "self-dismemberment" (144), accepting that is "grace" which "arrives only when God and the self are dead and history is over" (157). "Extravagant expenditure" (142), "perpetual displacement" (156), "festive discharge, carnivalesque release" (161) . . . "endlessly" (143).

Let me offer four observations about such a description of the "non-self."

First, along with Taylor, I do not believe there is any hope of resuscitating the Cartesian self or any of its remnants. But it is well to recognize that that is no real loss, for it never existed in the first place, but was an illusory product of reason. Put in the language of psychotherapy, the self of reason is a false self, defensively created out of fear,[26] that needs to be undone and broken through if I am to come to terms with my true self. This suggests that the death of the self of reason and the death of the god of reason reveals not the death of self and God, but the failure of reason. From this perspective, the death of God, and now self, marks the dethronement of reason and the collapse of its house of being.

Second, the fact that the modern self of absolute agency is an illusion does not demonstrate that there is no such entity as a self. Indeed, I suspect the postmodern non-self will be shown to be as mythical as its predecessor, another adapted, false self. There is still room for an agent self that is not absolute, with no claims to self-authorization and full presence, but a gifted/called self, gifted with agency and called to co-agency by an *Other*. It is true that would demand breaking with the radical immanentism and autonomy of modern philosophy. But this is the very kind of thinking that is precisely being called into question by thinkers such as Emmanuel Levinas. I suspect that as long as postmodernism champions the non-self (as the negation of the modern self), it still, regrettably, remains in hostage to logocentrism.

Third, Taylor's erring wanderer is a scary, sad, desolate figure, nameless, impersonal, and incurably wounded. Can such a postmod-

ern person, without home and without purpose, be called to responsibility? And is not such an anonymous person a difference that makes
no difference—a difference that is the same, because there is no longer
any uniqueness? Even more troubling, Taylor has only tears—tears
and wounds. What about healing, mending, and hope? Taylor seems
to collapse a healthy self/other tension (which includes mutually en-
hancing interactions as well as alienating ones) into a determinism of
sorts, in which relations are unavoidably only wounding and tearing.

Fourth, it will not be easy to talk of self and God in new ways
because talk of self and God, certainly philosophically and theologically, has been so tied to an ontology of being that to speak of self and
God is almost unavoidably to invoke echoes of these illusions. Can
nothing be said? Are we left speech-less? Is silence the only answer?
Echoes of Wittgenstein's "What we cannot speak about we must pass
over in silence"? That also was Heidegger's response: "Someone who
has experienced theology in his own roots, both the theology of the
Christian faith and that of philosophy, would today rather remain silent about god when he is speaking in the realm of thinking."[27] But
even then we need to say something, because silence bespeaks sometimes joy, sometimes contempt, sometimes pleasure, sometimes fear,
sometimes consent, sometimes renunciation, sometimes impotence,
sometimes honor. There is the ultimate silence of death. And there is
the silence that has to do with God, with what Pseudo-Dionysius had
in mind when he exhorted us "to honor the ineffable with a wise silence."[28]

DERRIDA: REMAINING ON THE THRESHOLD

Indeed, it is because of the recognized difficulties of the *via positiva* in
talking about God, amplified in recent times by the deconstructionist
critique, that there is today increased interest in the *via negativa*. The
question is even being asked if deconstructionism itself is a form of
negative theology. Does all negative theology have a "superessen-
tiality"—a supreme being beyond being—or does it, at least in some
versions, have a God who transcends all conceptions of being as presence? Does negative theology use language under erasure in a fashion
similar to deconstructionism?[29] Though the verdict is still out, it does
seem clear that deconstruction is atheistic in the sense that it de-centers
and does away with God as the center of a system[30] (but as Kevin Hart

makes clear, only in that sense[31]). Whether Derrida or other deconstructionists have faith in God is entirely another matter. And about
that, Derrida is, at least to my knowledge, silent.

It is in what is perhaps his most confessional essay, "How to Avoid
Speaking: Denials,"[32] that Jacques Derrida in 1987 directly addressed
the supposed connections between his thinking of *trace* and *différance*
and negative theology. There is much debate on whether he delivers
on his promise or continues to defer.

In the end, Derrida's denials, or denegations, as Taylor aptly trans-
lates,[33] seem neither to assert nor to deny. They circle around in a
cacophony of sounds. However, strikingly, in and through the verbal
clatter, there is the internal desert of silence. In Derrida's words, "We
are still on the threshold."[34] And he remains on the threshold, always.
That threshold is a "place of passage, this time, to give access to what
is no longer a place,"[35] and seemingly he is unable to ever cross over
with Eckhart to the "threshold that gives access to God."[36]

On the threshold he talks as if having no secret is the secret. "There
is no secret as *such*; I deny it. And this is what I confide in secret. . . .
The name of God (I do not say God, but how to avoid saying God
here, from the moment when I say the name of God?) can only be
said in the modality of this secret denial: above all, I did not want to
say that."[37]

Derrida then proceeds to treat negative theology in terms of three
paradigms—Greek, Christian, and neither Greek nor Christian. He
does so, he notes, "to avoid speaking of a question that I will be unable
to treat; to deny it in some way, or to speak of it without speaking of
it"—the question of the relation of negative theology to Jewish and
Islamic thought.[38] That this is an important void for Derrida is clear
not only because he goes out of his way to remind his readers of the
omission two more times, but because Derrida is himself a displaced
North African Jew. It is in this context that he talks of the "internal
desert": "In everything that I will say, a certain void, the place of an
internal desert, will perhaps allow this question to resonate. . . . a
resonant space of which nothing, almost nothing will ever be said."

Derrida pleads silence—almost. For then, in a telling footnote at
precisely this point, he begins to self-disclose in a way which almost
breaks the silence—but not without the hint of untold secrets and pain,
even much pain:

> Despite this silence, or in fact because of it, one will perhaps permit me
> to interpret this lecture as the most "autobiographical" speech I have

ever risked. . . . But if one day I had to tell my story, nothing in this narrative would start to speak of the thing itself if I did not come up against this fact: for lack of capacity, competence, or self-authorization, I have never been able to speak of what my birth says should have been closest to me: the Jew, the Arab. This small piece of autobiography confirms it obliquely. It is performed in all of my foreign languages: French, English, German, Greek, Latin, the philosophic, the metaphilosophic, Christian, etc.[39]

Taylor, in commenting on this essay, perceptively notes: "For many years at least since *Glas*, and I suspect long before, perhaps even from the beginning—Derrida has been struggling with the question of autobiography. . . . I begin to suspect that Derrida's deepest desire is to write an 'autobiography.' " He concludes: "Derrida could (or would) no more write an autobiography than he could (or would) write a theology."[40]

Derrida remains on the threshold.[41] No matter how strong his desire,[42] he cannot cross over and come home and tell his story.[43] He is the exile, the outsider, remaining always deliberately in/determinate and un/decidable. Do his constant deferrals on the threshold deliver us only to a gaping silence? Or does the work of Derrida perhaps open up a silent space before and beyond all metaphysical embarrassments, an interspace of in/finite im/possibility?

That this is a real im/possibility is clearly evident in his preoccupation, also in "Denials," with place and space. In his treatment of the Greek paradigm he treats at some length the "absolutely necessary space" which Plato in the *Timaeus* calls the *khôra*,[44] as the place making possible the formation of the cosmos. This *khôra*—place, spacing, receptacle—is not to be talked of "as of 'something' that is or is not, that could be present or absent, intelligible, sensible, or both at once, active or passive, the Good . . . or the Evil, God or man, the living or the nonliving."[45] *Khôra* is "radically nonhuman and atheological . . . radically ahistorical,". . . "nothing positive or negative. It is impassive, but it is neither passive nor active."[46] As "absolutely necessary space," *khôra* cannot be spoken of, but, at the same time, it cannot not be spoken of.

When Derrida moves on from the Greek paradigm to the Christian, he treats Eckhart, who conceives of Being as a place, "[s]olely a threshold, but a sacred place, the outer sanctuary (*parvis*) of the temple,"[47] which gives access to God in what is beyond place. He suggests that Heidegger's viewpoint represents a paradigm neither Greek nor Christian. He calls attention to Heidegger's posing the question as to whether "a *wholly* other place" is a "place of Being" or is rather "*a place of the wholly other.*"[48]

Finally, in his *Post-Scriptum* to the Calgary Symposium, recently published under the title *Derrida and Negative Theology*, he raises the issue of place once more. In negative theology, "[t]here remains the question of . . . the place opened for this play between God and his creation."[49] Is it a place opened or created by God, by the name of God? Or is it " 'older' than the time of creation, than time itself, than history, narrative, word, etc.," in order to make both God and his play possible? Is it a friendly place "opened by appeal" or is it a preceding space which remains "impassively foreign, like *Khôra*, to everything that takes its place and replaces itself and plays within this place, including what is named God"?[50]

He asks whether we need to choose between the two. He wonders if it's even possible. But—and this heightens the stakes—he immediately adds: "But it is true that these two 'places,' these two experiences of place, these two ways are no doubt of an absolute heterogeneity. One place excludes the other, one surpasses the other, one does without the other, one is, absolutely, without the other."[51]

Although faced with this un/decidability, ever wary of choosing, Derrida, ironically, precisely because his commitment to undecidability goes all the way down,[52] has to de-fer from the first space, which is primed in a certain way (I call it the with-space of creation,[53] the lovespace), and opt for the un/primed second space, the without place, the " 'something' without thing, like an indeconstructible *Khôra* . . . as the very spacing of de-construction,"[54] the spacing of *différance*. The space is held to be more primordial, more neutral, a kind of nontemporal "abyss without bottom or surface, an absolute impassibility (neither life nor death) that gives rise to everything that it is not."[55]

No doubt Derrida's staying on the threshold faithfully reflects his preference for un/decidability. At the same time, it may also leave him inadvertently under the bewitching spell of logocentrism. For, when all is said and done, if one tarries silent on the threshold because metaphysical claims to certainty and warrants for power are illusions to be overcome, have we really overcome them? To presume that we need to give up on any sense of a founded or grounded decision because the modernist tradition confuses/conflates giving logical reasons and grounding seems questionable. Grounding is much more and wider than logical grounding. Experiences of empathy, trust, and belonging, for example, are everyday sources of existential grounding.[56]

To repeat: I do believe that Derrida goes a long way in showing that language and metaphysics cannot provide privileged access to self-present meaning. But does that mean access to the mysterious, sacred desert place is impossible? Perhaps there are other ways and means to enter that space beyond or before. Can we can agree with Derrida that another philosophy/theology will not help? Reason is im/potent. But what about an approach that sees access as a non-philosophical/non-theological gift[57] to be received rather than a way to be engineered?

As Derrida describes it, to cross the threshold is, for Meister Eckhart, to use the power of the eye as a sieve. This new eye, for the mystics, is the eye of love, an eye that opens up a place beyond words, where words are no longer necessary. There may be homecoming.[58]

But Derrida remains poised on the threshold: although he wants to come home and tell his story, he cannot. He remains on the outside, an exile, displaced, wanting to break through. In her summary comments at the Calgary Symposium Morny Joy touches the heart of the matter: "The eye of love is foreign to the forays of his deconstruction."[59] For Derrida it seems as if once Reason has been dethroned, there is no other possibility for providing direction and hope. So we remain wandering, sometimes dwelling in the threshold of the temple, but we can never cross over and enter.

But perhaps there is a new eye: a new eye of love which, with the death of the metaphysical concepts of god, espies a space open for God free from ontotheological apron-strings. It is a space prior to the theoretical space defined by metaphysical thought. However, it is also, as a with-space, the space of and for love, not the neutral "without" space of *différance*. The god that appears would have nothing to do with the god of the philosophers.[60] In this space (to play on Paul Ricoeur's famous phrase) "love gives rise to thought," discourse is reborn, not for purposes of mastery or limitation or hemming in with conditions, but for connection. Because God as love (and love as God) is an overflowing, an excess, an emptying going beyond its own limits, a letting go, life and discourse can be connective, celebrative, communicative.

CROSSING THE THRESHOLD: A VISION OF LOVE

Lingering in this space, and wending my way to a provisional end, I offer a few fleeting glimpses of the far-ranging implications of replacing an ontology of being not with a deconstructed de/ontology, but with a (rediscovered)[61] vision of love.

In the first place, and of fundamental importance, "To be or not to be" is no longer the sum of the matter. Nor is the deconstructionist version on target: "to be *and* not to be, for to be is not to be, and not to be is to be."[62] Rather, the supreme question is: "To love or not to love." In other words, love replaces being-as-power as the highest category. For in the degree that one is not in love, one is deficient in being. God's love comes as a gift, an overflowing, an "excess," which calls us forth—luring, inviting, sustaining.[63] Being is liberated from its fixation on power and freed for love. As a result, in the phrasing of Jean-Luc Marion, "The fundamental ontic difference between what is and what is not becomes indifferent—for everything becomes indifferent before the difference that God marks with the world."[64]

Instead of the Cartesian self-grounding of "I think, therefore, I am," beginning with God's love means "I am loved, therefore I am." The birth of a self and an identity is a bestowal of the love of others, birthed in and through the love shown by others. The human self is intersubjective: in the we there is the I; in the I there is the we. The self finds its center in mutuality. Consequently, the healthy decentering of the modernist self as self-centering need not lead to the postmodern nonself, but to a recentering of the self in relations of love in community.

The passive "am loved" also suggests that whether or not we are existentially able to love is inextricably related to whether we were first loved. Enfolded within the bosom of "to love or not to love" is the question "To be loved or not to be loved." This pivotal interconnection between receiving love and giving love is one of the important emphases of all post-Freudian psychotherapeutic developmental theories since Erikson. Insofar as a child has not received what D. W. Winnicott calls "good-enough"[65] mothering, the child is handicapped in its ability to genuinely love and care for others. By the same token, healing, restoration, and empowerment of a fragmented self is best nourished in relationships of empathy and love.

The gift *of* love is also a gift *for* love; the gift is simultaneously a call. It is the birth of human agency as response-ability for the gift. Therefore, I love in order to be.[66] The process of receiving identity is at the same time a process of constituting one's identity in relation to others. A self is born not only in and through (receiving) love, but equally, reciprocally, in and through (giving) love to others. The two sides belong inextricably together. In this understanding of identity and

agency, not as self-creation or self-certification but as a received empowerment, a call to live out and fulfill, it remains important to talk
(in contrast to postmodernism) of a core self of continuity, coherence,
and agency.[67] This core self—not, it is true, the Cartesian unitary self
of reason—expands and contracts in the vicissitudes of its experience.
It is crucial in helping us to make sense out of the multiplicity of
experiences that both surround us and inhabit us. When we do not
have a bounded and gendered core experience of ourselves, instead of
being able to celebrate postmodern multiplicity, we suffer from fragmentation of self, sometimes to the point of psychosis or multiple personality.[68]

Indeed, I believe it is a fragmented sense of core identity, or even a
lack of such a sense of core identity, that brings many (most?) people
to therapy. Those who celebrate the fluid self as "effect" seem, as Jane
Flax puts it, "self-deceptively naïve and unaware of the basic cohesion
within themselves that makes the fragmentation of experiences something other than a terrifying slide into psychosis."[69] Only when a person has some sense of core self can s/he enter the inter-space and reach
out to a neighbor, not only with a sense of dread and fear of domination, but also with hope for connection, enrichment, and expansion.

Is it entirely coincidental that just when many women are attaining
a sense of agency and selfhood, postmodernism, largely male and middle-class, questions the very existence of self?[70] It is even more disturb-
ing, speaking psychotherapeutically, to realize that the kind of
multiplicity which certain forms of postmodernism champion results
from the very patriarchal domination and abuse that it sets out to challenge. No wonder postmodern feminists such as Julia Kristeva and
Luce Irigaray treat the issue of multiplicity with more sensitivity than
many postmodernists.[71]

Those who think it best to abandon the subject altogether as a fic-
tion, or who see the subject as a position in language or effect of discourse, may be adopting, wittingly or unwittingly, yet another strategy
to avoid facing their deeper selves. Is it, asks Flax, yet another way "to
evade, deny, or repress the importance of early childhood experiences,
especially mother–child relationships, in the constitution of self and
the culture more generally[?] Perhaps it is less threatening to have no
self than one pervaded by memories of, longing for, suppressed identification with, or terror of the powerful mother of infancy."[72] Descartes,
afraid of women and his body, retreated to the supposed certitude and
splendid isolation of his ego. Is the postmodern espousal of the non-

self a similar attempt to continue to repress, deny, or dull the pain? Perhaps the postmodern non-self is yet another version of the adapted or "false self" which needs to be abandoned in a dark night of the soul in order that the core or "true self" may emerge from hiding and begin the process of remembering and healing.

Beginning with love as an overflowing, an invitation (not a coercion) that is realized intersubjectively (not individualistically), opens up a new understanding of the spaces between self and other. In the big dichotomies that have defined the history of metaphysics since the Greeks, mind, culture, form, and intellect have been considered "male"; body, nature, matter, and sentiment, "female." And, of special interest here, *techne*, time, and same have connoted the male; physis, space, and the other, the female.[73] The "only way to give language to Nature, to Space, has been through the *techne*—through technique . . . as the active, masculine aspect . . . giving a narrative to [female, passive] *physis*."[74] The result has been the master narratives by which those in power dominate and exclude "the spaces of the *en-soi*, Other, without history—the feminine . . . [the] unknown, terrifying, monstrous, . . . the mad, the unconscious, improper, unclean, non-sensical, oriental, profane."[75] The breakdown of these master narratives has generated new ways of recognizing and renaming the other-than ourselves—the space, now unbound, coded feminine, outside the logic of modernity, not made possible by its structures, and thus sacred. Kristeva, in fact, calls this sacred place "a place of passage, a threshold where 'nature' confronts 'culture.' "[76]

Buber names this sacred interspace the "the sphere of 'between.' "[77] I prefer the term the "wild"[78] spaces, to emphasize that it is a space as free for love as it has been despoiled by control. "On the narrow ridge, where *I* and *Thou* meet, there is the realm of 'between.' "[79] It is a space "conceptually still uncomprehended . . . not an auxiliary construction, but the real place and bearer of what happens between. . . . [I]t does not exhibit a smooth continuity, but is ever and again reconstituted in accordance with [people's] meetings with one another."[80]

Love as gift creates a space-which-is-meeting, inviting partnership and co-birthing, and fundamentally calling into question the deconstructive idea that structures are necessarily always violent. It suggests a new thematization of meaning and truth as good connections, in contrast to both modernity's power, control, judgment, and postmodernism's disruption and dissemination of any claim of entitlement to

meaning and truth. Narratives are possible, not as grand control devices, but as tales of (broken) love co-authored in community. There
are countless narratives of endless suffering and horror, but there are
also wonderful tales (small, subversive stories)[81] of meeting, healing,
and suffering love in the midst of and in spite of suffering.

This is not an encouragement to retrench and build fixed residences
in the domesticity of modernity. Neither does it, in postmodern rejection of the modern, need to mean exile in the desert (expulsion and
wandering), perpetual homelessness. Rather, we have an invitation to
meet and sojourn together in the wild spaces of love as alternatives
both to modernist distancing or domination and to postmodern fluid-
ity and fusion. Connection rather than control is the dominant metaphor. In the interstices of love, Nygren's antithesis of *eros* and *agape*
notwithstanding, mutuality can be a sojourn together in which loving
self and loving other need not be in opposition but may be mutually
enriching.

In making room for a mutuality ethos, a vision of love re-envisions
Eros, not as the urge to unite, but as the urge to connect. Therefore,
Eros would no longer be a nostalgic but feared wish to return to a
primal, undifferentiated state, as it is with Freud (and even Heidegger).
For Freud, both individual and social history moves from undifferentiation (birth) to differentiation and back again to undifferentiation
(death). In this way *Eros* (love) and *thanatos* (death), although opposing instincts, end up turning into each other: fusion as the realization
of *Eros* is the death of the individual self.

With the focus on *Eros* as the desire to connect, as the passion for
mutuality and right relation, we have the possibility for non-possessive,
non-competitive (i.e., non-violent) connecting, co-partnering, co-
birthing, in the interspaces of love and creativity.[82] Tragically, such
spaces are often the abysses of the wounded, the labyrinths of the lost.
But they can also be places of healing and meeting. Tears, no doubt,
but also laughter; tears, but also mending.

The priority of love, with its impulse for mutuality over being, with
its focus on survival and power, does not mean there will be no conflict; nor does it suggest a resigned toleration of whatever demons of
oppression and domination are afoot. In fact, when we begin from a
self created in, with, and for love, choosing not to resist injustice further injures and diminishes the self. Acts of resistance against injustice
are acts of love. Beginning with a vision of love means that domination
and alienation need not be inevitable. There is also the possibility of

mutual recognition, empowerment, and pleasure. Transformation is possible. Healing can be as real as rending. Power need not always be meted out as power-over or power-under. Power relations can be transformed into power-with relations, relations of love.

If I read Foucault correctly, this belief goes along with his treatment of power, and then goes a step farther. For Foucault, when power relations are fixed and no longer in constant struggle, there is no power but violence and slavery. Power relations always imply the possibility of reversal. In my view this possibility of reversal, when seen through the eyes of love, can become not only a continual reversal of who is in control, but also a transformation of the power dynamics of conflict to one of shared connection. Power-with as an alternative to hierarchical power-over also opens up the possibility of ecological partnership with the earth and all its creatures, copartnership in the cosmic family so that the cosmos may be a love-place—a home rather than a deserted and ravaged desert.

Love is the difference that matters. And suddenly suffering has a different place, a legitimate place. It is no longer a diminution of being, a suffering-from, which detracts from who we are, but a very different suffering-with, a voluntary being-with which comforts and heals, enriching and transforming everyone and everything it touches.[83] Love as excess—without a why—overflows onto the plains and meadows of life as a celebrating-with. It seeps into life's cracks and fissures as suffering-with.

Beginning with love as a creative power (making something out of nothing) gives new place to love as forgiveness (making nothing out of something). In the experience of forgiveness there is release, a letting go, a freeing to new starts and new creations. Love turns us to the other, not as diminution of being, but as enrichment, hospitality, and celebration.[84]

Letting be (Gelassenheit) is the way of God. Since the way of God is love, this letting be is not simply a Heideggerian releasement to things; nor is it a meditative waiting for and remaining open for the miracle of Being's advent. It is a proactive being-with, especially with those who suffer, and, when appropriate, a robust pursuit of justice for the oppressed and a planetary ecological ethic for all creatures. In other words, such letting be is not ethically neutral, as it is with Heidegger, in which both the "hale" and the "evil" appear equally in the clearing of Being.[85]

At the same time, since love cannot be controlled, the Gelassenheit of love eschews control. And giving up control demands faith and trust, in spite of. *Gelassenheit* is a surrender of our will to control, a giving over, an Eckhartian abandonment to the cosmic wave of God's love. Such surrender is not forced. It is a voluntary movement of empowerment which releases to the energies alive in other people, in the world, and in God.

In closing, I trade on two of Julia Kristeva's titles. We do not simply have the "powers of horror"; we have also "tales of love." Instead of a Heideggerian *Dasein* facing the otherness of death, we have persons facing each other

> crossing the threshold, despite . . .
> taking the risk, despite . . .
> not trying (always to counter),
> not (always) fusing or fleeing,
> but sometimes meeting-in-the-middle spaces of love,
> not always wandering in labyrinths,
> or falling into abysses,
> yet not smugly settled, serenely ensconced,
> but journeying together . . .
> sojourning in the wild spaces of love, despite and in spite of
> > Zarathustra's laughter,
> > in spite of the killing fields . . .
> Faith is always despite . . .
> We sojourn not alone.
> God tents, tabernacles—sojourns—with us.[86]

> The ways of Love are strange,
> As those who have followed them well know,
> For, unexpectedly, She withdraws Her consolation.
> > He whom Love touches
> > Can enjoy no stability.
> > And he will taste
> > Many a nameless hour.
>
> >   *   *   *
>
> Sometimes burning and sometimes cold,
> Sometimes timid and sometimes bold,
> The whims of Love are manifold.
> > She reminds us all
> > Of our great debt
> > To Her lofty power
> > Which draws us to Herself alone.

Sometimes gracious and sometimes cruel,
Sometimes far and sometimes near
He who grasps Her in faithful love
> Reaches jubilation.
> Oh, how Love
> With one sole act
> Both strikes and embraces!

Sometimes humble, sometimes haughty,
Sometimes hidden and sometimes revealed;
To be finally overwhelmed by Love,
> Great adventures must be risked
> Before one can reach
> The place where is tasted
> The nature of Love.

Sometimes light, sometimes heavy,
Sometimes somber and sometimes bright,
In freeing consolation, in stifling anguish,
In taking and in giving,
Thus live the spirits
Who wander here below,
Along the paths of Love.[87]

NOTES

This is an edited version of a 1993 Canadian Theological Society Presidential Address which was published in *Toronto Journal of Theology* 11/1 (1995), 39–57.

1. Mark C. Taylor, "Think Naught," in *Negation and Theology*, ed. Robert Scharlemann (Charlottesville: University Press of Virginia, 1992), p. 37.

2. Mark C. Taylor, *Erring* (Chicago: University of Chicago Press, 1984), p. 6.

3. Taylor, "Think Naught," p. 36.

4. Ibid., p. 37.

5. See David Tracy's discussion of "limit" in Chapter 5 of *Blessed Rage for Order* (New York: Seabury Press, 1975), pp. 91–119.

6. For Taylor the "death of God is at the same time the death of the self" (*Erring*, p. 20).

7. Although Jean-Luc Marion, in his *God Without Being* (trans. T. Carlson [Chicago: University of Chicago Press, 1991]), makes a similar proposal

in respect to God, he continues (questionably, in my view) to see "to be or not to be" as "the first and indispensable question" for every creature (p. xx).

8. Martin Heidegger, *Identity and Difference*, trans. Joan Stambaugh (New York: Harper & Row, 1969), pp. 60, 72.

9. Ibid., p. 72.

10. Ibid.

11. Martin Heidegger, *Nietzsche*, Vol. 2, trans. David Krell (New York: Harper & Row, 1984), p. 106.

12. As quoted in Marion, *God Without Being*, p. 61, who gives the German text of Heidegger, pp. 211–12. Derrida discusses it in "How to Avoid Speaking: Denials," in *Derrida and Negative Theology*, ed. Harold Coward and Toby Foshay (Albany: State University of New York Press, 1992), pp. 126ff.

13. Two recent discussions have been especially helpful: Marion, *God Without Being*, chaps. 2 and 3, and Theo De Boer, *De God van de filosofen and de God van Pascal* ('s-Gravenhage: Meinema, 1989), pp. 49–58.

14. Benedict de Spinoza, *Ethics*, in *The Chief Works of Benedict de Spinoza* trans. R. Elwes (New York: Dover Publications, 1955), Part III, Proposition 6, p. 136.

15. Ibid., Part I, Proposition 34, p. 74.

16. " 'I think' comes down to 'I can.' . . . . Ontology as first philosophy is a philosophy of power . . . a philosophy of injustice" (Emmanuel Levinas, *Totality and Infinity*, trans. A. Lingis [Pittsburgh: Duquesne University Press, 1969], p. 46).

17. In *Positions*, trans. Alan Bass (Chicago: University of Chicago Press, 1981), p. 64, Derrida terms this totalizing "motif of homogeneity, the theological motif *par excellence.*" As Kevin Hart (*The Trespass of the Sign* [Cambridge: Cambridge University Press, 1989], p. 32) points out, in Derrida's sense, a theological discourse need not involve God, it only needs something that functions as an agent of totalization.

18. In this context, I cannot resist alluding to Walter Wink's *Engaging the Powers* (Minneapolis: Fortress Press, 1992), where he insists that the heart of Jesus' life and message was challenging the "domination system."

19. For an excellent analysis of the "problem of domination," see Jessica Benjamin, *The Bonds of Love* (New York: Pantheon Books, 1989).

20. Paul Tillich, *The Courage to Be* (New Haven, Conn.: Yale University Press, 1952), p. 179.

21. Theologically, I think this is one (perhaps *the*) compelling reason why the philosophical idea of the impassibility of God has historically often prevailed over the suffering love of God.

22. Spinoza, *Ethics*, Part III, Definition 3, p. 174.

23. Martin Heidegger, *On the Way to Language*, trans. P. Hertz (New York: Harper & Row, 1971), p. 181; and *Poetry, Language, Thought*, trans.

A. Hofstadter (New York: Harper & Row, 1971), p. 205. See John D. Caputo, "Thinking, Poetry and Pain," in *The Southern Journal of Philosophy*, 28, Supplement (1989), 55–81.

24. Gilles Deleuze and Felix Guattari, *Anti-Oedipus Capitalism and Schizophrenia*, trans. R. Hurly, M. Seem, and H. Lane (London: Athlone Press, 1977), p. 340.

25. All references to *Erring* (note 2) in this paragraph are included in text.

26. To take a classic example, we have discovered that Descartes' "ideal of the *cogito*, of the *matheis universalis* means *denial*, a defense against the flesh because the flesh is synonymous with anguish; and the clean fission between mind and body is an *isolation*, a setting apart and rendering innocuous of all that which spells dread" (Karl Stern, *The Flight from Women* [New York: Noonday Press, 1965], p. 101).

27. Heidegger, *Identity*, pp. 54–55.

28. Quoted in Marion, *God Without Being*, p. 54.

29. See especially Kevin Hart, *The Trespass of the Sign*; and two recent books of relevance: Scharlemann, *Negation and Theology*; and *Derrida and Negative Theology*, ed. Coward and Foshay.

30. For Derrida, "God is the name and element of that which makes possible an absolutely pure and absolutely self-present self-knowledge" (*Of Grammatology*, trans. G. Spivak [Baltimore: Johns Hopkins University Press, 1976], p. 98).

31. Hart, *Trespass of the Sign*, pp. 29, 30.

32. Reprinted in *Derrida and Negative Theology*, pp. 73–142. See note 39.

33. Mark C. Taylor, "nO nOt nO," in ibid., pp. 174–75.

34. Derrida, "Denials," p. 96.

35. Ibid., p. 121.

36. Ibid., p. 128.

37. Ibid., p. 95.

38. Ibid., p. 100.

39. Ibid., p. 135. Derrida wrote these words in 1987. After this speech was first delivered, I discovered that Derrida in 1991 surprisingly published a very moving, personal text—reflecting on his childhood and his mother's death and including also a commentary on St. Augustine's *Confessions*—called *Circumfession* as part of a dual text written with Geoffrey Bennington under the title *Jacques Derrida*, trans. G. Bennington (Chicago: University of Chicago Press, 1993). "[T]he constancy of God in my life is called by other names" (p. 155).

40. Taylor, "nO nOt nO," p. 195.

41. The threshold image is just one of the many un/decidability images which flood Derrida's work. Others include the hinge, breast, fold, valley, Plato's *pharmakon*, Mallarmé's hymen.

42. In his *Post-Scriptum* (in *Derrida and Negative Theology*, p. 318) Der-

rida sees a special connection between "desert" and "desire": "One has more and more the feeling that desert is the other name, if not the proper place, of desire."

43. My colleague Brian Walsh alerted me to the catchy line of Amos Wilder: "We cross the threshold into the story-world" ("Story and Story-World," *Interpretation* 37, 4 [1983], 355).

44. Derrida, "Denials," p. 104

45. Ibid., p. 106.

46. Ibid., p. 106/7.

47. Ibid., p. 121.

48. Ibid., p. 123.

49. Derrida, "Post-Scriptum," p. 314.

50. Ibid.

51. Ibid. Derrida points out that "what still relates them to each other is this strange preposition, this strange with-without or without-with, *without*."

52. At the same time, I admit to wondering if Derrida's "choice" for the second space does not precisely call into question whether undecidability can ever go all the way down.

53. In reference to the God-with-us (John I) by whom all things were created.

54. Derrida, "Post-Scriptum," p. 318.

55. Ibid., p. 315. It is important to note that this does not mean ethical neutrality for Derrida. Undecidability is a kind of quasi-transcendental condition, calling for decisions. Deconstruction is an intensification of responsibility, "a positive response to an alterity which necessarily calls, summons or motivates it. Deconstruction is therefore a vocation—a response to a call. . . . It is possible to see deconstruction as being produced in a space where the prophets are not far away" ("Deconstruction and the Others: An Interview with Derrida," in *Dialogues with Contemporary Continental Thinkers: The Phenomenological Heritage* (ed. R. Kearney [Manchester: Manchester University Press, 1984], pp. 118, 119). See James Olthuis, "An Ethics of Compassion," in *What Right Does Ethics Have?* (ed. S. Griffioen [Amsterdam: VU University Press, 1990], pp. 125–46).

56. For a valuable discussion of logical and existential grounding in the work of Richard Rorty and John Dewey, see Carroll Guen Hart, *Grounding without Foundations* (Toronto: The Patmos Press, 1993).

57. Derrida is now emphasizing that faith is presupposed by any deconstructive gesture. "I don't know, one has to believe" (*Memoirs of the Blind*, trans. Pascale-Anne Broult and Michael Naas [Chicago: University of Chicago Press, 1993], p. 129).

58. "Homecoming is not a return to the past but it is a becoming into the future" (Charles Winquist, *Homecoming: Interpretation, Transformation and Individuation* [Missoula, Mont.: Scholars Press, 1978], p. 9).

59. Morny Joy, "Conclusion: Divine Reservations," in *Derrida and Negative Theology*, p. 263.

60. Marion, *God Without Being*, p. 52.

61. Rediscovered, not only because it harks back to the love mysticism of St. Bernard, Meister Eckhart, John of the Cross, or Ruysbroeck the Admirable, but also because the important work of women mystics such as the twelfth-century Hildegard of Bingen and the Rheno-Flemish Beguines of the thirteenth century is coming to light. Eckhart's famous expression about the gratuitous nature of Divine Love, *without a why*, appears for the first time in the work of the Cistercian nun, Beatrice of Nazareth, and later in the writings of the Beguines. See Emilie Zum Brunn and Georgette Epiney-Burgard, *Women Mystics in Medieval Europe* (New York: Paragon House, 1989), p. xxxi.

62. Mark C. Taylor, *De-constructing Theology* (New York: Crossroad Publishers, 1982), p. 56.

63. Like Marion, I want to carefully distinguish between beginning with a gift given by God from Heidegger's impersonal *es gibt*, in which the gift is the giving without starting from any giver. See Marion, *God Without Being*, pp. 102–107.

64. Ibid., p. 88. See Marion's discussion of Romans 4:17 and I Cor. 1:28, where God calls "nonbeings to become beings . . . , [and] calls the nonbeings as if they were beings" (ibid., pp. 88–95).

65. Donald Winnicott, *The Maturational Processes and the Facilitating Environment* (New York: International Universities Press, 1965), p. 145.

66. "*I am to the extent that I am loved, therefore I love in order to be.*" According to French feminist literary critic Julia Kristeva, this saying is "for the medieval thinker . . . an implict definition of the subject's being" (*Tales of Love*, trans. L. Roudiez [New York: Columbia University Press, 1987], p. 171).

67. In his ground-breaking clinical study *The Interpersonal World of the Infant* (New York: Basic Books, 1985), Daniel Stern concludes that infants between two and seven months form a sense of core self—self-agency, self-coherence, self-affectivity, and self-history.

68. In fact, James Glass, in *Shattered Selves* (Ithaca: Cornell University Press, 1993), critiques the postmodern celebration of multiplicity by demonstrating that for the many people who suffer from schizophrenia and multiple personality, multiciplicity is unadulterated anguish.

69. Jane Flax, *Thinking Fragments* (Los Angeles: University of California Press, 1990), p. 218–19.

70. See Patricia Waugh, "Postmodernism," in *Feminism and Psychoanlyis: A Critical Dictionary*, ed. E. Wright (Oxford: Basil Blackwell, 1992), p. 344.

71. Toril Moi, in her introduction to *The Kristeva Reader* (ed. T. Moi

[New York: Columbia University Press, 1986], p. 13), sees Kristeva doing a "balancing act between a position which would deconstruct subjectivity and identity altogether, and one that would try to capture these entities in an essentialist or humanist mould."

72. Flax, *Thinking Fragments*, p. 232.

73. According to Kristeva, the connotations of space and the feminine go back at least to Plato's *khôra*, and "the 'other' is the 'other sex' " (*La révolution du langage poétique*, p. 326, quoted in Alice Jardine, *Gynesis* [Ithaca: Cornell University Press, 1985], p. 114).

74. Ibid., p. 73.

75. Ibid, pp. 72–73.

76. Julia Kristeva, *Desire in Language*, ed. Leon Roudiez, trans. T. Gora, A. Jardine, and L. Roudiez (New York: Columbia University Press, 1980), p. 238. For Kristeva, the undifferentiated space shared by mother and child is called *khôra* (p. 133).

77. Martin Buber, *Between Man and Man*, trans. G. Smith (London: Collins, 1947), p. 244.

78. I distinguish my use of "wild" in reference to interspace from Julia Kristeva's discussion in *Tales of Love* (pp. 1, 2) of a love "aptly called *wild . . .* a crucible of contradictions and misunderstandings." For me, love is the primal force both gifting to and calling for good ordering (i.e., good connections). Kristeva's wild, semiotic love is over against and subversive of the symbolic rule of the law of the Father even as it is subject to it.

79. Buber, *Between Man and Man*, p. 246.

80. Ibid., pp. 244–45.

81. De Boer contrasts the Grand Stories of domination with the "small story . . . of Abraham, Issac, Jacob and Jesus Christ" (De God, p. 152). Brian Walsh works out the idea of the Gospel as subversive in *Subversive Christianity* (Bristol: The Regius Press, 1992).

82. See Christian feminist Carter Heyward's inspired revisioning of Eros along these lines in *Touching Our Strength: The Erotic as Power and the Love of God* (San Francisco: Harper & Row, 1989).

83. According to Romans 8:17, suffering-with goes along with being an heir of Christ.

84. In *Post-Scriptum*, p. 317, Derrida notes: "To let passage to the other, to the totally other, is hospitality."

85. "With healing, evil appears all the more in the lighting of Being. The essence of evil . . . consist[s] . . . in the malice of rage. Both of these, however, healing and raging, can essentially occur only in Being, insofar as Being itself is what is contested" (Martin Heidegger, "Letter on Humanism," in *Basic Writings*, ed. D. Krell [New York: Harper & Row, 1977], p. 237). For neutrality as a property of traditional ontologies of being, see De Boer, *De God*, pp. 49–52. In contemporary philosophy Levinas, in particular, pro-

tested that such neutrality is in fact oppressive. Paul Ricoeur's *Oneself as Another* (trans. K. Blamey [Chicago: University of Chicago Press, 1992]) is also a recent eloquent plea against ethically neutral ontologies. I want to emphasize again that Derrida intends his priniciple of undecidability to intensify ethical responsibility. See John D. Caputo's *Radical Hermeneutics* (Bloomington: Indiana University Press, 1987, chaps. 9 & 10) and *Against Ethics* (Bloomington: Indiana University Press, 1993) for a Derridean ethics of dissemination which contrasts with Taylor's more Nietzschean approach. See also Simon Critchley's *The Ethics of Deconstruction* (Oxford: Blackwell, 1992).

86. Leviticus 26:11, Rev. 21:3, John 1:14.

87. Hadewijch of Antwerp, most of thirteenth-century Stanzaic Poem V, quoted in Zum Brunn and Epiney-Burgard, *Women Mystics*, pp. 113–14.

INDEX OF NAMES

INDEX OF SUBJECTS

NOTES ON CONTRIBUTORS

JEFFREY DUDIAK is a Ph.D. candidate in Philosophical Theology in the co-joint doctoral program of the Vrije Universiteit (Free University) in Amsterdam and the Institute for Christian Studies in Toronto. He is writing a dissertation on the idea of discourse in the thought of Emmanuel Levinas. He is a Quaker, and lives with his wife, Julie Robinson, in Toronto.

CARROLL GUEN HART is Director of Worldview Studies at the Institute for Christian Studies. She is the author of *Grounding Without Foundations, a Conversation Between Richard Rorty and John Dewey* (Patmos Press, 1993). She is currently developing programs, in a partnership with other community organizations, which focus on faith and science, calling and professionalism, and cultural studies. Other interests include reading novels, designing clothing, and involvement in the Homes First Society, which houses street people.

HENDRIK HART is Professor of Philosophy at the Institute for Christian Studies, where he has taught since 1966. He has published *Communal Certainty and Authorized Truth*; *Understanding Our World*; *Setting Our Sights by the Morning Star*; and (with Kai Nelson) *Search for Community in a Withering Tradition*.

RONALD A. KUIPERS is a Ph.D. candidate in Philosophy at the Institute for Christian Studies. His concentrations are Richard Rorty, Pragmatism, Feminism, and Continental Philosophy. He is an active advocate for the bicycle lobby in Toronto, and is a member of a non-profit housing cooperative. He has authored a forthcoming book on the philosophy of Richard Rorty.

JAMES H. OLTHUIS is a Professor of Philosophical Theology at the Institute for Christian Studies, where he has taught since 1968. He is the author of *Facts, Values, and Ethics*; *I Pledge You My Troth*; *Keeping our Troth: Staying in Love During the Five Stages of Marriage*; and A

Hermeneutics of Ultimacy: Peril or Promise. He is also a psychotherapist in private practice in Toronto.

JAMIE SMITH received his M.Phil. from the Institute of Christian Studies and is now a Ph.D. candidate at Villanova University, where he also teaches philosophy of religion and health-care ethics. He has published articles in *Studies in Religion/Sciences Religieuses, Faith and Philosophy*, and *The Journal of Pentecostal Theology*.

JANET CATHERINE WESSELIUS is a Ph.D. candidate in Philosophy at the Institute for Christian Studies. She is writing a dissertation on notions of objectivity in feminist epistemology. She has taught courses in feminist philosophy, women's studies, and world religions. She is currently on the Board of Directors of an alternative housing co-operative in Toronto.